LEADING
STANDARDS-BASED
LEARNING
An Implementation Guide
for Schools and Districts

TAMMY HEFLEBOWER

JAN K. HOEGH

PHILIP B. WARRICK

MARZANO
Resources

555 North Morton Street
Bloomington, IN 47404
888.849.0851
FAX: 866.801.1447

email: info@MarzanoResources.com
MarzanoResources.com

Visit **MarzanoResources.com/reproducibles** to download the free reproducibles in this book.

Printed in the United States of America

Library of Congress Cataloging-in-Publication Data

Names: Heflebower, Tammy, author. | Hoegh, Jan K., author. | Warrick,
    Philip B., author.
Title: Leading standards-based learning : an implementation guide for
    schools and districts / Tammy Heflebower, Jan K. Hoegh, Philip B.
    Warrick.
Description: Bloomington, IN : Marzano Resources, [2021] | Includes
    bibliographical references and index.
Identifiers: LCCN 2020030389 (print) | LCCN 2020030390 (ebook) | ISBN
    9781943360376 (paperback) | ISBN 9781943360383 (ebook)
Subjects: LCSH: Education--Standards.
Classification: LCC LB3060.82 .H44 2021 (print) | LCC LB3060.82 (ebook) |
    DDC 379.1/58--dc23
LC record available at https://lccn.loc.gov/2020030389
LC ebook record available at https://lccn.loc.gov/2020030390

Production Team
President and Publisher: Douglas M. Rife
Associate Publisher: Sarah Payne-Mills
Art Director: Rian Anderson
Managing Production Editor: Kendra Slayton
Copy Chief: Jessi Finn
Production Editor: Laurel Hecker
Content Development Specialist: Amy Rubenstein
Copy Editor: Mark Hain
Editorial Assistants: Sarah Ludwig and Elijah Oates

Acknowledgments

The authors give special thanks to the schools, districts, and school support agencies high-lighted throughout this resource.

Anoka-Hennepin School District, Anoka, Minnesota

The Anoka-Hennepin School District is one of Minnesota's largest, serving approximately 38,000 students and 248,000 residents. Spread out across 172 square miles, the district is made up of thirteen suburban communities north of the Twin Cities of Minneapolis and St. Paul. Anoka-Hennepin has twenty-six elementary schools, six middle schools, and five traditional high schools, plus alternative middle and high school sites, in addition to an award-winning community education program.

Columbus Public Schools, Columbus, Nebraska

Columbus Public Schools is a public school district located in Columbus, Nebraska. It has 3,928 students in grades preK–12 with a student-teacher ratio of sixteen to one. The district is comprised of five elementary schools, one middle school, and one high school. Located in a midwestern community of twenty-five thousand people, Columbus Public Schools offers the advantages of larger school districts with a small-town atmosphere.

Deer Creek Public Schools, Oklahoma City and Edmond, Oklahoma

Deer Creek Public Schools encompasses seventy-two square miles and includes portions of three counties (Oklahoma, Logan, and Canadian) and two cities (Oklahoma City and Edmond). Deer Creek is known for its community-centered atmosphere, excellent staff, strong parental involvement, and focus on the growth of students both academically and personally. Deer Creek is one of the top school districts in the state of Oklahoma and is proud of the many student accomplishments that occur each year. Deer Creek has implemented standards-referenced reporting in all elementary schools and as of 2020 is implementing the pilot for the intermediate school.

Empower Learning

Empower Learning is a learning management system and electronic gradebook provider. The roots of Empower stretch back nearly twenty years, with founder Scott Bacon creating a platform purpose-built to support standards-based grading and competency-based education. The platform integrates the use of proficiency scales to house a system's guaranteed and viable curriculum, measure student progress, deliver instruction at an individual student's point of need, and provide reporting tools to inform data-driven decisions. The company's goal is to democratize human potential by empowering all stakeholders with the technology to personalize learning.

Heartland Area Education Agency

Heartland Area Education Agency is located in central Iowa, one of nine such area education agencies (AEAs) in the state. Many, if not all, states have agencies such as this at a level between the state department of education and districts, but many of those work more closely with the department of education. In Iowa, AEAs work much more closely with public school districts and accredited nonpublic schools, often even embedding teams of consultants inside districts and buildings to support staffs at every level.

Jefferson County Public Schools, Golden, Colorado

Jefferson County Public Schools has been providing educational excellence for almost seventy years. Approximately 9 percent of all the K–12 students in Colorado attend a Jefferson County school. The district's mission is to provide a quality education that prepares all children for a successful future. Jefferson County consists of 155 schools and many programs on 168 campuses, including eighty-five elementary schools, five K–8 schools, seventeen middle schools, seventeen high schools, fifteen charter schools, twelve option schools (schools with students from other districts), two outdoor laboratory schools, one online school, and one career and technical education school.

The Schools of McKeel Academy, Lakeland, Florida

The Schools of McKeel Academy are a public, not-for-profit charter school system comprised of three campuses: McKeel Academy of Technology (7–12), McKeel Academy Central (preK–6), and South McKeel Academy (preK–6). Designated as a high-performance charter school system by the state of Florida, the flagship campus opened its doors to 360 students in 1995. As of 2020, McKeel Academy charter schools have an enrollment of over 3,200 students.

Monett R-1 School District, Monett, Missouri

Monett R-1 School District, located in Monett, Missouri, serves roughly 2,300 students in grades K–12. The diverse community is reflected in the student population where more than 30 percent of students entering kindergarten speak a language other than English and close to 70 percent qualify for free or reduced lunches. The school district provides a wide range of opportunities for students including a regional technology center and the Greater Ozarks Centers for Advanced Professional Studies.

Northwood Public School District, Northwood, North Dakota

The Northwood Public School District, located in Grand Forks County, serves approximately three hundred students in grades K–12. The K–6 elementary school and the 7–12 secondary school are housed in a shared facility. The district began its initial proficiency scale work and grading exploration through workshops hosted by the Red River Valley Education Cooperative.

Novato Unified School District, Novato, California

Novato Unified School District is a public school district located in Novato, California. It has 7,863 students in grades K–12 with a student-teacher ratio of twenty-one to one. According to state test scores, 47 percent of students are at least proficient in mathematics and 55 percent in reading.

NYOS Charter School, Austin, Texas

NYOS (Not Your Ordinary School) is a free public charter school established in Austin, Texas, in 1998. The NYOS school board comprises four teachers, four parents, up to five community or business members, and a nonvoting student member. NYOS is located on two separate campuses: the preK–3 Kramer campus and the 4–12 Lamar campus. NYOS elementary is part of the Marzano High Reliability Schools (HRS) network and in 2016 was recognized as a level 4 certified school for implementation of standards-referenced reporting. The school is currently in the process of moving to HRS level 5, competency-based grading and reporting.

Uinta County School District #1, Evanston, Wyoming

Uinta County School District #1 is located in Evanston, Wyoming. The district currently operates four elementary schools, two middle schools, one high school, and one alternative high school, amounting to a total of 987,510 square feet of educational space. Approximately three thousand preK–12 students are served in the district.

Wichita Public Schools, Wichita, Kansas

Wichita Public Schools is the largest school district in Kansas, with an enrollment of approximately fifty thousand diverse students. The district has fifty-four elementary schools, fifteen middle schools, three K–8 schools, nine high schools, nine special schools, and five special program locations. Of these school sites, twenty-four house magnet programs. Wichita Public Schools students come from ninety-seven countries, and more than 105 languages are spoken in the homes of district students.

Marzano Resources would like to thank the following reviewers:

Rebecca Goddard
Assessment Program Specialist
Fulton County Schools
Atlanta, Georgia

Jennifer Karnopp
Author and Educational Consultant
Bloomington, Indiana

Steve Mefford
Facilitator of Curriculum and
    Professional Learning
Urbandale Community School District
Urbandale, Iowa

Susan Silva
Executive Director of Curriculum and
    Instruction
Clear Creek Independent School District
League City, Texas

Toby West
Dean of Students
James Conger Elementary School
Delaware, Ohio

Table of Contents

Reproducibles are in italics

About the Authors xi

Foreword xiii
By Jennifer Steele and Cecily Klein

Introduction 1
    Build Your Knowledge and Understanding 4
    Clarify Terminology 5
    Craft a Multiphase Plan 8

PHASE 1
Curriculum and Communication 13
    Design a Guaranteed and Viable Curriculum for Core Content Areas 13
    Draft an Initial Implementation and Communication Plan 38
    Educate Key Leaders 47
    Assemble a Guiding Team 53
    Analyze Existing Grading Practices and Beliefs 56
    Establish Digital Storage for Standards and Scales 57
    Summary 59

PHASE 2
Alignment and Capacity Building 61
    Begin Rolling Out Standards and Scales for Core Content Areas 61
    Align Instruction and Assessment 71
    Expand Your Efforts 84
    Share Information 87
    Monitor Implementation 99
    Summary 101

PHASE 3

Universal Implementation, Communication, and Reporting Systems 103
    Expand Work in Non-Core Content Areas 103
    Align Scales for Core Content Areas 106
    Include Teachers of Exceptional Learners 107
    Plan and Initiate the Rollout 112
    Prepare for Reporting Systems 117
    Summary 123

PHASE 4

Continuation, Revision, and Expansion 125
    Seek Feedback From Teachers About Classroom Assessments in Core Content Areas 125
    Continue the Implementation Rollout 126
    Continue Work in Non-Core Content Areas 129
    Communicate With Stakeholders 131
    Implement New Reporting Systems for Selected Grades 136
    Summary 141

PHASE 5

Monitoring, Tracking Student Achievement, and Celebrating 143
    Expand Implementation to Additional Content Areas or Grade Levels 143
    Continue Tracking Student Achievement Data 146
    Train Incoming Stakeholders 147
    Celebrate Success 150
    Summary 151

Epilogue 153

Appendix A: Additional Resources for Chapter 1 155
    Proficiency Scales 155
    Consensus Building 162
    Staff Learning Opportunities 165

Appendix B: Additional Resources for Chapter 2 167
    Leveled Assessments 167
    Implementation Plan 172
    Communication Toolkit 173
    Support for Standards-Based Reporting in Higher Education 175

Appendix C: Additional Resources for Chapter 3 177
  Vertical Alignment 177
  Vertical Alignment Process, Phase I 179
  Vertical Alignment Process, Phases II and III 180
  A Parent's Guide to Standards-Based Grading 181
  Sample Presentation to Parents 183

Appendix D: Additional Resources for Chapter 4 187
  Focus Group Protocol 187
  Standards-Based Report Cards 190
  Parent FAQs 194

Appendix E: Additional Resources for Chapter 5 199
  Active Progress Monitoring 199

References and Resources 205

Index 211

About the Authors

**Tammy Heflebower, EdD**, is a highly sought-after school leader and consultant with vast experiences in urban, rural, and suburban districts throughout the United States, Australia, Canada, Denmark, Great Britain, and the Netherlands. She has served as an award-winning classroom teacher, building leader, district leader, regional professional development director, and national and international trainer. She has also been an adjunct professor of curriculum, instruction, and assessment at several universities, and a prominent member and leader of numerous statewide and national educational organizations. She was vice president and then senior scholar at Marzano Resources and continues to work as an author and associate with Marzano Resources and Solution Tree. In addition, Tammy is the CEO of her own company, !nspire Inc.: Education and Business Solutions, specializing in powerful presentation and facilitation techniques, which she writes about and shares worldwide.

Tammy is sole author of the *Presenting Perfected* book series and lead author of *Crafting Your Message: An Educator's Guide to Perfect Presentations*. She is also lead author of the award-winning bestseller *A School Leader's Guide to Standards-Based Grading*, lead author of the award-finalist *A Teacher's Guide to Standards-Based Learning*, and coauthor of *Collaborative Teams That Transform Schools: The Next Step in PLCs* and *Teaching and Assessing 21st Century Skills*. She is a contributing author to over a dozen other books and publications, many of which have been translated into multiple languages and are referenced internationally.

Tammy holds a bachelor of arts from Hastings College where she was honored as Outstanding Young Alumna and her volleyball team was inducted into the athletic hall of fame. She has a master of arts from the University of Nebraska Omaha, and she received her educational administrative endorsement and doctorate from the University of Nebraska–Lincoln.

Jan K. Hoegh has been an educator for over thirty years and an author and associate for Marzano Resources since 2010. Prior to joining the Marzano team, she was a classroom teacher, building leader, professional development specialist, high school assistant principal, curriculum coordinator, and assistant director of statewide assessment for the Nebraska Department of Education, where her primary focus was Nebraska State Accountability test development. Jan has served on a variety of statewide and national standards and assessment committees and has presented at numerous conferences around the world.

As an associate with Marzano Resources, Jan works with educators across the United States and beyond as they strive to improve student achievement. Her passion for education, combined with extensive knowledge of curriculum, instruction, and assessment, provides credible support for teachers, leaders, schools, and districts. High-quality classroom assessment and grading practices are her primary training focuses. She is coauthor of *Collaborative Teams That Transform Schools*, *A School Leader's Guide to Standards-Based Grading*, *A Teacher's Guide to Standards-Based Learning*, and *A Handbook for Developing and Using Proficiency Scales in the Classroom*, as well as other publications.

Jan holds a bachelor of arts in elementary education and a master of arts in educational administration, both from the University of Nebraska at Kearney. She also earned a specialization in assessment from the University of Nebraska–Lincoln.

Philip B. Warrick, EdD, spent the first twenty-five years of his education career as a teacher, assistant principal, principal, and superintendent and has experience leading schools in the states of Nebraska and Texas. He was named 1998 Nebraska Outstanding New Principal of the Year and was the 2005 Nebraska State High School Principal of the Year. In 2003, he was one of the initial participants to attend the Nebraska Educational Leadership Institute, conducted by the Gallup organization at Gallup University in Omaha. In 2008, Phil was hired as the campus principal at Round Rock High School in Round Rock, Texas. In 2010, he was invited to be an inaugural participant in the Texas Principals' Visioning Institute, where he collaborated with other principals from the state of Texas to develop a vision for effective practices in Texas schools. In 2011, Phil joined the Solution Tree–Marzano Resources team and works as an author and global consultant in the areas of high reliability school leadership, instruction and instructional coaching, assessment, grading, and collaborative teaming.

He earned a bachelor of science from Chadron State College in Chadron, Nebraska, and earned his master's and doctoral degrees from the University of Nebraska–Lincoln.

Foreword

By Jennifer Steele and Cecily Klein
Department of Curriculum and Instruction, Jefferson County Public Schools, Colorado

For years, educators have been discussing how to manage and fulfill all of the standards and expectations set forth by state and provincial departments of education. Being in Colorado, a local control state, our district needed to determine a process to ensure our students meet or exceed state academic expectations each year. Jefferson County Public Schools is a large system with over 84,000 students, 4,700 teachers, and 155 school campuses, so calibration was critical to student success for every child. It was important to us that we supported teachers in understanding the essential learnings in each content area and in each grade level along with the progression of learning needed to get there. With 31 percent of our students living in poverty, such calibration would create and solidify a true guaranteed and viable curriculum for each and every child.

Not only did we intend to provide teachers and students with clarity about what was requested for students to know and be able to do, but our district needed to define ways to communicate learning, which included defining what grades truly mean. We had received multiple requests from key stakeholders to redesign our grading practices and report card. Expectations of academic success were inconsistent among our schools as each school was determining its own definition of proficiency for each academic standard. We quickly discovered that we could not identify a grade if we didn't have a consistent way to ensure calibration of what students needed to know and be able to demonstrate.

We then asked ourselves, "What resources, supports, and professional learning would assist teachers in developing clarity about the expectations housed in the Colorado Academic Standards?" The research that followed brought us to develop our strong relationships with Tammy Heflebower and Jan Hoegh. They partnered with us to assess, develop, and facilitate learning for our organization around proficiency-based teaching and learning. This handbook offers the teacher clarity that is needed in order to systemically calibrate learning expectations for all students. The tools and resources will inspire educators everywhere to calibrate expectations throughout the teaching and learning cycle (plan, teach, assess, reflect).

In this new book, Heflebower, Hoegh, and Warrick provide support through a comprehensive plan that welcomes multiple entries to support educators wherever they may be. The guidance, scales, and resources that are provided in this book have been developed by educators across the United States, in districts such as ours. Those familiar with standards-based education will recognize many familiar tools and will discover many new resources to support them in their own journey. The path forward can be a bit daunting, especially in a large district, but with these tools and supports, clarity for educators and students can be achieved and enacted.

Introduction

Grading needs reform. The educational community has witnessed a vast number of changes, including but not limited to providing meals for needy students, new and improved technology, longer school days, inclusion of and services for students with special learning and behavioral needs, the suggestion then requirement to teach a set of vastly more complex and numerous standards, an increased focus on student mindfulness and social-emotional learning, accountability demands and statewide assessments, and so on. Even with the myriad of well-meaning innovations, educational grading practices have changed little. Many schools (especially secondary schools) still grade traditionally. That is, grades are based on calculations of points on a one hundred–point scale accrued for various assignments, averaged, and translated into a letter grade (A–F). Often, student behaviors are included—points taken off for late work and missing assignments, or bonus points added for more positive behaviors, like having the syllabi signed or bringing in classroom supplies. The points in a student's grade often have more to do with compliance than learning. Grading practices, instructional focus, and even curricula are often inconsistent between different teachers teaching the same courses within their own school, district, or state.

The expanding knowledge of how students learn best and how schools can help all students succeed has raised intriguing questions about feedback, tracking progress, grading, grade point averages (GPAs), and what really constitutes learning. In the limited time teachers have with students, what is *really* essential for students to know and understand in this course or grade level? How can individual teachers and teams of teachers who are teaching the same or similar standards score students more consistently? How might teachers rethink the traditional approach of students accumulating a myriad of points (some related to learning, some not so much) as the basis for doling out grades? Are grades accurate? Are grades even necessary? In addition, as online and self-guided modes play a larger and larger role in education—whether due to improvements in technology, the expansion of personalized learning, or urgent and unusual situations like the COVID-19 pandemic—questions specific to these formats arise. For example, how many online comments constitute an A in the participation percentage of the grade? How might teachers provide useful feedback through the internet? As educators learn new ways to provide meaningful learning opportunities to students, now is a perfect time to rethink the importance and precision of grades.

Standards-based learning (SBL), the approach we advocate in this book, addresses many of these problems. Much has been written about the what, why, and how of standards-based or standards-referenced grading and learning and from a variety of perspectives (Gobble, Onuscheck, Reibel, & Twadell, 2016; Guskey & Bailey, 2001; Heflebower, Hoegh, & Warrick, 2014; Heflebower, Hoegh, Warrick, & Flygare, 2019; Marzano, 2010; O'Connor, 2009a; Reeves, 2011; Schimmer, 2016; Wiggins, 1996; Wormeli, 2006b). Readers familiar with other works on this topic will note similarities to the discussion in this book, though perhaps with somewhat different phrases and descriptions. Different authors espouse varied terminology for similar processes. For example, Heflebower and colleagues (2014) summarized a few commonly used phrases:

> Grant Wiggins (1993, 1996) and [Robert] Marzano (2010) described *standards-referenced grading* as a system in which teachers give students feedback about their proficiency on a set of defined standards and schools report students' levels of performance on the grade-level standards, but students are not moved forward (or backward) to a different set of standards based on their level of competence
>
> *Standards-based grading* is a system of assessing and reporting that describes student progress in relation to standards. In a standards-based system, a student can demonstrate mastery of a set of standards and move immediately to a more challenging set of standards. . . . [A]s soon as a student demonstrates competency with all of the standards for a specific level and subject area, he or she immediately begins working on the next level of standards for that subject area. (pp. 3–4)

An example of this idea might include the following description.

> This means that if a third-grade student masters the entire set of third-grade mathematics standards in two months, that student immediately begins to work on fourth-grade mathematics standards. The same principle applies to all grade levels and subject areas: as soon as a student demonstrates competency with all the standards for a specific level and subject area, he or she immediately begins working on the next level of standards for that subject area. At the same time, a student who does not achieve proficiency on the standards continues to work on those standards until he or she reaches proficiency. Thus, standards-based grading is the process teachers also use for moving toward *competency-based* or *proficiency-based learning and reporting*. (Heflebower et al., 2019, pp. 4–5)

Standards-based learning is similar to competency-based education (CBE) in that students advance or remediate based on their levels of mastery on prioritized standards, and teachers use flexible groupings to do so. In SBL, teachers might pull standards from various grade levels to better match student needs within the existing grade-level structure. In CBE, individualized learning goals and objectives, as well as learner profiles, accompany students in a structure that is more fluid and often involves students being assigned to a grade band (K–2, 3–5, 6–8, 9–10, 11–12), rather than a particular grade level. What we espouse can still be obtained within most existing educational structures.

For our purposes, we will primarily use the more comprehensive term *standards-based learning* (Heflebower et al., 2019). This signifies a culmination for some schools and districts, and a transition to competency-based education for others. The rationale for this broader term is simple. When teachers, schools, and districts move to a standards-based system, it encompasses more than grading. Rather, SBL takes into account modifying curricula, aligning assessments, tracking progress, setting goals with students, providing students with feedback, and aligning instruction, as well as grading and reporting. Please note, however, that the examples from various schools and districts we cite in this book may use various terms according to their local entities. Regardless of the terminology used, each sample we present contributes to the overall implementation of SBL components.

Throughout this resource, we will more thoroughly explain the major components essential for implementing SBL. Briefly, though, modifying curricula simply means that schools and districts must ensure that they define a consistent set of content that can reasonably be taught in the instructional time available. Often, this requires schools and districts to review existing state or provincial standards documents to narrow the foci to those most essential (prioritized) to each grade level and content area or course. Next, developing or revising proficiency scales will bring those prioritized standards to life in the classroom. Proficiency scales organize the prioritized standards into simple, more complex, and most complex knowledge and skills—a learning progression. These help teachers focus planning, instruction, assessment, and feedback to students. They also provide students with clear learning targets against which to track their own learning. Proficiency scales also become the basis for assessment and feedback. Thus, grades truly reflect learning, rather than a simple accumulation of points.

Although the idea of standards-based education is commonplace in many states, provinces, and nations, schools and districts have often implemented it with insufficient attention and contemplation regarding the necessary changes to reporting and grading. Often, schools and districts jump into the deep end by modifying the report card as an initial step. Doing so may create unwarranted angst and misunderstandings by all of those involved (teachers, parents, students). Some schools or districts try to prioritize every single standard equally, which can overburden teachers and inadvertently foster an emphasis on covering material, instead of deeply learning it. Furthermore, rushing too quickly to the evaluation and grading side of SBL may convolute and confuse stakeholders. Slowing the process to prioritize standards; create, revise, and field-test proficiency scales; and revamp classroom assessments will be worth the time and effort.

As a resource, this book will primarily focus on the leader's role in guiding the important work of implementing SBL within your school, district, or both. There is no one right way to adopt SBL practices, but you will obtain well-researched and documented information to assist you in transforming how grading is considered, applied, and shared within your system. We also share thoughtful guidance, samples, and suggestions throughout this handbook—examples gleaned by leading this work in our own schools and districts and the hundreds of educators and students we have worked with around the world.

As leaders, our role is to provide comprehensive efforts within or across our systems, while improving those systems with new learning and information. We think philosopher Alfred North Whitehead (Forbes Quotes, n.d.) described it best when he said, "The art of progress is to preserve order amid change and to preserve change amid order." In fact, transitioning to SBL is a systemic change, commonly referred to as a *second-order change*. It is not merely incremental tweaks to an already-existing system (that is, first-order change). Rather, it involves more significant, substantial changes to the system itself (Marzano, Waters, & McNulty, 2005). It requires educators, students, and parents to rethink and reframe beliefs about grading that they have held for many years. This systemic shift requires reflection, new learning, and changes in practice. Second-order change is rarely if ever linear. It requires flexibility and sometimes involves taking two steps back in order to take ten steps forward. Thus, the first steps a leader must take are to build his or her own knowledge and understanding of SBL, clarify terminology, and craft a multiphase plan.

Build Your Knowledge and Understanding

As building and district leaders, you must be well versed in SBL, and all that it entails. This is no small change—the shift to SBL is exciting, challenging, trying, rewarding, frustrating, and extremely gratifying. It may be the most transformational change on which you ever embark. Attend conferences, read publications, connect with personal learning networks, and build and use associations of colleagues as you lead and monitor this endeavor. See page 50, as well as the references and resources list (page 205) of this book, for recommended resources that provide a foundation of information, research, and perspectives.

As previously mentioned, the focus of this resource is on what leaders need to consider for *leading* the myriad of strategic processes and products that serve as the foundation for solid SBL. We advise you to consider six major components of standards-based systems when building your knowledge prior to implementation.

1. Identifying the priority standards most essential for monitoring and reporting purposes

2. Creating detailed proficiency scales to ensure systemwide understanding of the varying degrees of proficiency

3. Ensuring teachers use proficiency scales for planning instruction, providing students with meaningful feedback, tracking their learning progress, and creating student-focused learning goals

4. Considering how this work affects exceptional students within your system, including both special education and gifted and talented programs

5. Monitoring how students are progressing toward the priority standards through the use of quality common classroom assessments

6. Consistently applying SBL reporting and grading practices, including any conversions back to an existing one hundred–point or A–F scale

All of these essential components serve as the groundwork for SBL. Without attention to these six components, your progress will be limited and may even be counterproductive. In other words, if significant parts are omitted, you may find yourself instigating turmoil without thorough implementation and follow-through, creating a hurricane over otherwise calm waters. For instance, if you neglect to ensure that teachers are using proficiency scales, you may find that consistency is lacking from teacher to teacher within the same grade or course. If some teachers continue business as usual, it will stall larger SBL efforts. The absence of proficiency scales also limits effectiveness in unit planning, quality feedback, and classroom assessments.

As you work through these efforts, be mindful of controlling what you can. Ideally, the work encompassed in items 1, 2, 4, and 6 should be done at a district level. It is important that the priority standards are consistent from school to school, as well as the use of proficiency scales and ways in which exceptional students will be addressed. If you find yourself in a situation where districtwide work is not in your purview, then certainly begin this work within your own building—items 3 and 5 in the previous list are excellent starting points for individual schools. Yet, be cautious that adjustments may be warranted later on, when a district focus comes into play. How different principals guarantee that priority standards, proficiency scales, and common assessments are used with students may look a bit differently based on structures in their schools, grade levels served, and the number of students and staff in their buildings. The way each local school monitors student progress may also fluctuate. The greater the consistency across schools in a district, however, the better.

Clarify Terminology

Closely related to building your knowledge and understanding is clarifying terminology. It is essential for a school or district to use language consistently and establish shared definitions to support common understanding and common practice.

> It is important as a leader to decide on and clarify the language you will consistently use in your school (or district). You need language for the standards you will continually reference and report about. You may also need terminology for the classroom components that specify learning for students, as well as for assessment components. For instance, you may elect to use the language of *prioritized standards* (Heflebower et al., 2014), *power standards* (Ainsworth, 2003), *learning targets* (Moss & Brookhart, 2012), or *essential learnings* (Wiggins & McTighe, 2005), to name a few. Decide on the terminology you will use, share it, and use it consistently. Do not underestimate this step. If school personnel continually interchange the curriculum and assessment language, teachers, parents, and students may perceive changes to the content or processes when there are none. (Heflebower, 2020, p. 198)

As noted previously, many of the concepts central to SBL have several different names. Before beginning this work, establish the set of terms that your district or site will use. Figure I.1 (page 6) provides a glossary of the commonly used terms to assist you in deciding on your common language.

Figure I.2 (page 8) shares an additional sample set of definitions from Heartland Area Education Agency in Iowa. This example was part of a set of documents the agency provided to area districts in support of SBL work.

These sample definitions may be useful as you create or compare your own documents. Always consider clarity, consistency, and communication. Sharing such definitions with your system will add clarity and coherence in verbiage throughout your school or district.

Curriculum Terms	*Curriculum:* Guaranteed course of study and learning objectives that integrates standards, instructional strategies, materials, and assessments to ensure that all students are able to achieve standards
	Resources: Materials used for instruction that may include teachers' editions, websites, and other print and online sources
	Pacing guide: A document that provides sequenced grade-level expectations over the four quarters of a school year
	Priority standard: A learning standard that a school district determined to be of particular importance for the students based on data and professional judgment to be important in life, in school, and on the state assessment. Priority standards are standards that endure over time, give students leverage in other content areas, and prepare them for the next grade. Priority standards are revisited on an annual basis so that revisions can be made as new data are available (also known as a *power standard*).
	Proficiency scale: A defined learning progression or set of learning targets for a specific topic, relative to a given standard. It shows teachers and students what proficiency looks like, what knowledge and skills students need to achieve proficiency, and how students might go beyond proficiency (Heflebower et al., 2019).
	Learning targets: Classroom objectives you will teach most likely in a lesson or series of a few lessons. These are directly linked to your priority standards, and they are often found as elements on your proficiency scales.
	Progress monitoring: Regular use of student achievement information to track students' progress toward a goal, or a school's or district's progress toward a goal for increased student achievement
	Response to Intervention (RTI): A framework used by educators to help students who are struggling with a set of skills or concepts; every teacher will use various interventions (teaching procedures) with any student to help them succeed in the classroom—not just students with special needs or learning disabilities.
	Tier 1 indicators: Specific indicators used to determine whether state and district learning expectations have been achieved as evidenced by student achievement information.
	Tier 1 interventions: The general education core curriculum, instruction, and social and behavioral supports for all students, with adequate differentiation of instruction
	Tier 2 indicators: Specific actions taken by adults to elicit student achievement outcomes (for example, 100 percent of faculty, student support staff, and administrators will participate in the review of student achievement data)
	Tier 2 interventions: Short-term interventions for struggling students who have not responded adequately to the Tier I core curriculum and differentiation of instruction. These interventions are part of the general education system.
	Tier 3 indicators: Narrative analysis of relationship between Tiers 1 and 2. These indicators can include conclusions, questions raised, next steps, and so on.
	Tier 3 interventions: More intensive or individualized short-term interventions for students who fail to respond adequately to the Tier 1 core curriculum and differentiation of instruction. These interventions are part of the general education system.
Large Cycle Assessments	**Summative** Summative assessments are generally given at the end of the course, unit, or lesson. Summative assessments provide students the opportunity to demonstrate what they have learned. Summative assessments are usually given one time per year and are often used for accountability purposes. Examples include state or provincial assessments, ACT, SAT, and end-of-course exams.
Short Cycle Assessments	**Formative** Formative assessments are generally given during instruction with the primary goal of improving or modifying instruction to promote student achievement of intended learning outcomes. Formative assessment occurs minute-to-minute or day-to-day. Examples include checking for understanding, quality questioning and listening, use of writing prompts, use of clickers, and self-reflection.

Mid-Cycle (Interim) Assessments	Interim assessments fall between large cycle and small cycle and are intended to (1) evaluate students' knowledge and skills relative to a specific set of academic goals (prioritized standards) and (2) inform decisions both at and beyond the classroom level (school, feeder, and district).
	Interim assessments are usually given three to six times per year at the essential learning and indicator(s) level. Examples include interim assessments, Measures of Academic Progress (MAP) assessments, and Developmental Reading Assessment (DRA).
Predictive Assessments	Some assessments are given primarily to predict success on other high-stakes assessments. For example, the PLAN exam predicts success on the ACT exam.
Required State Assessments	These are state funded and supported, they must be conducted, and data are collected at the state and district level.
	English language assessments are required for students who have been identified as having a language background other than English. The assessment measures the progress of students in attaining English proficiency in comprehension, speaking, listening, reading, and writing. Results are used for summative and formative purposes.
	Statewide assessments required per mandate that all public schools align to the state standards. In most states, students in grades 3–10 are tested every year in reading, mathematics, and writing, and grades 5, 8, and 10 are also often tested in science and social studies. Some states also require end-of-course (EOC) exams to fulfill requirements of the Every Student Succeeds Act (2015). Results for such exams are used both for summative and formative purposes.
	Statewide alternative assessments are the alternate version of the statewide assessment designed for students with severe cognitive disabilities. Results are used for summative and formative purposes.
Required District Assessments	These are district required and funded.
	Classroom-based measures (CBMs) are progress-monitoring assessments used for students who have been identified as needing targeted or intensive services under the RTI model.
	ACT-PLAN is currently sometimes required for certain grade levels in certain states. This assessment predicts success on the ACT exam and also identifies career preparation for students. Results are used mostly for predictive purposes.
	The Preliminary SAT, also known as the PSAT/NMSQT (National Merit Scholarship Qualifying Test), is a practice version of the SAT exam and tests skills in reading, writing, and mathematics.
	Cognitive Abilities Test (CogAT) is sometimes required for all students who are recommended for gifted-and-talented services. This test measures students' abilities in reasoning and problem solving using verbal, quantitative, and nonverbal (spatial) symbols. This test is administered to students at the end of specific grades or beginning of others or as determined by local districts. Results are used for predictive purposes.
	Developmental Reading Assessment (DRA) is sometimes used as an assessment to meet the requirements mandating that all students are reading at grade-level proficiency by the end of third grade and that those who are not at grade level are put on an individualized literacy plan (ILP). DRA2 results are used for summative, formative, and predictive purposes.
	End of Course (EOC) assessment is required by some districts for all students enrolled in specific high school courses. Results are used for both summative and formative purposes. In addition to interim assessments, end of course assessments should be developed to standardize outcome expectations for honors courses to allow for weighting of grades.
	Interim assessments will be required in core content areas as they are developed. These quality assessments will be developed to measure student learning of the district prioritized standards. Results will be used for summative and formative purposes—with an emphasis on formative.
	Northwest Evaluation Association's Measurement of Academic Progress (MAP). These computerized tests are adaptive and offered in reading, language usage, science, and mathematics. When taking a MAP test, the difficulty of each question is based on how well the student answers all of the previous questions. If the student answers correctly, questions become more difficult. If the student answers incorrectly, the questions become easier. In an optimal test, a student answers approximately half the items correctly and half incorrectly. The final score is an estimate of the student's achievement level.

Source: © 2007 by Tammy Heflebower.

Figure I.1: Sample definitions.

Accommodations, Modifications, and Interventions	*Accommodations:* Accommodations do not change the expectations for students. They simply provide opportunities for more equitable access to grade-level content. An example might be more space on the page, more time to complete a task, or moving to a quiet location. Available to all students.
	Modifications: The learning target or standard is modified so the expectations for the student are changed. Modification is done by a student's individualized education plan (IEP) team only.
	Interventions: Focused instruction on a targeted performance deficit, identified through diagnostic assessment. Interventions are provided in addition to the core curriculum with the intent of improving a student's proficiency.
Assessments	Tasks that allow students to show what they know and can do against established learning targets and goals.
Summative Assessment	Tasks that allow students to show what they know and can do against established learning targets and goals. They are often given at the end of a period of learning to signify the summation of learning and mark where a student is at a given time in relation to a standard or learning target.
Formative Assessment	Instruments and processes used to gather information to adjust teaching and learning as needed. Formative assessments can be used before, during, and after learning. Their most typical use is during instruction so teachers can make adjustments to improve learning. Often referred to as *formative assessment practices* or *processes* to denote that formative assessment is not a piece of paper but a process that involves different types of gathering evidence.
Screening Assessment	A component used in standards-based or -referenced learning. It is often an assessment task that is used as a preassessment in order to determine where to begin instruction for a student group of students. In order to know if the system is healthy, we need to identify that at least 80 percent of students can be successful with no additional supports or interventions.
Diagnostic Assessment	Another component of standards-based or -referenced learning. In order to apply appropriate interventions, the practitioner must be able to diagnostically assess, often using a preassessment for individual students, where the student's skill deficit occurs within the learning progression. These may be used by all teachers or for those students moving in from other districts.
Progress Monitoring	Used to assess students' academic performance, to quantify a student's rate of improvement or responsiveness to instruction, and to evaluate the effectiveness of instruction.
Communication Plan	Facilitates effective communications with the various audiences having a stake in the project. It describes how communication will occur and generally includes the following. • Communication objectives • Communication method and frequency • Target audiences and key content for the communications
Consensus Building	A process used to bring stakeholders to a common understanding or commitment regarding a topic; competencies, resources, and motivation for attainment of knowledge and skills. It ultimately culminates in common agreements among the group.
Curriculum: Intended, Enacted, Assessed	*Intended:* Curriculum that was written to be used in the classroom. *Enacted:* Curriculum that was actually taught in the classroom. *Assessed:* Curriculum that was assessed through the formative and summative assessment processes.

Source: © 2020 by Heartland Area Education Agency. Used with permission.

Figure I.2: Definitions for standards-based learning and grading.

Craft a Multiphase Plan

In order to enact the six aforementioned components (page 4), a leader must thoughtfully craft a multiphase plan, as well as a corresponding timeline for all phases of SBL implementation. As previously mentioned, implementing SBL requires a thorough and thoughtful set of processes and products. We recommend reviewing and revising your multiphase plan throughout your implementation efforts. You will likely find places within it for slowing down your efforts and others for expediting the components within your plan. Having a plan signifies a seriousness about the work. It helps all staff better understand the time frames and expectations of your SBL efforts.

The multiphase process we suggest in this book has five stages, which address all six components of SBL in a workable manner.

- Phase 1: Curriculum and Communication

- Phase 2: Alignment and Capacity Building

- Phase 3: Universal Implementation, Communication, and Reporting Systems

- Phase 4: Continuation, Revision, and Expansion

- Phase 5: Monitoring, Tracking Student Achievement, and Celebrating

The work begins in phase 1 with a careful process for clarifying which standards are most important. Once priority standards are determined, those standards are expanded into learning progressions, or proficiency scales. Phase 1 encapsulates the first two SBL components and provides a greater degree of specificity about each prioritized standard. Phase 2 is about alignment and capacity building. During this phase, work occurs on aligning classroom instruction and assessments to the proficiency scales. This alignment among standards, instruction, and assessment is foundational for students to be able to track their progress, obtain meaningful feedback, and set learning goals. It captures much of SBL components 3 and 5. This curriculum work is somewhat arduous, but a select group of teachers, known as a design team, can efficiently draft priority standards, proficiency scales, and aligned assessments (Heflebower et al., 2014). Alternatively, existing grade-level or content-area teams, such as collaborative teams within a professional learning community (PLC), could undertake this work. This is particularly applicable if an individual school (rather than a district) is shifting toward SBL.

All the while, you are building capacity within your system for not only doing the initial work, but sharing it and obtaining feedback from your system. Most often, this occurs in the core areas of mathematics, English language arts (ELA), science, and social studies, but this approach can be modified based on local needs. During phase 3, prioritization, proficiency scales, and aligned assessments are completed for the remaining content areas. Additionally, the needs of exceptional learners are addressed (SBL component 4), and your implementation plan is underway. In phase 3, you also prepare for any modifications of your reporting systems. In phase 4, your implementation efforts are continued, and revisions are enacted. SBL component 5, modifying reporting documents, is in progress during this phase and piloted with specific grade levels or content areas. Phase 5 culminates your work by ensuring you monitor implementation efforts, track student achievement (connecting it to local, state, and national assessments as warranted), and celebrate your many successes at instituting a SBL system and mindset. Figure I.3 (page 10) displays the multiphase plan with a detailed list of activities for each phase. Within this book, we dedicate a chapter to each phase and explicitly describe the components listed within each phase in greater detail.

Phase 1 Curriculum and Communication	Phase 2 Alignment and Capacity Building	Phase 3 Universal Implementation, Communication, and Reporting Systems	Phase 4 Continuation, Revision, and Expansion	Phase 5 Monitoring, Tracking Student Achievement, and Celebrating
Design a guaranteed and viable curriculum. • Priority standards • Proficiency scales • Feedback and revision • Pacing guides **Draft an initial implementation and communication plan.** **Educate key leaders.** • Board of education • Staff leaders **Assemble a guiding team.** **Analyze existing grading practices.** **Establish digital storage for standards and scales.**	**Begin rolling out standards and scales.** • Seek feedback from teachers. • Review and incorporate teacher feedback. • Begin field-testing standards and scales. **Align instruction and assessment.** • Align proficiency scales with instructional activities and resources. • Share methods for using scales for feedback and goal setting. • Train teacher design teams on assessment literacy. • Align quality classroom assessments. • Train teachers on inter-rater reliability processes. • Share strategies for intra-rater reliability. **Expand your efforts.** • Continue revising proficiency scales for core content areas. • Prioritize standards and draft proficiency scales for all other content areas. • Continue working with technology for storage and access.	**Expand work in non-core content areas.** • Align quality classroom assessments with standards and scales. • Request that design teams field-test standards and scales. • Obtain feedback from design teams and revise. • Solicit feedback from teachers not on design teams and revise. **Continue to train staff on assessment literacy.** **Include teachers of exceptional learners.** **Plan and initiate the rollout.** • Decide the progression of the rollout. • Announce the implementation plan. • Require teachers to use proficiency scales. • Continue to educate and update the board of education. **Prepare for reporting systems.** • Finalize technology for electronic reporting. • Field-test the gradebook.	**Seek feedback from teachers about classroom assessments in core content areas.** **Begin the implementation rollout.** • Announce and share written plans with all staff. • Implement proficiency scales in selected grade levels. • Implement common classroom assessments in selected grade levels. **Continue preparation in non-core content areas.** • Revise proficiency scales as needed. • Align quality classroom assessments with standards and scales. • Train non-core teachers on inter-rater reliability processes. • Share intra-rater reliability strategies. **Communicate with stakeholders.** • Organize learning opportunities for all staff. • Share belief statements. • Conduct focus groups with students and parents.	**Expand implementation to additional grade levels.** • Proficiency scales • Common classroom assessments • New reporting systems • Focus groups with students and parents **Continue tracking correlations among scores.** **Train incoming stakeholders.** • New staff • New parents • New board members **Celebrate success.**

	Share information. • Engage in learning opportunities for additional learning leaders. • Communicate initial implementation plan to key leaders. • Establish core beliefs with teacher and leader teams. • Send scouts to learn from other schools and districts. • Continue to educate the board of education. • Educate parents. **Monitor implementation.**		• Provide board members opportunities to observe new systems in action. **Implement new reporting systems for selected grades.** • Ensure families understand new reporting practices. • Finalize technology needs. • Track correlations among scales, common assessments, and state assessments.	

Source: Adapted from Heflebower, 2020; Heflebower et al., 2014.

Figure I.3: The complete multiphase plan.

While this multiphase plan is purposeful and quite effective, you can and should customize it to your school or district. You may find that you need additional components or phases, or that you can omit some of the activities suggested throughout this book. Such adaptations may be completely appropriate for your local setting and your specific needs. The multiphase plan is a multiyear undertaking. For example, depending on your starting point and the size of your district, phase 1 might take one or two years. Phase 2 often lasts two years; if some components (such as proficiency scales) were already in existence or underway, it might only take one year. It is important to note that your local setting may move faster or slower than suggested, accelerating or decelerating any of the mentioned components. If in doubt, go slower rather than faster. Remember, this is a mammoth change that affects all staff, students, and stakeholders, and it may feel overwhelming at times. In each chapter, we recommend ways to lean on consultants, networks, and associations for guidance and support.

As you craft and follow your multiphase plan, there are many ways to use this book. If you have already implemented some aspects of SBL, you might compare your previous work to the activities shown in figure I.3. Check off components completed in your building or district, then denote practices or products currently underway, and yet other components that may be new to you, or to which you may need to attend in the future. It may be most useful for you to read selected sections of this book related to those new and unaddressed components you identify in such a review. Perhaps you simply want to see how other districts communicated or created documents helpful to implementation. Not only will you find examples from schools and districts throughout the phases and corresponding chapters, but also in the various appendices. If you are just starting out with SBL, you might proceed in a more thorough and sequential manner, and thus use this book as a procedural guide. Whatever way best suits your needs, we hope you find this book practical and valuable.

PHASE 1
Curriculum and Communication

In phase 1, you will review existing efforts and jump into some of the most central components of SBL. Some districts will find they have done a great deal of work in phase 1, so crafting proficiency scales may be the biggest undertaking. Others may find themselves in a major overhaul and remain in this phase for quite a while. Either way, take the time you need to do quality work. For most districts, the proficiency scale development will be a yearlong process. Whatever your situation, keep in mind that such a transformational change will require monitoring and reflecting. Check in with staff often to ensure the pacing is appropriate and the workload manageable.

To begin SBL implementation, this chapter highlights the following activities.

- Design a guaranteed and viable curriculum for core content areas.
- Draft an initial implementation and communication plan.
- Educate key leaders.
- Assemble a guiding team.
- Analyze existing grading practices and beliefs.
- Establish digital storage for standards and scales.

These activities within the phase are not necessarily sequential; you might work on several components concurrently.

Design a Guaranteed and Viable Curriculum for Core Content Areas

One of the major activities in phase 1 is designing a *guaranteed and viable curriculum* for core content areas. This term, coined by Robert J. Marzano (2003; Eaker & Marzano, 2020), simply refers to a set of essential content in a certain grade level or course that all students will learn (guaranteed) and that can be taught within the amount of time provided (viable). Because most standards documents include far more content than a teacher could possibly cover in a school year, schools and districts need to prioritize and select the standards that all students in each grade level or course will learn. This makes the curriculum manageable and eliminates variance between classrooms. To facilitate teaching and learning, a guaranteed and viable curriculum should also include proficiency scales or learning progressions that describe levels of knowledge and skill within each standard or set of closely related standards. Students then receive instruction, assessment, and feedback based on these scales.

A guaranteed and viable curriculum is the foundational step for SBL because in most states and provinces, there are still far too many, often repetitive, standards. This process not only helps clarify the most essential sets of knowledge and skills for students, but also helps ensure teachers possess a deep understanding of those specific sets of knowledge and skills. As they review the curriculum throughout the prioritization and proficiency scale processes, teachers often remark, "I now better understand the standards I teach." That deep understanding helps as they design units and tailor instructional activities to align to the expectations of the prioritized standards.

The best time to conduct curriculum work is when your state, province, or other education agency is updating or modifying its standards. Most localities review and revise educational standards every few years, so this is a convenient time to engage in prioritization and scale design. Completing this initial work in tandem with that review makes great sense and will also refrain from signifying monumental school or district changes at that point and time. This is not to imply that standards prioritization and scale design are secretive or subversive. We simply argue that there is no need to cause angst within your system by announcing a massive grading change at this point in time. In fact, doing so might actually hijack your efforts and cause negativity or pushback because the changes are so radically different from the present system. The curriculum and assessment components of the work—incremental steps toward the ultimate goal of a holistic standards-based system—can be conducted for their own sake before broadening the scope of the changes to SBL. However, if you cannot or will not wait for a naturally occurring standards-revision cycle, then begin the work as you see fit. Students deserve our very best, and engaging in this work may not perfectly coincide with a state or provincial edict.

The following sections provide additional guidance on prioritizing standards, drafting proficiency scales, soliciting feedback on the curriculum, and creating pacing guides.

Priority Standards

Begin by identifying your priority standards. *Priority standards* are the ones on which teachers focus instruction, assessment, and feedback in SBL. These are also the standards that will be reported in your standards-referenced reporting document (that is, the report card). In other words, the work of prioritization determines which standards are the most essential, meaning those that you will ensure all students attain. Selecting a focused set of standards on which teachers can feasibly provide instruction in the time available is what makes a curriculum viable. To ensure the curriculum is guaranteed, leaders must coordinate teams of teachers to do this work on a schoolwide or districtwide level so that the instructional focus does not vary from classroom to classroom. During phase 1, most districts focus on the core content areas—mathematics, English language arts, science, and social studies. Even more specifically, we recommend beginning with a more linear content area like mathematics, as teachers are not only prioritizing the standards but also learning the process of prioritization. This may expedite the work as generalist teachers in elementary levels work on multiple sets of content areas throughout the phases.

The remaining standards not deemed priorities are identified as supporting standards. *Supporting standards* (also known as *supplementary standards*) are still taught and may or may not be assessed, but the priority standards are the basis of assessing and reporting student performance (Heflebower et al., 2019). Although it is still important to teach standards that are not deemed priority, teachers devote significant time and resources to ensuring that all students master the priority standards. For example, if thirty standards are listed in your state standards documents for a grade level or course, teachers might prioritize fifteen of those and teach the remaining fifteen as subcomponents of the prioritized ones. Alternatively, teachers might teach low-priority standards independently (that is, as the focus of a lesson) but spend less time on them.

Ideally, decisions about which standards are prioritized will be made collaboratively by teacher teams at the school or district level. The process of identifying priority standards is best conducted by a *design team* of forty to fifty teachers from across the district. If the work is being done by a single smaller school, all teachers may be involved. If your school is quite large in size, consider a subset of teachers (perhaps three per grade level or course) to conduct the work. During this process, content-area expert teachers will review existing state standards, use a vetting process to determine the priority standards, and conduct horizontal and vertical alignment. Thus, the team should be representative of the grade levels and content areas in your school or district. Obviously, if you are a very small district, you may involve most or all teachers in certain grade levels and content areas. If this is your situation, you might initiate collaboration with other smaller districts, either directly or through the leadership of an intermediate agency within your region.

Within any educational agency, there are some teachers who really like curriculum and assessment work and thrive in discussions of what they teach and how they assess it. Plain and simple, they are well-versed local experts, ideally positioned to perform this work. However, involving too many teachers (more than fifty) early in the process will not only slow the progress of the initial work, but also strain the system with the need to find time for the work, hire substitute teachers, and so on. Instead, consider this design team as the first in a series of district committees. This team will draft the first version of the priority standards before obtaining feedback from other teachers. Later, additional teachers may elect or be recruited to join the teams that conduct other components of the process, such as assessment and instructional alignment (see page 71). This way, an increasing number of teachers are involved throughout the process, yet the burden of time and effort at any given point remains manageable.

Our recommended approach to prioritizing standards involves (1) analyzing standards documents to identify critical content, (2) selecting a preliminary set of prioritized standards, (3) categorizing the standards by topic or theme, and (4) reviewing the final categories to avoid significant omissions of knowledge and skills. These four steps provide a structure for school leaders to explain the process to teachers and monitor teams' progress.

While this basic process works well in most situations, individuals and teams may have unique needs that require adjustments. For example, if some teachers have performed prioritization work before or are extremely experienced content experts, you can differentiate the process to acknowledge what they bring to the table. Table 1.1 presents variations for these situations. In essence, these modifications honor teachers' knowledge and expertise during the initial part of the process to capture increased support and buy-in.

TABLE 1.1: DIFFERENTIATING THE PRIORITIZATION PROCESS

Use the basic four-step process if . . .	Differentiate the basic process in order to value previous work if . . .	Differentiate the basic process to value teacher experience and content expertise if . . .
You have less experienced teachers on the team or you have a very tight timeline. You are not as concerned about drawing out the content expertise of your teachers. You simply want to get the work completed. You have few, if any, meeting structures in place. You may have to get this done during a limited number of workdays. You don't have a teachers' union, or your union is typically supportive of your efforts around curriculum.	Your school or district has identified priority standards in the past but needs to align them to new standards, such as the Common Core State Standards or Next Generation Science Standards. Your staff are already very familiar with your state's standards documents. You have structures and processes already in place for engaging in collaborative work. You have an involved teachers' union, and its members are amenable to the alignment work that is necessary.	You have very experienced staff members on the team. Teachers have done curriculum work before and are content experts. You have structures and processes already in place for engaging in collaborative work. You have a strong teachers' union and must often defend curriculum work and get buy-in for structures and processes.

Source: Heflebower et al., 2014, p. 21.

Before the prioritization process, establish the criteria that the design team should consider when evaluating standards. Consider these five criteria to determine which standards to prioritize.

1. **Endurance:** Knowledge and skills that will last beyond a class period or course

2. **Leverage:** Knowledge and skills that cross over into many domains of learning

3. **Readiness:** Knowledge and skills important to subsequent content or courses

4. **Teacher judgment:** Knowledge of content area and ability to identify more- and less-important content

5. **Assessment:** Student opportunity to learn content that will be assessed (Heflebower et al., 2014, p. 18)

Next, allocate time and space for the work to happen. Although time and space may seem like straightforward concerns, ensuring that teachers have time for important conversations and space with the appropriate materials for their work is extremely important to the successful completion of prioritization work. Paying attention to these details communicates to teachers that their work is important and prevents small problems or time constraints from hindering efforts.

Ideally, standards prioritization and proficiency scale creation (see page 25) is done one content area at a time. Although scales should ultimately be written for all content areas, we recommend beginning with mathematics since it is quite linear in nature, which will provide momentum for the process and give educators valuable experience. Once teachers and leaders are familiar with the process, they can address the remaining content areas. For each content area (mathematics, ELA, social studies, science, and so on), plan for one and a half to two full days (ten to twelve hours) of concentrated team time to identify priority standards. If you are prioritizing standards in several content areas simultaneously, you can compress the amount of time needed by training all the content area teams together and then splitting them into content teams for the rest of the work. The sample plan in figure 1.1 was created for Jefferson County Public Schools in Colorado. Here you will notice the estimated number of days for facilitating prioritization of standards, using the Marzano Resources Critical Concepts (see page 21 for more details), the projected outcomes for each session, and the possible related resources to enhance the work.

Day and Time	Topic	Responsibility	Possible Resources
Day 1 Morning	• Direct instruction regarding the big picture of the project, including prioritization, proficiency scales, and quality classroom assessment design – Sometimes we elect to do an abbreviated overview with more complete direct instruction on each component right before the team completes that portion of the work. • Direct instruction on the *what*, *why*, and *how* of standards prioritization		• Handout and presentation • *A School Leader's Guide to Standards-Based Grading*
Day 1 Afternoon	• Work time for teams to determine prioritized standards and create measurement topics with guided practice Or • Work time to review and revise Critical Concepts measurement topics with guided practice	Content teams	• Colorado Academic Standards for mathematics • Critical Concepts for mathematics • Electronic prioritization template • Tech support available or on call
Day 2 Morning	• Work time to complete prioritization process and move toward vertical reviews	Trainers	• Computers with electronic templates loaded • Cloud-based documents for simultaneous drafting and revisions • Chart paper and markers

Source: © 2018 by Tammy Heflebower.

Figure 1.1: Prioritization and proficiency scales development process agenda.

It is best if work in each content area can be finished in one continuous session. However, we recognize that this is not always possible. If continuous time is not available, leaders can use existing meeting times, such as collaborative team meetings, after-school meetings, monthly curriculum meetings, or professional development meetings. When using a series of short meetings, it is important to keep in mind that the work may take longer. For example, work that could be accomplished in five or six consecutive hours will probably take seven or eight one-hour meetings.

Whichever meeting structure they use, leaders can facilitate the work by providing appropriate space and materials for each team. It is best if each grade-level group has a space in which to collaborate (for example, a round table for each group). Each grade-level group should also have access to the following supplies.

- A copy of existing state standards documents for the content area of focus for each member of the group

- Note paper

- A copy of your state or provincial assessment frameworks documents

- Highlighters

- Scissors

- Sticky notes

- Chart paper and markers

As noted previously, the design team uses a four-step process to navigate the actual prioritization of the standards. Here, we explain each step of the basic process and provide differentiation strategies for the unique needs of various groups. Ideally, the process described here will be used by teams of teachers. However, individual teachers can also use the process to prioritize standards on their own.

Step 1: Analyze Standards Documents

Prior to the first meeting, distribute copies of applicable content-area state standards documents to the teachers on the team and request that they read through the documents and become familiar with the content before coming to the first meeting. If it is impossible for teachers to complete this work beforehand, allow about an hour for teachers to read the documents at the first meeting. Because all teachers involved in the process must have a firm understanding of the current standards documents and reading through them is the only way for team members to gain that understanding, all groups of teachers, regardless of previous prioritization work or teachers' levels of experience, *must* complete this step. However, if teachers are already very familiar with the standards documents, allocate a shorter amount of time for reading them. Additionally, when working with highly experienced teachers, postpone this step until after step 2 in order to *first* draw on experienced teachers' expertise regarding what content is essential in their courses. Have them draft an initial set of prioritized standards before comparing that work to state or provincial standards documents.

Step 2: Select Preliminary Priority Standards

After reading the standards documents, teachers independently identify two levels of content in the documents: (1) priority standards and (2) supporting standards. Limit the time spent on this task to thirty to forty minutes. This will keep teachers from deliberating too long over any one standard; the goal is to get a gut reaction about the importance of each standard. Remind teachers that their first impression is probably the most reliable at this stage.

After they complete their individual selections, teachers form grade-level or course-specific groups. Teachers compare their ratings with those of others in their group and explain their decisions. Then the team considers the criteria of endurance, leverage, readiness, teacher judgment, and assessments (see page 16). This allows the teachers to check their initial judgments against the criteria and examine their thinking. The goal is for groups to reach a general consensus about which standards should be prioritized for their grade level or course, and which are secondary. This step takes approximately one to two hours.

If your school has an existing set of prioritized content and needs to check its alignment to new standards documents, such as revised state standards, teams can use a highlighting procedure to identify various levels of alignment (rather than importance) between existing priority standards and the new standards. Select different colors (for example, green, yellow, and red) to denote the following levels of alignment.

- Content that appears in the same course at the same grade level in existing priority standards and new standards. These strongly aligned standards likely do not need to change.

- Content that is present in both the school's priority standards and the new standards documents but at a different grade level or in a different course. These standards will need to move to the grade level at which they appear in the new standards documents, since students will ultimately be assessed at the new grade level.

- Content represented in the new standards but not in existing standards. These standards are then evaluated according to the criteria for prioritizing standards. Those added to the existing priority standards should be added at the grade level in which they appear within the new standards.

As in the basic process, the end goal is for grade-level or course-level teams to reach consensus about which standards should be prioritized for each grade level.

If your team consists of highly experienced teachers, have them use their professional judgment to independently list important content for students to learn at their grade level or in their courses *before* they look at any standards documents. Next, have them discuss their lists with other grade-level or course teammates, explaining what they listed and why. Here, the goal is for teachers to agree on which standards should be most important at their grade level *before* they look at any standards documents. Then, distribute copies of the standards documents to each teacher for his or her grade level or course and give teachers time to read the documents. Ask teachers to compare their lists of important content to the standards documents and fill in any important content or information that they initially failed to list. They should also cross out information in their lists that does not appear in the standards documents. Again, the goal is for each grade-level team to agree on which standards should be prioritized.

The example in figure 1.2 represents a portion of a document that is the result of multiple conversations about standards among horizontal grade-level teachers as well as vertical reviews from teachers of adjacent grade levels. Please note that the teachers assigned a label of *priority* or *supporting* to all grade-level standards (indicated in bold font), but not individual indicators within standards (indicated by nonbold font).

Teachers should also address the amount of time necessary to teach all of the standards noted for each grade level. Each grade-level team should discuss and denote the number of days that will be required to teach each prioritized standard to mastery, with one class period equaling one day. Noting the time required to teach next to each standard will help the team further prioritize the standards: those that take more time to develop conceptual understanding will obviously require more time for teaching. Teams should consider whether any standards can be combined, and which standards should be less emphasized according to the criteria previously discussed (endurance, leverage, readiness, teacher judgment, and assessment). Revisiting these criteria during revision throughout the process of identifying priorities can help teams further clarify and affirm, and sometimes change, their initial decisions.

Step 3: Categorize Priority Standards

Steps 3 and 4 always take place sequentially regardless of whether previous work has been completed or teachers are experienced. These steps occur after the standards have been prioritized and agreed on by each grade-level or course group. In this step, teams create categories of standards. We recommend writing each standard on a sticky note or slip of paper to facilitate this work. To save time, teachers can cut apart the chart paper where they identified the priority standards. Once each prioritized standard has been cut from standards documents, teams group the standards into common themes by arranging the prioritized standards into categories. This should only take about fifteen to thirty minutes. A group prioritizing standards in ELA, for example, might organize their standards within the CCSS strands (Reading Foundations, Reading of Literary Text, Reading of Informational Text, Writing, Speaking and Listening, and Language; NGA & CCSSO, 2010a). A group working in mathematics might organize the standards into the CCSS domains (Operations and Algebraic Thinking, Number and Operations in Base Ten, Fractions, Measurement and Data, Geometry; NGA & CCSSO, 2010b).

Another resource that can guide categorization of priority standards is the lists of measurement topics that are available as part of the Critical Concepts (Simms, 2016)—a focused set of topics that encompass standards for the core content areas in grades K–12 developed by analysts at Marzano Resources. The measurement topics for each content area and grade band provide a manageable set of broad categories of content based on analysis of the Common Core and other standards documents. As an example, figure 1.3 (page 22) lists the measurement topics for middle school mathematics. Predeveloped resources such as this can expedite the process of prioritizing and categorizing standards. A school or district could begin with these measurement topics and scales and

SECOND GRADE		
DOMAIN: Reading Standards for Literature		
Standard Code	**Strand: Key Ideas and Details (KID)**	**Rating**
2.RL.KID.1	**1. Ask and answer such questions as *who, what, where, when, why,* and *how* to demonstrate understanding of key details in a text.**	Priority
2.RL.KID.1.1.b	Ask questions to demonstrate understanding of key details in a story or poem.	
2.RL.KID.1.2.c	Respond to questions about key details in a story or poem.	
2.RL.KID.2	**2. Recount stories, including fables and folktales from diverse cultures, and determine their central message, lesson, or moral.**	Supporting
2.RL.KID.2.1.b	Retell a story, fable, or folktale from diverse cultures using key details.	
2.RL.KID.2.2.b	Identify a main idea or lesson of a story, fable, or folktale from diverse cultures.	
2.RL.KID.3	**3. Describe how characters in a story respond to major events and challenges.**	Priority
2.RL.KID.3.1.b	Describe the response of characters in a story to major events.	
2.RL.KID.3.2.b	Describe the response of characters in a story to challenges.	
OSC Code	**Strand: Craft and Structure (CAS)**	**Rating**
2.RL.CAS.4	**4. Describe how words and phrases (for example, regular beats, alliteration, rhymes, repeated lines) supply rhythm and meaning to a story, poem, or song.**	Supporting
2.RL.CAS.4.1.b	Relate the author's choice of words and phrases to the rhythm of a story, poem, or song.	
2.RL.CAS.4.2.b	Relate the author's choice of rhythm, words, and phrases to the meaning of a story, poem, or song.	
2.RL.CAS.4.3.a	Identify the use of regular beats, alliteration, rhymes, and repeated lines in a story, poem, or song.	
2.RL.CAS.5	**5. Describe the overall structure of a story, including how the beginning introduces the story and the ending concludes the action.**	Priority
2.RL.CAS.5.1.a	Identify the beginning, middle, and ending of a story.	
2.RL.CAS.5.2.a	Identify the setting, characters, problem, and resolution in a story.	
2.RL.CAS.5.3.b	Describe the introduction to a story through its setting, characters, and problem.	
2.RL.CAS.5.4.b	Describe the conclusion to a story through its setting, characters, and resolution to a problem.	
2.RL.CAS.5.5.b	Describe the changes in the setting, characters, and problem over the course of a story.	
2.RL.CAS.6	**6. Acknowledge differences in the points of view of characters, including by speaking in a different voice for each character when reading dialogue aloud.**	Supporting
2.RL.CAS.6.1.a	Identify the point of view from which a character tells a story in a story, poem, drama, or song.	
2.RL.CAS.6.2.b	Describe the different points of view of characters in a story, poem, drama, or song.	
OSC Code	**Strand: Integration of Knowledge and Ideas (IKI)**	**Rating**
2.RL.IKI.7	**7. Use information gained from the illustrations and words in a print or digital text to demonstrate understanding of its characters, setting, or plot.**	Priority
2.RL.IKI.7.1.b	Explain the characters, setting, or plot in a story by using illustrations.	
2.RL.IKI.7.2.b	Describe the characters, settings, and problems in a story by using words from the text.	
2.RL.IKI.8	**8. Compare and contrast two or more versions of the same story (for example, Cinderella stories) by different authors or from different cultures.**	Supporting
2.RL.IKI.8.1.a	Compare and contrast two or more versions of the same story written by authors from different cultures.	

Source: © 2017 by Archdiocese of Chicago. Used with permission.

Figure 1.2: Benchmark report for English language arts, grade 2.

personalize them for the local level. See www.marzanoresources.com/educational-services /critical-concepts for more details defining and outlining the Critical Concepts, as well as step-by-step processes for leading this work.

Once the priority standards have been categorized, teams should list the categories and priority standards on separate pieces of chart paper, printing the grade level or course at the top of each chart page. Figures 1.4 and 1.5 (page 24) exemplify a science team's vertical review from Jefferson County Public Schools. The teachers have cut apart the state standards and categorized the standards by posting the slips on chart paper. They then distilled the standards statements into concise learning targets.

Grade 8	
Exponents	Linear Functions
Cube and Square Roots	Volume
Scientific Notation	Transformations, Similarity, and Congruence
Rational and Irrational Numbers	Angles of Two-Dimensional Figures
Linear Equations	Line and Angle Constructions
Systems of Linear Equations	Pythagorean Theorem
Quadratic Equations	Bivariate Categorical Data
Concept of Functions	Bivariate Measurement Data
Grade 7	
Signed Numbers and Absolute Value	Angle Relationships
Converting Fractions, Decimals, and Percentages	Constructing Triangles
Linear Equations	Circles
Proportional Relationships	Comparing Distributions
Inequalities	Representative Samples
Area and Volume	Simple Probability Models
Analyzing Geometric Figures	Probability of Compound Events
Transformations of Geometric Figures	
Grade 6	
Signed Numbers and Absolute Value	Independent and Dependent Variables
Factors and Multiples	Measurement Conversions
Long Division	Area and Volume
Fraction Division	Coordinate Plane
Evaluating Algebraic Expressions	Measures of Central Tendency
Ratios, Rates, and Percentages	Measures of Variability
Algebraic Equations	Deploying Distributions
Inequalities	Analyzing Distributions

Source: Adapted from Simms, 2016.

Figure 1.3: Measurement topics for mathematics, grades 6–8.

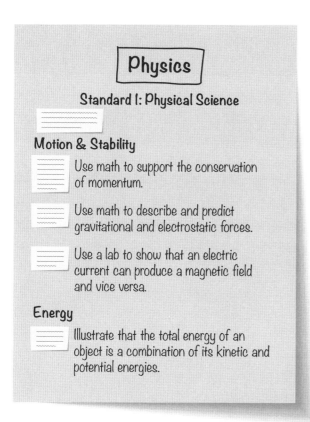

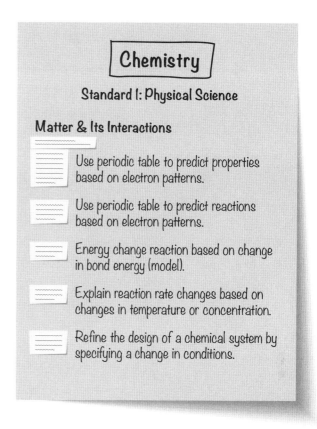

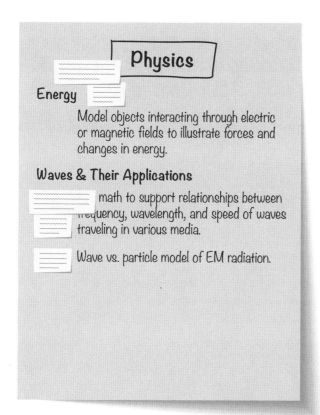

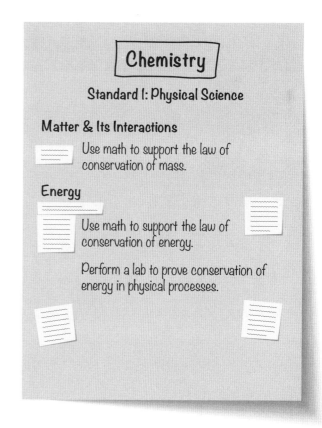

Source: © 2020 by Jefferson County Public Schools. Used with permission.

Figure 1.4: Categories of priority standards for high school science.

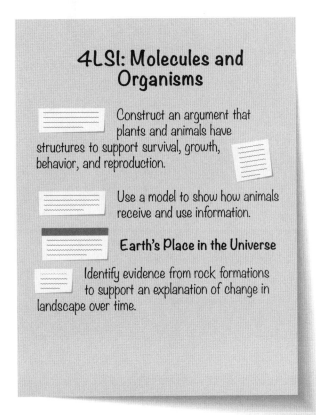

4LSI: Molecules and Organisms

Construct an argument that plants and animals have structures to support survival, growth, behavior, and reproduction.

Use a model to show how animals receive and use information.

Earth's Place in the Universe

Identify evidence from rock formations to support an explanation of change in landscape over time.

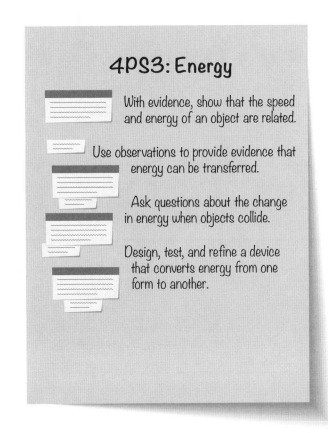

4PS3: Energy

With evidence, show that the speed and energy of an object are related.

Use observations to provide evidence that energy can be transferred.

Ask questions about the change in energy when objects collide.

Design, test, and refine a device that converts energy from one form to another.

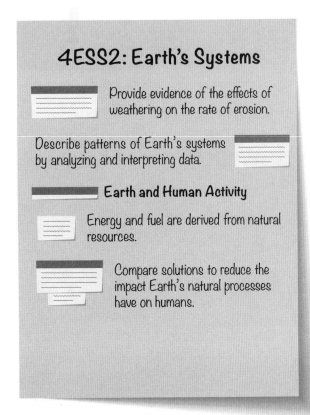

4ESS2: Earth's Systems

Provide evidence of the effects of weathering on the rate of erosion.

Describe patterns of Earth's systems by analyzing and interpreting data.

Earth and Human Activity

Energy and fuel are derived from natural resources.

Compare solutions to reduce the impact Earth's natural processes have on humans.

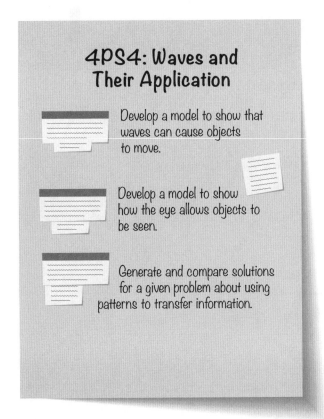

4PS4: Waves and Their Application

Develop a model to show that waves can cause objects to move.

Develop a model to show how the eye allows objects to be seen.

Generate and compare solutions for a given problem about using patterns to transfer information.

Source: © 2020 by Jefferson County Public Schools. Used with permission.

Figure 1.5: Categories of priority standards for fourth-grade science.

Step 4: Review the Final Categories

Begin step 4 by displaying the charts of priority standards from step 3 around the room. Use a rotating review strategy (Kagan & Kagan, 2009) to give teams the chance to review other grade-level or course-specific groups' lists, particularly at grade levels above and below or for courses taken before or after their own. Topics often spiral up through the grade levels, as you can see in figures 1.4 and 1.5 with the fourth-grade and high school versions of "waves and their applications," highlighting the importance of this review. Each team assigns one person (called the chart leader) from the team to remain at his or her team's own chart to explain which standards were identified as priority standards and why. The other team members rotate to review the other charts. Every three to five minutes, the administrator or leader prompts groups to rotate to a new chart, prompts the chart leader at each chart to explain his or her group's decisions and rationale, and prompts groups at each chart to ask questions of and offer suggestions to the chart leader, which the chart leader then records. This strategy allows teachers to see how the priority standards fit together and where topics or standards may require further separation or inclusion.

As mentioned previously, it is especially important that grade-level or course teams review the levels above and below their own. Leaders can decide whether or not to have the teams rotate to every chart or just those adjacent to their own grade levels. After completion of the rotating review, each team returns to its own chart to review and revise its work based on comments received. Teams should track each accepted revision as well as revisions that were declined by the group, along with the rationale for accepting or declining each revision. These notes can become the basis for a frequently asked questions (FAQ) document. This review-and-revision part of the process takes approximately one hour.

In order to use priority standards for additional phases, teams will need to type and save the lists of priority standards as electronic documents. Leaders can arrange for this to be done outside of group work time or can ask teachers to type and save their final lists of priority standards at the end of step 4. If all of the teachers in a district or school have access to a shared drive on a network, we suggest that leaders create a folder for each content area on that shared drive. Within each content-area folder, there should be separate folders for each grade level. All priority standards lists should be saved in the appropriate folders. If a district or school does not have a shared drive or network, all electronic lists of priority standards should be emailed to one individual responsible for organizing and archiving the files. This is often one individual team member for each grade level or course. This may also be done by support staff, if available.

Proficiency Scales

After prioritizing standards, it will be appropriate and necessary to embark on the creation or revision of proficiency scales for the core content areas of English language arts, mathematics, science, and social studies. This entails teachers expanding each prioritized standard into a progression of knowledge by clearly articulating the simple, target, and complex knowledge and skills within the standard. These levels of knowledge are matched to numeric scores to create a proficiency scale. Proficiency scales serve as the hub for teaching and learning in a standards-based system, as figure 1.6 (page 26) depicts. Everything in a standards-based system revolves around proficiency scales. Consider an airline hub, such as Chicago O'Hare or Denver International. Throughout the day, flights are coming into and leaving these airports. An airport hub is a constant stream of activity. The same is true of proficiency scales. Proficiency scales are used by multiple stakeholders, including teachers, students, and parents. Additionally, many classroom practices link to proficiency scales—planning, instruction, assessment, and feedback. In essence, proficiency scales are in the center of an SBL environment.

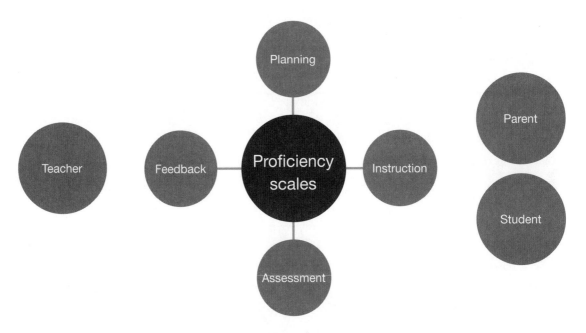

Source: Adapted from Heflebower et al., 2019.

Figure 1.6: Proficiency scales as the hub of the teaching and learning process.

Due to proficiency scales' central role in the system, it is paramount that all educators—but especially leaders and teachers on design teams—come to understand what scales are and how to create them. A proficiency scale is a tool, intended for use by teachers, students, and parents, that presents a collection of related learning targets and scores for determining a student's current level of performance. A primary purpose for proficiency scales is to clarify for teachers, students, and other stakeholders what knowledge and skills students must attain for mastery. Figure 1.7 presents the generic form of the scale with a description of each level.

Score	Description
4.0	Complex content—a performance beyond what a standard requires
3.0	Target content—the level of learning required for all students
2.0	Simple content—basic knowledge or skill necessary for mastering the target content
1.0	With help, partial success with score 2.0 content and score 3.0 content
0.0	Even with help, no success

Source: Adapted from Heflebower et al., 2019.

Figure 1.7: Generic form of a proficiency scale.

In order to ensure success when developing proficiency scales, it is paramount that participants understand each of the scale levels. Consider the following descriptions of each level, which expand on the generic form of the scale.

Score 4.0: The *complex content* on a proficiency scale represents knowledge or skill that goes beyond the score 3.0 expectations. It is a performance that requires a student to *apply* his or her understanding of the content at score 3.0—that is, to do something with the knowledge or skill.

Score 3.0: The *target content* on a proficiency scale is what all students must know and be able to do by the end of the year or course. This level most closely aligns to the original standard.

Score 2.0: The *simple content* is foundational knowledge that a student must acquire in order to master the target content. This level includes both academic vocabulary and prerequisite knowledge and skills.

Score 1.0: Score 1.0 does not include academic content. Instead, it is a description of performance where the student requires instructional support or help in order to demonstrate any knowledge or skill from score 2.0 or score 3.0.

Score 0.0: This level represents a learner who is unable to demonstrate any knowledge or skill represented on the proficiency scale, even when instructional supports are implemented.

Proficiency scales are "a powerful means of clarifying what students must know and be able to do by the end of an academic year or course" (Hoegh, 2020, p. 4). Consider the following situation. A second-grade team of teachers has examined each ELA standard and determined the following standard is a priority: "The student will use text features to locate information and gain meaning from a grade-level text." While the standards-prioritization process clarifies which standards receive strong instructional focus, the team must go one step further to define the knowledge and skills within individual priority standards. This is the role of the proficiency scale: to articulate a progression of knowledge for the standard. The proficiency scale in figure 1.8 (page 28) presents this progression for the second-grade text features standard. Note that the standard appears in the scale as the target content. Additional sample scales appear in appendix A (page 155).

When beginning to develop scales, your school or district must make three decisions about the format of the scale.

1. Will we include score 0.0 on our scales?

2. Will we include half-point scores on our scales?

3. How will we approach score 4.0 content on our scales?

While score 0.0 is helpful for indicating when a student demonstrates no knowledge of a topic, there is the potential for confusing this score of 0.0 with a traditional zero, typically used to indicate work not submitted. Thus, some educators choose to omit it from their scales. This is perfectly fine because score 1.0 and score 2.0 still exist to communicate to a student that he or she has not yet mastered the target content.

ENGLISH LANGUAGE ARTS	
Grade 2 Text Features	
Score 4.0 **Complex Content**	The student will: • Suggest an additional text feature to a grade-appropriate text and provide a rationale for this decision
Score 3.0 **Target Content**	The student will: • Use text features to locate information in a grade-level text • Use text features to gain meaning from a grade-level text
Score 2.0 **Simple Content**	The student will: • Identify text features, such as illustrations, diagrams, glossary, headings, bold print, captions, graphs, and table of contents
Score 1.0	The student will: • Demonstrate partial success with help on score 2.0 and score 3.0 content
Score 0.0	The student will: • Demonstrate little or no success with help on score 2.0 content

Source: Adapted from Hoegh, 2020.

Figure 1.8: Proficiency scale for text features, grade 2.

The second decision is whether to include half-point increments (0.5, 1.5, 2.5, and 3.5) on the proficiency scales. There is no right or wrong answer. The inclusion of the half-point scores gives more options for grading student progress and makes growth more visible to students themselves. With half-point scores, students see their scores increase more often, providing recognition and motivation. For example, consider a student who has proven mastery of all the content at score 2.0 on the scale and most of the score 3.0 content, but is struggling to understand one particular learning target at score 3.0. With the half-point increment, this student could receive a score of 2.5 and the following feedback from a teacher in relation to the text features scale: "You can clearly identify the different text features on our scale, and some of the time you are able to use them to locate information and better understand the text. Currently, your performance on this scale is 2.5. Let's really focus on getting more consistent with using the different text features. With some effort, I believe it won't be long before you are proficient on this scale!" Figure 1.9 is an expanded version of the generic form of a proficiency scale presented in figure 1.7 (page 26), including the half-point increments.

The third decision relates to the content of score 4.0 on the scale. A few authors disagree with placing level 4.0 content and knowledge on the proficiency scales; they believe the scale should stop at 3.0 (O'Connor, 2018; Schimmer, 2016). We, however, believe it is imperative to have a 4.0 level. Without the option for students to demonstrate deeper learning, we may inadvertently hold back higher-achieving students, and thus refrain from differentiating our teaching and learning experiences for students. By including 4.0 content and knowledge, teachers gain support and additional thinking about ways to take students beyond the proficient level. Without specifying one level below and above proficiency, we limit the implementation of the priority standards by assuming all teachers know and have the guidance for a more comprehensive learning experience. Moving students to and beyond the standard is an important consideration when planning a unit.

Score	Description
4.0	Complex content—a performance beyond what a standard requires
3.5	In addition to score 3.0 performance, partial success with score 4.0 content
3.0	Target content—the level of learning required for all students
2.5	No major errors or omissions regarding score 2.0 content and partial success with score 3.0 content
2.0	Simple content—basic knowledge or skill necessary for mastering the target content
1.5	Partial success with score 2.0 content and major errors or omissions regarding score 3.0 content
1.0	With help, partial success with score 2.0 content and score 3.0 content
0.5	With help, partial success with score 2.0 content but not with score 3.0 content
0.0	Even with help, no success

Source: Adapted from Heflebower et al., 2014.

Figure 1.9: Generic form of the proficiency scale with half-point scores.

With these concepts and decisions in place, it is time to actually develop the scales. It is typical for teacher teams to develop a proficiency scale for each prioritized standard. However, that is not a hard-and-fast rule. Sometimes a proficiency scale includes several related standards. At the end of the scale development process, there will likely be between ten and fifteen proficiency scales for each grade level or course within a content area. There are numerous ways teams of teachers can successfully develop scales; here we provide an overview of some options. For more details related to this important work, see *A Handbook for Developing and Using Proficiency Scales in the Classroom* (Hoegh, 2020) and *A School Leader's Guide to Standards-Based Grading* (Heflebower et al., 2014).

Customize Existing Scales

One option is to customize existing scales. It is important that any teacher or team of teachers considers scales from an outside source as *starter scales*, meaning that they need to be customized for the team's particular school or district. If you are just beginning the scale-development process, you might work with another school or district that has already developed scales, perhaps even using some of their scales as a starting point for your own work. Alternatively, there are commercially available scales, such as those associated with the Marzano Resources Critical Concepts (Simms, 2016). These are topic-based proficiency scales that require customization of the score 2.0 content. To illustrate, figures 1.10 and 1.11 (pages 30 and 31) present the original and customized versions of the kindergarten scale for Print Concepts.

Customizing the Critical Concepts or other existing scales can expedite the scale-development process. In this case, rather than writing scales from scratch, teams simply review existing scales and modify the language to personalize them to their respective school or district. In most situations, they are making minor tweaks to the wording or content, as opposed to large-scale overhauls. Jefferson County Public Schools used the customization approach in 2019–2020. The plan in figure 1.12 (page 32) shows how the Jefferson County leadership team scheduled scale-development work for various content areas and levels. You will also note that *teachers on special assignment* (TOSAs) worked with teams in the prioritization and proficiency scale tasks, as well as facilitated the work beyond formal training and work session dates. TOSAs are teachers who are recognized for their content expertise. They are often part of curriculum departments in large school districts. Their role in this process was to help add deep content-area expertise to the grade-level and course discussions.

4.0	The student will: • Test the idea that the letters in a word must be written in a specific order for it to be understood (for example, write the letters from the word *rainbow* in several different orders, including the correct order, and ask an adult which one means *a colorful arch in the sky*)
3.5	In addition to score 3.0 performance, partial success at score 4.0 content
3.0	The student will: **PC1**—Explain how written words are organized on pages (for example, when given a printed book or booklet of blank pages, explain which words in the book would be read first, next, and last and where in the booklet words would be written first, next, and last) **PC2**—Write sentences when told how to spell individual words (for example, when told that the sentence *I went to the store* has five words, and when each word is spelled orally by an adult who indicates uppercase and lowercase letters, write down the sentence using correct spacing and proper formation of each letter)
2.5	No major errors or omissions regarding score 2.0 content, and partial success at score 3.0 content
2.0	**PC1**—The student will recognize or recall specific vocabulary (for example, *back cover*, *book*, *bottom*, *front cover*, *left*, *page*, *right*, *top*, *word*) and perform basic processes such as: • State that words are written from left to right on a page • State that words are written from top to bottom on a page • State that words are read from left to right on a page • State that words are read from top to bottom on a page • State that pages in a book are read in order from the front cover to the back cover **PC2**—The student will recognize or recall specific vocabulary (for example, *alphabet*, *letter*, *lowercase*, *sentence*, *space*, *spell*, *uppercase*, *word*) and perform basic processes such as: • State that spoken words are represented in written language by specific sequences of letters • State that words are separated by spaces when they are written down • Point to spaces between words • Name all uppercase letters of the alphabet • Name all lowercase letters of the alphabet • Write all uppercase letters of the alphabet • Write all lowercase letters of the alphabet
1.5	Partial success at score 2.0 content, and major errors or omissions regarding score 3.0 content
1.0	With help, partial success at score 2.0 content and score 3.0 content
0.5	With help, partial success at score 2.0 content but not at score 3.0 content
0.0	Even with help, no success

Source: Adapted from Simms, 2016.

Figure 1.10: Original Print Concepts scale for kindergarten English language arts.

4.0	The student will:
	• Write several sentences to explain important information about a text
3.5	In addition to score 3.0 performance, partial success at score 4.0 content
3.0	The student will:
	PC1—Explain how written words are organized on pages
	PC2—Write sentences when told how to spell individual words
2.5	No major errors or omissions regarding score 2.0 content, and partial success at score 3.0 content
2.0	**PC1**—The student will recognize or recall specific vocabulary (for example, *back cover, bottom, front cover, left, page, right, top*) and perform basic processes such as: • State that pages in a book are read in order from the front cover to the back cover **PC2**—The student will recognize or recall specific vocabulary (for example, *alphabet, letter, lowercase, sentence, space, uppercase, word*) and perform basic processes such as: • State that words are made up of letters • State that words are separated by spaces when they are written down • Name the letters of the alphabet • Write the letters of the alphabet
1.5	Partial success at score 2.0 content, and major errors or omissions regarding score 3.0 content
1.0	With help, partial success at score 2.0 content and score 3.0 content
0.5	With help, partial success at score 2.0 content but not at score 3.0 content
0.0	Even with help, no success

Source: Adapted from Simms, 2016.

Figure 1.11: Customized Print Concepts scale for kindergarten English language arts.

In the plan in figure 1.12 (page 32), each content-area and level team has identified the days they will meet, what they will work on each day, and the numbers of teachers and TOSAs assigned to the work. There is a great deal of variety across the different teams. For instance, fourteen of the district's music teachers (one music teacher per building) participated to increase involvement and deepen application across the district. Some of the teams planned their work in more detail than others. In some areas, you will note more or less involvement by teachers and TOSAs, which was a function of the district's ability to obtain substitutes. As leaders are aware, you will make modifications as your best hopes meet reality.

Create New Scales Using the Standards as Target Content

While customizing existing proficiency scales is an effective method for scale development, another option is creating your own proficiency scales from scratch. One common method is to simply record the priority standard at the score 3.0 level on the proficiency scale. From there, a team of teachers can work collaboratively to determine critical vocabulary and other simple content and record it at score 2.0. Lastly, the team would generate a sample application task for score 4.0. The scale in figure 1.13 (page 33) resulted from this particular scale-development method.

Content Area and Level	Work Days				Total Teacher Days	Total TOSA Days
ELA Elementary	June 10 Grades K–5 scales **Teachers:** 3 **TOSAs:** 3		June 11 Vocabulary alignment, grades K–5 **Teachers:** 3 **TOSAs:** 3		10	8
ELA Secondary	May 29 Grades 6–12 scales and vocabulary (Analyzing Narratives and Generating Narratives) **Teachers:** 2 **TOSAs:** 1		May 31 Grades 6–12 scales and vocabulary (Analyzing Narratives and Generating Narratives) **Teachers:** 2 **TOSAs:** 1			
Mathematics Elementary	May 31 Grades K–5 scales **Teachers:** 4 **TOSAs:** 4		June 3 K–12 vocabulary **Teachers:** 5 elementary, 6 secondary **TOSAs:** 6		21	21
Mathematics Secondary	June 5 Grades 6–12 scales **Teachers:** 6 **TOSAs:** 3					
Science	May 29 Elementary scales Secondary scales High school earth science scales High school biology scales **Teachers:** 1 elementary, 4 secondary **TOSAs:** 5	May 30 K–12 science vocabulary **Teachers:** 1 elementary, 3 secondary **TOSAs:** 4	June 13 Sixth-grade science scales to meet new standards **TOSAs:** 4	June 14 Sixth-grade science scales to meet new standards **TOSAs:** 4	9	17
Social Studies Elementary	June 13 Scale drafting **TOSAs:** 4		June 14 Scale drafting **TOSAs:** 4		14	8
Social Studies Secondary	May 29 Seventh-grade scales and vocabulary **Teachers:** 2 **TOSAs:** 1	June 4 World history scales and vocabulary **Teachers:** 1 **TOSAs:** 1	June 12 Sixth-grade scales and vocabulary **Teachers:** 2 **TOSAs:** 1			
Music (K–12)	May 31 Finalize two proficiency scales **Teachers:** 14				14	0
Spanish Language Arts Secondary	June and July work. World Language teachers. Some TOSAs.					

Source: © 2019 by Jefferson County Public Schools. Used with permission.

Figure 1.12: Plan for scale development.

READING
Story Elements
Grade 3

Score 4.0	In addition to score 3.0 performance, the student demonstrates in-depth inferences and applications that go beyond what was taught.	
	Score 3.5	*In addition to score 3.0 performance, partial success at score 4.0 content*
Score 3.0	The student will: • Describe characters in a grade-appropriate story (e.g., their traits, motivations, or feelings) and explain how their actions contribute to the sequence of events (RL.3.3)	
	Score 2.5	*No major errors or omissions regarding score 2.0 content, and partial success at score 3.0 content*
Score 2.0	The student will recognize or recall specific vocabulary, such as: • *action, character, contribute, feeling, motivation, sequence of events, story, trait* **The student will perform basic processes, such as:** • Recognize or recall the characters' traits, motivations, and feelings from a grade-appropriate story	
	Score 1.5	*Partial success at score 2.0 content, and major errors or omissions regarding score 3.0 content*
Score 1.0	With help, partial success at score 2.0 content and score 3.0 content	

Source: Adapted from Marzano, Yanoski, Hoegh, & Simms, 2013.

Figure 1.13: Sample scale using the priority standard as score 3.0 content.

Create New Scales Using a Five-Step Process

Another scale-development method involves using a five-step process to determine each score level on the proficiency scale. This method of developing proficiency scales often works very well because it presents a concrete, step-by-step means of developing a well-constructed learning progression based on a prioritized standard. An important feature of this method is that each learning target on the scale is a single-idea statement of knowledge or skill. This often helps teachers, students, and parents better understand what must be learned at each level on the scale. The following steps are included in this method (Hoegh, 2020).

1. Determine the topic of the proficiency scale.

2. Determine the language of score 3.0 (the target content).

3. Determine vocabulary related to the target content and record it in score 2.0 (the simple content).

4. Determine additional simple content and record it in score 2.0.

5. Identify an example or two of how a student might demonstrate a score 4.0 performance (the complex content).

Imagine a grade 2 ELA standard that reads, "The student will use text features to locate information and gain meaning from a grade-level text." Using the five-step process to create a scale for this standard might proceed as follows.

1. **Determine the topic of the proficiency scale:** "This standard is all about using text features. Therefore, it makes sense to call this scale 'Using Text Features.'"

2. **Determine the language of score 3.0:** "The language of the standard works well for this level, except it might be helpful to create two single-idea learning targets at this level, one about locating information and the other about gaining meaning."

3. **Determine vocabulary related to the target content and record it in score 2.0:** "There are numerous text features students will need to know in order to master this standard. However, let's just include the term *text feature* as vocabulary. The different types of text features can be part of a separate learning goal."

4. **Determine additional simple content and record it in score 2.0:** "Students will definitely need to identify a pretty inclusive set of text features, such as illustrations, diagrams, glossary, headings, bold print, captions, graphs, and table of contents in order to attain mastery of score 3.0."

5. **Identify an example or two of how a student might demonstrate a score 4.0 performance:** "There are numerous ways a student could demonstrate a performance at this level. What if we asked students to suggest an additional text feature to a grade-appropriate text and provide a rationale for this decision? That definitely requires a student to apply understanding of the target content."

See figure 1.8 (page 28) for the text features proficiency scale that might result.

When a school or district tackles the development of proficiency scales from scratch, it is typical to plan for a full academic year for the completion of this work. Of course, the amount of progress made is dependent on the amount of time allotted. There are instances when a school or district plans for two or three consecutive summer days for scale development. This can result in the initial development of all of the intended scales for a grade level or course, and can possibly even include a scale revision process. Other schools might choose to do the work more incrementally, a few hours at a time, throughout an entire year. Most important to understand proficiency scales is that they evolve over time. Scales that are drafted and even revised typically get better as a result of teachers using the scales. Ultimately, it is common for a scale revision to occur on a yearly basis in an effort to continue improving these important classroom tools.

Pacing Guides

After proficiency scale development is complete, it is time for teacher teams to draft a yearlong or course-long pacing guide. This document offers valuable guidance to teachers regarding the order of the content on the proficiency scales, as well as the amount of time to spend on each topic. Just as proficiency scales are best created at the district level, the same can be said about pacing guides. This is to ensure that teachers in all schools teach the content in a similar manner and spend a similar amount of time teaching the content. This is important for giving students a consistent education, and it is especially advantageous when students move between schools within the district. In this case, teachers from across schools would collaborate on this important work. A team of three to five teachers per grade level or course is adequate for this districtwide team, as this development team will only be generating a draft. Feedback for revisions will be collected after the pacing guide has been piloted in classrooms.

The format of a pacing guide may vary from one content area to another in order to honor the preferences of individual teacher teams and the differences across content areas. For example, figure 1.14 (page 36) is an example for fourth-grade mathematics. The format reflects the linear nature of mathematics (as opposed to the spiraling nature of English language arts, for instance). Each proficiency scale is presented in the left-hand column along with an approximate number of days for teaching the content on the scale. It is important to note that a span of days is provided in order to accommodate variance in different groups of students. The standards related to each proficiency scale are presented in the next two columns, including both priority and supporting standards. Finally, the guide indicates the academic quarters in which the scales will be taught and reinforced. While each proficiency scale receives prominent instructional focus during a particular quarter of the academic year, each proficiency scale is also reinforced periodically during the remainder of the year. This is to ensure that all students have adequate opportunities to learn the content on each scale, and also to ensure that students' memory systems retain this important information.

Figure 1.15 (page 37) is a pacing guide example for the content area of science for sixth grade. This district's pacing guide is a digital file that also serves as an *anchor document* for everything related to the standards for these teachers. In addition to pacing information (approximate number of days that will be spent teaching the content), it includes links to additional resources (for example, proficiency scales, unit plans, and assessments).

Regardless of the format of the pacing guide, it will be important to establish a revision process for these guidance documents. Teachers learn a lot about how long it takes to teach content as initial documents are used. For this reason, leaders in the school or district will want to request that teachers keep detailed notes about teaching the content on proficiency scales. This important information will be considered at a later time when revision to the documents occurs.

Clearly, the work of attaining clarity about the standards is an important starting place in any SBL environment. When teachers clearly understand what students must know and be able to do, they can plan for how to pass that clarity on to students. This communication is discussed in the following section.

What is *so important* in this grade level and content area or course that it is identified as a priority?				
Topics and Approximate Time Required to Teach	**Priority Standard Number or Indicator**	**Supporting Standard Number or Indicator**	**Quarter Taught**	**Quarter Reinforced**
Place Value 15 to 17 days	**4.NBT.2** Read and write multidigit whole numbers using base-ten numerals, number names, and expanded form. Compare two multidigit numbers based on meanings of the digits in each place, using >, =, and < symbols to record the results of comparisons.	**4.NBT.1** Recognize that in a multidigit whole number, a digit in one place represents ten times what it represents in the place to its right.	First	Second, third, fourth
Addition and Subtraction 12 to 15 days	**4.OA.3** Solve a variety of problems based on the multiplication principle of counting.	**4.NBT.4** Fluently add and subtract multidigit whole numbers using the standard algorithm.	First	Second, third, fourth
Multiplication 9 to 11 days	**4.OA.1** Interpret a multiplication equation as a comparison. Represent verbal statements of multiplicative comparisons as multiplication equations.	**4.OA.2** Multiply to solve word problems involving multiplicative comparison.	Second	Third, fourth
Division 13 to 17 days	**4.OA.4** Find all factor pairs for a whole number in the range 1–100. Recognize that a whole number is a multiple of each of its factors.		Second	Third, fourth
Factors and Multiples 7 to 9 days	**4.OA.4** Determine whether a given whole number in the range 1–100 is a multiple of a given one-digit number.	**4.OA.4** Determine whether a given whole number in the range 1–100 is prime or composite.	Second	Third, fourth
Equivalent Fractions 10 to 12 days	**4.NF.2** Compare two fractions with different numerators and different denominators using <, >, and =; justify the comparison.	**4.NF.1** Explain why a fraction $\frac{a}{b}$ is equivalent to a fraction $(n \times a) / (n \times b)$ by using visual fraction models, with attention to how the number and size of the parts differ even though the two fractions themselves are the same size. Use this principle to recognize and generate equivalent fractions.	Third	Fourth
Fraction Addition and Subtraction 13 to 15 days	**4.NF.3** Understand a fraction $\frac{a}{b}$ with $a > 1$ as a sum of fractions $\frac{1}{b}$.	**4.NF.3.A** Understand addition and subtraction of fractions as joining and separating parts of referring to the same whole. **4.NF.3.B** Decompose a fraction into a sum of fractions with the same denominator in more than one way.	Third	Fourth
Fraction Multiplication 10 to 12 days	**4.NF.4.C** Solve word problems involving multiplication of a fraction by a whole number, by using visual fraction models and equations to represent the problem.	**4.NF.4.A** Understand a fraction $\frac{a}{b}$ as a multiple of $\frac{1}{b}$.	Third	Fourth

Topics and Approximate Time Required to Teach	Priority Standard Number or Indicator	Supporting Standard Number or Indicator	Quarter Taught	Quarter Reinforced
Decimal Fractions 10 to 12 days	**4.NF.5** Express a fraction with denominator *10* as an equivalent fraction with denominator *100*, and use this technique to add two fractions with respective denominators *10* and *100*.		Fourth	Fourth
Measurement Conversions 10 to 12 days	**4.MD.4** Solve problems involving addition and subtraction of fractions by using information presented in line plots.	**4.MD.4** Make a line plot to display a data set of measurements in fractions of a unit.	Fourth	Fourth

Source: Adapted from Hoegh, 2020.

Figure 1.14: Grade 4 mathematics pacing guide.

	Unit and Standard	Pacing	Materials	Supplemental
Q1	**Human Energy** **MS-PS3-1.** Construct and interpret graphical displays of data to describe the relationships of kinetic energy to the mass of an object, and to the speed of an object. **MS-PS3-2.** Develop a model to describe that when the arrangement of objects interacting at a distance changes, different amounts of potential energy are stored in the system.	15 days Proficiency scale HE unit plan HE level 2 test	**Amplify** Plot predictions lab	**Scientist report** Scientist outline
	MS-PS3-5. Construct, use, and present arguments to support the claim that when the kinetic energy of an object changes, energy is transferred to or from the object. **Force and Motion** **MS-PS2-1.** Apply Newton's third law to design a solution to a problem involving the motion of two colliding objects.	25 days Proficiency scale FM unit plan FM level 2 test	**Amplify** Speed and motion lab Heel-toe Physics Education Technology simulation (gravity and space; gravity and orbits)	
Q2	**Force and Motion (continued)** **Thermal Energy** **MS-PS1-1.** Develop models to describe the atomic composition of simple molecules and extended structures. **MS-PS1-4.** Develop a model that predicts and describes changes in particle motion, temperature, and state of a pure substance when thermal energy is added or removed. **MS-PS2-1.** Apply Newton's third law to design a solution to a problem involving the motion of two colliding objects.	25 days Proficiency scale TE unit plan TE level 2 test	**Amplify** Energy transfer lab (spoons) Boiling water lab	**Natural resource** Natural resource outline

Source: © 2019 by Uinta County #1 School District. Used with permission.

Figure 1.15: Science pacing guide.

Draft an Initial Implementation and Communication Plan

Work as a leadership team to draft both implementation and communication plans. An implementation plan states which components of the phases will be applied and when. It is often displayed in a timeline format. A communication plan focuses on which constituent groups will be informed about the phases and when. It may include both push-out (sharing information) and pull-in (seeking input or feedback) components. Both are necessary for a comprehensive rollout. Remember, the implementation and communication plans will be fluid documents. They must be flexible enough to respond to increased or decreased pacing of the suggested components in the multiphase plan. For example, you may find that you can complete implementation faster at the secondary level, where teachers are focused on one content area rather than many content areas at once as elementary teachers often are. You may have efforts already underway at certain levels, allowing those teachers or schools to move faster.

A draft implementation plan helps teachers and leaders see commitment to SBL implementation. It also communicates deadlines for work completion and use. Decide on the rollout—the expected implementation in specific grade levels and content areas. Will this be in stages or all at once? For example, it is common to begin rolling out new systems in grades K–2 first, then 3–5, then 6–8, and finally 9–12. It is also helpful to think of the implementation plan in terms of products. For example, you may decide that teams will complete the prioritization work in June and July, with feedback being sought in August and September. Next, proficiency scale work would get underway in September through November of that same year; another feedback loop would occur in November and December. Assessment development might then begin in January of the next year and last until March. Again, a feedback loop would follow in April, so teams can finalize the scales in May and June for a rollout in the following school year.

The sample implementation plan in figure 1.16 comes from Novato Unified School District in Novato, California. This district uses the term *proficiency-based learning* in place of SBL. Its comprehensive plan includes the use of a teacher leadership team (TLT) consisting of teacher leaders from each site in the district who have been instrumental in deepening learning for other teachers, seeking input, and partnering with the district and consultants in training and implementation efforts. Novato centered its plan on a five-year goal that all students achieve mastery of the content and demonstrate the district's six Cs: collaboration, communication, critical thinking, conscientious learning, cultural competence, and character.

Novato Unified School District's VISION 2023 (2018–2023): By 2023, all students will demonstrate standards-based proficiency of the Graduate Profile that includes the Novato Unified School District's six Cs and content-based mastery.

2018–2019

- Initial learning targets established for each grade level in
    - All content areas grades 6–12
    - Math, ELA, physical education, and music grades TK (transitional kindergarten)–5
- Essential standards established for each grade level in
    - All content areas grades 6–12
    - Math, ELA, physical education, and music grades TK–5
- District or school teams work with Marzano Research Group to guide work
- Establish teacher leadership team to facilitate system shift to proficiency-based education (PBE), forty participants
    - Representative of all school sites
    - Representative of all grade levels preK–12
    - Representative of all content areas
    - Representative of all specialized programs (SPED, EL, GATE)
- TLT participates in initial three-tier training
    - Tier 1: Team Building and Vision Development
    - Tier 2: Proficiency-Based Education (Marzano)
    - Tier 3: Explicit Leadership Training (facilitation, adult learning models, engaging in difficult conversation, meeting-planning practices)
- New standards-based elementary school report card piloted
- Middle school digital portfolios introduced
- Elementary teachers introduced to Data Matters

2019–2020

1. Proficiency scales developed for each essential standard
2. Preliminary common assessments created and piloted
3. TLT continues three-tier training
4. TLT plans and facilitates all district-wide professional development
5. All district-wide professional development focused on PBE
    a. Three days in content or grade-level teams districtwide
    b. Four days in school teams split by content or grade-level teams
6. PBE community outreach and education
    a. Monthly newsletter to all Novato Unified School District (NUSD) community members
    b. Parent education nights at all schools
7. Expand TLT to include up to an additional forty participants
8. Learning maps created for all elementary ELA and mathematics essential standards
9. Elementary school report card revisions based on pilot results
10. New elementary school report card adopted and implemented
11. Elementary student-led conferences implemented (fifth grade)
12. Middle school digital portfolios implemented (eighth grade)
13. High school Graduate Profile defense introduced (twelfth grade)
14. Secondary teachers introduced to Data Matters

Figure 1.16: Sample implementation plan.

continued →

2020–2021
• Proficiency scales implemented in all secondary content areas
• Proficiency scales implemented in elementary ELA, math, music, and physical education
• Common assessments implemented or piloted in all content areas
• Essential standards established in science grades TK–5
• Proficiency scales written for all science essential standards
• Secondary schools begin to explore proficiency-based reporting systems
• Task force established to align PBE practice with NUSD board policies
• Task force introduces first reading of proposed NUSD board policy and makes recommendation for adoption
• TLT Year 1 participants shift focus to new teacher training and support
• TLT Year 2 participants continue three-tier training
• *All* TLTs continue to facilitate and model PBE implementation in content or grade-level teams *and* school teams

• PBE community outreach and education continue
   – Quarterly newsletter to all NUSD community members
   – Parent education nights at all schools
   – Community meeting to include an expert panel representing community and postsecondary partners

• First group of high school seniors participate in the Graduate Profile defense
• NUSD high schools no longer identified as ranking high schools
• The recognition of *Distinguished Students* will replace the recognition of   – Valedictorian and salutatorian
2021–2022

• Proficiency scales and common assessments implemented in
   – All content areas grades 6–12
   – Math, ELA, science, physical education, and music grades TK–5

• Essential standards established in social studies grades TK–5
• Task force brings final proposal of updated NUSD board policy for adoption
• All schools pilot proficiency-based reporting system(s)
• All TLTs continue to facilitate and model PBE implementation
2022–2023
• New proficiency-based reporting system adopted and implemented   – Gradual implementation of grade-reporting system to support a smooth and consistent transition for students and family
• Full implementations of all components
• Reflection and refinement

Source: © 2018 by Novato Unified School District. Used with permission.

In addition to the drafted implementation plan, compose a preliminary communication plan to be used internally. Such a plan signifies who needs to know what by when. Strategic communication with students, parents, teachers, and community about the concept of SBL is one of the most important aspects of the entire implementation process. A district's communication on this topic needs to be ongoing and designed to inform and educate two different publics. The first public is the internal public—staff, students, and the board of education. The second is the external public—parents and community members. Strategic communication begins with a core message that consistently and efficiently communicates the basic ideals of the implementation to both publics. For this purpose, districts should begin by developing an "elevator speech" about the concept and rationale for the move to SBL. The power of an elevator speech—so called because it is only the length of an elevator ride—is that it distills a message down to the most important elements. The elevator speech is used for mass distribution of a universal message that can be easily incorporated into newsletters, on websites, during faculty meetings, with school improvement teams, and even in discussions with individuals. Figure 1.17 shows the elevator speech examples developed for the McKeel Academy charter schools in Lakeland, Florida. The McKeel leadership team created two versions of an elevator speech, a print version and a spoken version. Both contain the key messages about their SBL and SBG implementation.

SBG and SBL Elevator Speech—for print

Our teachers are dedicated to teaching and providing students opportunities to become skillful learners who take ownership in their learning. As a charter school, we have the ability to operate and implement programs that rise above the status quo. Standards-based learning, complemented by standards-based grading, is one of those programs. This program helps to provide both students and parents a clearer indication of what has been learned, while also developing a stronger foundation for our students' future learning as they move to the next grade level.

SBG and SBL Elevator Speech—for speaking

Our teachers are dedicated to providing students with opportunities to become skillful learners who take ownership in their learning (work). Let's remember, as a charter school, we have greater flexibility in how we operate, as well as in the types of programs we implement that rise above the status quo . . . it's the core of who we are. Standards-based learning complemented by standards-based grading is one of those programs. It helps to provide kids and their parents a clearer indication of what has been learned while also developing a stronger foundation for our students' future learning as they move to the next grade level.

Source: © 2020 by The Schools of the McKeel Academy. Used with permission.

Figure 1.17: McKeel Academy written and spoken elevator speech examples.

While you will have some universal messages, like the elevator speech, you must also consider various constituents and their specific needs for information. Teachers are the first users of standards, proficiency scales, and aligned assessments. Students are next, and parents follow. For example, teachers would need a detailed understanding of prioritized standards, proficiency scales, and aligned classroom assessments. Students would need student-friendly understanding (or versions) of proficiency scales, but they have less need to know about the concept of prioritized standards. Rather, they will experience them through the use of proficiency scales within the classroom. Parents will eventually need to understand what is reported about their children's learning—a set of the most essential standards for each grade level or course. They will also see their children using proficiency scales in classrooms to track their progress, obtain meaningful feedback, and set personalized learning goals. Parents may see proficiency scales referenced by their children throughout the year, especially at the end of reporting periods.

As you draft your communication plan, contemplate the various modes for sharing your message. These may include, but are not limited to, your school or district website, course syllabi, curriculum documents, classroom websites, written feedback documents, digital documents, newsletters, social media, and the like. Additional support for drafting a communication plan can be found in *A School Leader's Guide to Standards-Based Grading* (Heflebower et al., 2014, pp. 88–97) and *A Teacher's Guide to Standards-Based Learning* (Heflebower et al., 2019, pp. 121–127).

Figure 1.18 shows a communication plan from Wichita Public Schools. Note that this district uses the term *standards-referenced grading* to describe its grading and learning practices. Wichita leaders designated question-and-answer sessions specifically for parents, as well as corresponding presentation slides and documents. You also see the process they used for obtaining questions at the beginning and throughout the parent session. They expanded their constituents to include various community groups. They also made great use of social media platforms in communicating thoroughly. Furthermore, they provided a set of likely questions and possible responses to assist those in leading the outreach sessions, as well as suggestions for the processes inherent in adult learning sessions.

In addition to the overall communication plan, Wichita Public Schools crafted messaging documents for various stakeholder groups. The document for teachers to use in conversations with families, shown in figure 1.19 (page 44), covers likely questions from families, professional responses and talking points, and conversation skills to practice and use. This thorough plan helped support teachers, create consistent messaging, and provide district leaders and staff with thoughtful and well-articulated planning questions.

Figure 1.20 (page 45) is a sample of how Wichita Public Schools communicated to parents in both print and electronic formats. They shared examples and links to various explanatory documents.

Wichita Public Schools also created a brochure, shown in figure 1.21 (page 46), to communicate with parents about standards-referenced grading practices. You will notice it includes a brief overview of what standards-referenced grading entails, as well as a sample scale. The timeline for implementation is included, as well as a request for feedback and the website for more information.

Additionally, figure 1.22 (page 47) is a visual displayed on Wichita Public Schools' website, which communicates the timeline for implementing standards-referenced grading across the district.

Wichita Public Schools Communication Plan

We knew our challenge would be communicating effectively with all stakeholders—internal and external.

- Prior to our first year of implementation, we worked hard to develop documents that could be shared districtwide. (See SRG Communication Toolkit items.)

- We carefully designed a parent Q&A session format to ensure participants were able to ask their questions and learn about SRG at the same time. (See Parent Community Q&A Session slides and Parent Q&A document.)

  - We asked all those attending the Q&A sessions to write their questions on notecards at the beginning of the session and throughout the presentation.

  - During the presentation, one of the district members categorized the questions so the information shared made as much sense as possible.

  - Following the last session held, we posted all the questions and answers on our district website and provided the documents to administrators and instructional coaches who used the information to prepare for conferences. The most successful schools held their own parent Q&A sessions prior to conferences using the district's format and handouts.

- During the summer and into the fall of this year, we used the Q&A format to share our work with as many community partners as possible. Community partners included the following:

  - Reporters from multiple news outlets

  - State board of education members

  - Business association members

  - NAACP organization members

  - Key faculty members of local colleges and universities

  - Local non-profit organizations working closely with our schools

- Administrators were asked to include information in their monthly newsletters.

- Tweets introducing the change and guiding readers to our district website were sent weekly leading up to conferences this first year.

- Internal communication is also critical for implementation, especially in a larger district. We used the following strategies to communicate why we are making changes:

  - Regular presentations to the board of education

  - An internal website with a link to ask questions

  - Prior to implementing SRG for grades K–5 this year, we sent weekly emails to the entire district with updates to the website based on posted questions

  - We are currently sending monthly updates that include celebrations, new information, and updates to the website based on questions

  - Q&A sessions with union representatives, certified staff, classified staff, and substitute teachers

  - Q&A sessions with student-leadership organizations

Source: © 2019 by Wichita Public Schools. Used with permission.

Figure 1.18: Sample communication plan.

Supports for Teachers in Conversations With Families

This document is intended to support the teachers and staff in their efforts to communicate with families regarding the implementation of standards-referenced grading (SRG). Knowing that families are the "stage setters" for their children, our desire is to partner with them. We always think, "partnership." Our website for SRG has numerous resources for families; please encourage families to go there to learn more: www.USD259.org/Grading

1. Likely questions from families, with possible answers

Likely question	Possible answer
Where on the report card is the overall grade for my student?	An overall grade is simply an average of all the content your student has worked on, and so it really does not communicate what your student knows or is able to do. With standards-referenced grading, your student will receive scores for each learning target, or standard, we teach instead of an average of them all. This will help parents, students, and teachers know exactly what is mastered and what still needs work.
There are not many 3s. Is my student doing poorly?	The standards are expected to be mastered by the end of the year, and this is only the end of the first quarter. **We will expect to see lower scores as we first begin teaching the targets.** This student is doing very well! As you can see, there are several 2s and 2.5s already, indicating the student is progressing toward a 3 rather quickly.
Why is there a separate behavior grade?	We want to report, more clearly than ever, what your child knows and is able to do. Behavior and work habits are extremely important, as they put your child in the best possible position to succeed and grow as a student and as a person. We want to look at the whole child and separate out behavior and work habits from the academic grade so we can get a very clear picture of where your child is already successful, and where he or she may need extra support.
Where can I go to learn more?	Three places: 1. The district website: www.USD259.org/Grading 2. Setting the Stage for Student Success sessions—see the bottom of these pages for dates and places. 3. SRG Hotline for Families—each Tuesday, Wednesday, and Thursday in October from 5 p.m. to 7 p.m.

2. Professional responses, talking points

- Grading practices will focus on students' demonstration of their mastery of academic standards. This will help us better understand what students truly know and can do. Factors not based on academic learning such as extra credit, bonus points, student behavior, work ethic, and homework performance will no longer be combined with academic learning to help determine grades. Student behavior, work ethic, and homework performance will be communicated with families through progress reports.

- Your child will have many opportunities to demonstrate his or her mastery of standards.

- The proficiency scales will help your child understand how to focus his or her efforts at being able to succeed with each standard, by breaking down the standard into its foundational parts. This means your child will be better equipped to "own" his or her learning.

- We will be celebrating growth toward the standard; the proficiency scales help us all to see growth.

- A scale score of 3 means your child has demonstrated proficiency with that standard, which is our goal for each grade-level standard by the end of the school year.

- Behavior and work-habit grades help us to separate out behavior from mastery of academic skills as we evaluate and determine where your child might need extra support, and where he or she is successful.

- We have always had these academic standards; now we are operating with more clarity about them.

3. Conversation skills to practice and use

Skill	Note
Presuming positive intentions	Giving families credit in their thinking, for wanting the best for their children, enables you to respond with language that suggests partnership.
Pausing	You stand to gain credibility and confidence when you pause briefly to gather your thoughts. Pausing before responding facilitates your response from a place of thinking, as opposed to a place of feeling. We feel first and think second. Our responses from cognition increase our influence and our ability to speak partnership language.
Paraphrasing	Paraphrasing is the primary relationship-building tool. Paraphrasing communicates that you are invested in understanding the other person. Feeling understood creates a biochemical response in the brain. A good paraphrase communicates that you understand, without having to use the words *I understand*. Here are some possible paraphrasing sentence starters: So what's important to you is… You feel… You are concerned about… You want to be certain that… You mean… Tip: A good paraphrase does not include the word *I*.
Other sentence stems to support communication	Let me add this to your understanding… Let me assure you that… If this were my child, I would certainly want… Here is what we know… Because we want to communicate more clearly than ever about your child's progress, we…
Responding with evidence	Let's look together at the standards and where your child is…

Source: © 2019 by Wichita Public Schools. Used with permission.

Figure 1.19: Communication support document for teachers.

We want to communicate what your child knows and is able to do through standards-referenced grading. Wichita Public Schools now uses a 0–4-point grading scale. Progress reports have been updated to clearly reflect the standards students are working toward. Academic standards and behavior standards are graded separately. Standards-Referenced Grading practices are common across all WPS elementary schools. Your child's progress report will clearly communicate their success toward learning goals. Please visit with your child's teacher about your child's progress and if you have any questions. More information, including sample progress reports, can be found at www.usd259.org/Grading.

Source: © 2019 by Wichita Public Schools. Used with permission.

Figure 1.20: Sample parent communication.

Source: © 2019 by Wichita Public Schools. Used with permission.

Figure 1.21: Standards-referenced grading brochure for parents.

ROLL-OUT TIMELINE

STANDARDS REFERENCED GRADING

**Elementary School
PreK/Middle School**
High School

AUG 2019
Elementary School
Implementation (Grades K–5)

AUG 2020
PreK & Middle School
Implementation (Grade 6)

AUG 2021
Middle School Implementation
(Grades 7–8)

AUG 2022
High School
Implementation Begins

Elementary implementation of Standards-Referenced Grading began in the 2019–20 school year.

Middle school will begin implementation during the 2020–21 school year for sixth grade. Progress reports will reflect the new grading system for students in sixth grade during the first year of implementation. Progress reports will reflect the new grading system for students in seventh and eighth grade during the second year of middle school implementation, which is the 2021–22 school year.

High school will begin implementing the new grading system during the 2022–23 school year in entry-level courses.

Source: © 2019 by Wichita Public Schools. Used with permission.

Figure 1.22: Sample implementation time line.

Educate Key Leaders

Another key activity in phase 1 is to begin educating key leaders in your system. Leaders will receive the products the design teams produce and lead the implementation at their respective sites. Specifically, building leaders will consider existing processes in their schools related to the work of the design teams and obtaining pertinent feedback from their teachers. Instructional coaches may be able to assist with aligning the instructional supports necessary for teachers to see affiliation and realize results. Directors of special education and English learner (EL) services will make immediate connections for supporting the instructional needs of students they serve. Communications directors will assist in the outreach to the various constituents, and technology directors will see how this work requires connectivity to student learning management systems and electronic grading programs. Superintendents and assistant superintendents will use this information in board of education reports, guidance for teaching and learning, and designation of grants to support future funding. Two groups we recommend sharing information and resources with at this stage are boards of education and staff leaders. Additionally, a consensus-building tool appears in appendix A (page 162).

Board of Education

When implementing any new concept or program in a school or district, you must communicate regularly with the board of education and educate its members on the concept. Board members need to understand SBL to a level that gives them the ability to speak about it in an accurate and informed manner. Throughout the five phases of implementation described in this book, we identify different ideas for ongoing communication with the board of education. We realize, however, that different boards take on different personalities and prefer to be involved at different levels and times. Thus, these are only suggestions based on what has worked in our experience implementing SBL.

One of the first tasks for communicating with the board of education is to preview the concept of SBL and engage board members in some proactive education. During this previewing process, focus on why the change is important and what the change can do to enhance student learning. Consider reviewing the changes that have occurred in state, provincial, or national education policies that have prompted districts and other education agencies to examine and adapt their practices in the areas of curriculum, assessment, and grading. Accessing national and state- or province-level statutes provides an excellent starting place for this work with the board and a natural connection to make sure board policy is in fact compliant with current school law. As part of these conversations it will be important to bring forth the difference between norm-referenced (individual student progress is compared to other students' progress) and criterion-referenced (individual student progress is compared to objective criteria—the standards each student is expected to learn) approaches to education. As an example, consider the following points on criterion-referenced education in the United States.

- Criterion-referenced teaching and learning measure individual student performance against a set of criteria established as academic standards and indicate an individual student's level of proficiency in relation to specific standards that have been established both nationally and at the state level.

- The No Child Left Behind Act (NCLB), which Congress passed in 2001 and President George W. Bush signed into law on January 8, 2002, ushered in a new criterion-referenced era of education in the United States. This law required states to establish academic standards that all students were expected to meet. It also required states to implement assessment and reporting systems to measure student progress within the standards that were established.

- As the criterion-referenced era progressed, the Every Student Succeeds Act (ESSA) was passed in 2015, signed by President Barack Obama on December 10 of that year. According to the U.S. Department of Education (n.d.), ESSA "requires for the first time that all students in America be taught to high academic standards that will prepare them to succeed in college and careers."

- To meet ESSA requirements, schools and districts must define high levels of performance in academic standards and implement systems that clearly track students' performance. Standards-based learning does exactly this.

It is also helpful when communicating with the board of education to practice one of Stephen R. Covey's (2004) seven habits of highly effective people: beginning with the end in mind. Showing the board members what a standards-referenced or standards-based report card looks like and the information it conveys is an effective way to do this. Use the report card to show how the changes relate to the laws requiring schools to practice a criterion-referenced approach to education and how the new report cards provide more useful information to teachers, students, and parents. This conversation also creates opportunities to discuss the scope of work that will need to occur to reach that point, such as prioritization of standards, development of proficiency scales, and the need to train staff in these specific topics.

Prior to implementation, consider engaging the board in article or book studies for early learning about the concept. If your district is working with specific consultants in planning for this transition, have the consultants do a presentation for the board at a work session. As the early stages of the implementation begin to move forward, include board members in training sessions with educators to learn about and understand the concept from the ground up. Having a board member or two attend trainings to hear firsthand about the concept will provide a valuable, personal aspect of communication to the board of education.

Throughout the implementation, the board should receive information and presentations on the different aspects of SBL that are the focus of work at the time. It is important to retain these resources for the board in easily accessible, digital portfolios (for example, a set of folders on Google Drive) that keep each member organized regarding topics, activities, and how the SBL concept is beginning to take shape across the school or district. These portfolios might contain short articles about different aspects of the implementation work, artifacts of practice as the work begins to unfold, and videos of previous presentations. These portfolios become a record of the work and an ongoing tutorial for board members during the implementation. They can also help educate and update new board members who might be seated during the implementation process.

Staff Leaders

At this stage, you should also begin educating the additional key staff leaders (formal and informal leaders) who are not directly involved in the implementation. Building principals and assistant principals provide various and differentiated learning opportunities for teachers within their buildings. You might begin developing this understanding with book studies for collaborative teams. Some schools and districts make these book studies voluntary, others mandatory. Some books we recommend include the following.

- *Grading* (2nd ed.) by Susan Brookhart (2014)

- *How to Give Effective Feedback to Your Students* (2nd ed.) by Susan Brookhart (2017)

- *Practical Solutions for Serious Problems in Standards-Based Grading* by Thomas R. Guskey (2009c)

- *Answers to Essential Questions About Standards, Assessments, Grading, and Reporting* by Thomas R. Guskey and Lee Ann Jung (2013)

- *A School Leader's Guide to Standards-Based Grading* by Tammy Heflebower, Jan K. Hoegh, and Philip B. Warrick (2014)

- *A Teacher's Guide to Standards-Based Learning* by Tammy Heflebower, Jan K. Hoegh, Philip B. Warrick, and Jeff Flygare (2019)

- *A Handbook for Developing and Using Proficiency Scales in the Classroom* by Jan K. Hoegh (2020)

- *Rethinking Grading: Meaningful Assessment for Standards-Based Learning* by Cathy Vatterott (2015)

Consider what makes the most sense to your system. Some schools elect to center the study on various articles that staff leaders can easily obtain and read. The following list presents some possible articles and resources. It is by no means exhaustive.

- "Get It Right the First Time!" by Tammy Heflebower, Jan K. Hoegh, and Philip B. Warrick (*Phi Delta Kappan*, March 2017)

- "Making the Grade: When Do Kids Deserve As?" by Peg Tyre (*Family Circle*, February 2012)

- "What We Learn From Grades" by Marge Scherer (*Educational Leadership*, November 2011)

- "Five Obstacles to Grading Reform" by Thomas R. Guskey (*Educational Leadership*, November 2011)

- "Starting the Conversation About Grading" by Susan Brookhart (*Educational Leadership*, November 2011)

- "Redos and Retakes Done Right" by Rick Wormeli (*Educational Leadership*, November 2011)

- "The Case Against Grades" by Alfie Kohn (*Educational Leadership*, November 2011)

- "Grades That Show What Students Know" by Robert J. Marzano and Tammy Heflebower (*Educational Leadership*, November 2011)

- "Reporting Student Learning" by Ken O'Connor and Rick Wormeli (*Educational Leadership*, November 2011)

- "No Penalties for Practice" by Douglas Fisher, Nancy Frey, and Ian Pumpian (*Educational Leadership*, November 2011)

- "How Grading Reform Changed Our School" by Jeffrey A. Erickson (*Educational Leadership*, November 2011)

- "Seven Practices for Effective Learning" by Jay McTighe and Ken O'Connor (*Educational Leadership*, November 2011)

- "Grading Exceptional Learners" by Lee Ann Jung and Thomas R. Guskey (*Educational Leadership*, February 2010)

- "Reforming Grading Practices in Secondary Schools" by Ken O'Connor (*Principal's Research Review*, January 2009)

- "Seven Reasons for Standards-Based Grading" by Patricia Scriffiny (*Educational Leadership*, October 2008)

- "Effective Grading Practices" by Douglas Reeves (*Educational Leadership*, February 2008)

- "Standards-Based Grading and Reporting: A Model for Special Education" by Lee Ann Jung and Thomas R. Guskey (*Teaching Exceptional Children*, November 2007)

- "The Challenges of Standards-Based Grading" by Thomas R. Guskey and Lee Ann Jung (*Leadership Compass*, Winter 2006)

- "Accountability: Teaching Through Assessment and Feedback, Not Grading" by Rick Wormeli (*American Secondary Education*, Summer 2006)

- "Making High School Grades Meaningful" by Thomas R. Guskey (*Phi Delta Kappan*, May 2006)

- "Grading to Communicate" by Tony Winger (*Educational Leadership*, November 2005)

- "The Case Against the Zero" by Douglas Reeves (*Phi Delta Kappan*, December 2004)

- "Grading Policies That Work Against Standards . . . and How to Fix Them" by Thomas R. Guskey (*NASSP Bulletin*, December 2000)

Besides articles and books, staff leaders can learn about SBL at conferences, on-site professional development from consultants, or electronic links to video resources.

Figure 1.23 (page 52) shows how a smaller district might craft a yearlong plan for sharing information on standards-based grading. Here you will see district efforts for sharing information via a monthly newsletter, webinars, and book studies. This district also added in information for families and community members. An example of a letter alerting staff to training opportunities appears in appendix A (page 165).

STANDARDS-BASED GRADING AND ASSESSMENT-FOCUS ACTIVITIES Sample District					
District Efforts				Building Efforts	
Monthly Newsletter	Webinars	Book Study	Family and Community	Leadership Team Members Facilitate Faculty Activity	Collaborative Team Discussions
November: Separating Academics From Behavior December: Identifying Power Standards January: Writing Quality Proficiency Scales February: Busting the Myths of Standards-Based Grading and Assessment March: Aligning Assessments to Scales April: Honoring Most Recent Learning May: Rechallenges and Redos	Webinars with Dr. Tammy Heflebower November 2012: Administrative Team January 2013: Districtwide May 2013: Leadership Team	Administrators: *The Principal as Assessment Leader* (Guskey, 2009a) All certified staff: *The Teacher as Assessment Leader* (Guskey, 2009b)	Monthly newspaper article Taping of brief student and staff videos to post on district website or show at board meetings	Presentation and activity on monthly focus topic provided by curriculum director to leadership team	Guiding questions on *The Teacher as Assessment Leader* (Guskey, 2009b) provided in monthly newsletter

Figure 1.23: Plan for educating staff leaders.

Intermediate agencies can also be instrumental in providing learning opportunities for leaders and teachers. Many American states have agencies at a level between the state department of education and local school districts. Such agencies serve as intermediaries, helping local districts enact statewide mandates. They assist local districts by pooling resources and offering a myriad of services (professional development, special education direction and support, EL direction and support, and assistance with federal and statewide grant writing and oversight). Some are called area education agencies (AEAs), educational service units (ESUs), or boards of cooperative education services (BOCES). Some of those work more closely with the department of education. One example is Heartland AEA. Heartland AEA has an embedded team of consultants inside districts and buildings to support staff at every level K–12. As Becca Lindahl from Heartland AEA stated:

> We have created a document that we call *Framework: Standards-Based Learning Including Grading and Reporting*. This framework includes six components: standards-based learning; learning targets, scales, and rubrics; implementation considerations; beliefs about student learning; student management systems and grading/reporting; and internal/external capacity building. [Individual sections of the framework explain] what that component is about and then detail some information that allows readers to determine if their district or building is at a level of Foundational Essentials, Making Progress, or Optimized for that item. The details under each level hold descriptions of what's involved for districts and for educators in the classroom.

> Creating this framework has allowed us to lead learning over standards-based practices for educators in schools within our agency. We've

held day-long workshops over the last couple years with speakers and researchers such as Tammy Heflebower, Jan Chappuis, Myron Dueck, Tom Schimmer, Matt Townsley, and Carol Commodore. Also for a couple years now, on the afternoon of the first Friday of each month, we've held what we call Framework Fridays, using an ed-camp style workshop to draw educators in for conversation on a component in the framework. Our agency has realized the importance of helping our educators understand what standards-based learning, including grading and reporting, looks like as a responsible, student-centered method of changing and improving curriculum, instruction, and assessment for all our learners. (B. Lindahl, personal communication, January 2, 2020)

Heartland AEA, as well as many others, has proven instrumental in providing high-quality learning opportunities for local school districts.

As another approach to providing training to various district and building leaders, Jefferson County Public Schools used its existing Learning Network leadership meetings to provide training and share information. The Learning Network meets monthly, and in the 2019–2020 school year, it devoted four of its nine meetings to SBL. In those meetings, the curriculum design and learning innovation department shared the prioritization, proficiency scales, and some optional classroom assessments with building and district leaders. The trainings were designed in three-hour segments. The morning session was specifically tailored to district and site learning coaches, as well as other site support leaders; the afternoon session targeted building leaders. This format allowed some flexibility and choice in attendance, as well as a focus more related to the audience. Scheduling these learning sessions as part of existing leadership training days limited the burden for leaders; it did not require additional time away from their building or district responsibilities.

Assemble a Guiding Team

Assembling a guiding team is one of the most important steps a principal or district leader will take for his or her school early in the implementation. The notion that real change must be staff driven might be clichéd, but it holds true. As John Kotter and Holger Rathgeber (2005) advised, "make sure there is a powerful group guiding the change—one with leadership skills, credibility, communications ability, authority, analytical skills, and a sense of urgency" (p. 130). To that end, assembling a dedicated, knowledgeable, and enthusiastic guiding team is a crucial element of implementing SBL practices. The members of this team will read articles and books to strengthen their understanding of the work; they may also visit other schools or districts where many of these components are already in place. In short, they will become experts and lead the implementation and communication efforts. The guiding team essentially functions at the cabinet level of the implementation. As such, the selection of members to serve on this team needs to be strategic in multiple aspects.

The exact makeup of the guiding team is flexible but should have representation from all areas of operation in the district or school. It might even include students when it is age appropriate, although this is not a requirement. The size of the team will be relative to the size of the district or school. In smaller districts or schools, team members might handle dual responsibilities and therefore represent multiple perspectives on the guiding team. In larger districts or schools the team will be a bit larger as specialization of responsibility is more likely. The size of the team needs to be workable from a communication and meeting perspective. However, the most important aspect is to get the necessary people and areas of district or school operation on the team.

When considering the different areas of operation that might be represented on the team, you might consider some of the design team members who are drafting priority standards and proficiency scales. The guiding team should involve teacher leaders as well as some school-level leaders, instructional coaches, and district staff. It is also important to include a representative from the technology department since technology will be essential to storing and sharing resources and reporting grades. Technology options for SBL practices change rapidly, so a team member who can navigate current and future technology options is invaluable. As team members are selected, be sure to involve key people who are trusted, are good listeners, and possess the ability to communicate ideas in a compelling fashion. Additionally, this team provides an opportunity to include an influential "fence-sitter"—a respected staff member who often sits on the sidelines and observes curiously before jumping on board with an initiative—in a formal leadership role. So long as he or she does not resist or undermine initiatives, in our experience, an influential fence-sitter's involvement can speed up the rate at which other staff members accept and adopt SBL and grading ideas.

Another aspect to consider in the creation of the guiding team is the balance of strengths and talents each member can bring to the team. In the book *Strengths-Based Leadership*, Tom Rath and Barrie Conchie (2008) identified four domains of strength that bring balance and productivity to a leadership team: executing, influencing, relationship building, and strategic thinking. They provide a description of each of these domains and how each strengthens the effectiveness of the team:

> *Executing* know how to make things happen . . . *influencing* help their team reach a much broader audience . . . *relationship building* are the essential glue that holds the team together, and . . . *strategic thinking* are the ones who keep us all focused on what *could be*. (Rath & Conchie, 2008, pp. 24–26)

Ensuring that members represent a balanced mix of these strengths serves a team well.

Establishing the guiding team also includes developing norms, identifying dates and times for the team to meet, and establishing protocols for the team's operation. Often, this team meets more often at first (maybe once every two weeks), but can move to less frequent meetings (say, monthly) later in the process. Because of the nature of discussion and new learning this team will commit to doing, norms for this team might include statements such as agree and disagree with ideas, not people; what is said here stays here; and what is learned here leaves here.

One protocol we recommend is to implement a few "open chair" spots at guiding team meetings. That is, allow a few teachers not on the team to attend and participate in each meeting, which adds transparency to the process. Michael Fullan (2008) commented on this type of transparency:

By transparency I mean openness about results. I also mean openness about what practices are most strongly connected to successful outcomes. What is inside the black box of implementation? How can we help others learn about and understand the inner workings of implementation? (p. 57)

By offering the open chair option, the guiding team essentially eliminates the black box Fullan described and offers a clear look into the inner workings of the implementation for anyone who is interested. School leaders might offer the open chair spots on a first-come, first-served basis, use a formal sign-up process, or invite specific teachers they feel would benefit from the experience.

A key task of the guiding team during phase 1 is to build consensus around SBL:

Attention to consensus means that staff and administration understand the "why" behind change and have a voice to productively ask questions and participate in decision making. Consensus rests upon the belief that we are better together, and different perspectives make our action planning better. Consensus should be attended to throughout the continuous improvement process. (Iowa Area Education Agencies, n.d.)

Certain logistics or protocols, actions, and considerations must be built into consensus building across a district, school, and school community. Figure 1.24 is a sample consensus-building tool used by Heartland AEA. Heartland AEA used this process to develop consensus throughout the process with various stakeholder groups. To enable districts and schools to use this, Heartland AEA first used this scale with participants during an information session with interested district and school teams in attendance. The Heartland team introduced the scale, talked about the benefit of building consensus among stakeholders, and then had school teams discuss with their groups how this could work back in their own districts. Team members discussed what stakeholder groups should be included, when this should happen, what it might look like using this scale with groups, who might lead the process, how they would work with the results of the consensus gathering, and then how they could do ongoing monitoring once new processes about SBL and grading were in place. Teams not only knew they wanted to just begin the process of involving stakeholder groups to build consensus as they studied or implemented SBL and grading; they also knew they wanted to work toward reaching *optimized* on the scale.

Internal and External Capacity Building			
	Foundational Essentials	**Making Progress**	**Optimized**
Consensus Building	The district or building makes efforts to uncover current beliefs and attitudes about grading. District or building educators share the belief that all students can learn.	The majority of stakeholders, as determined by the Guiding Team, is in agreement of being able to commit to or support standards-based or -referenced learning and grading. District or building consensus is reached on purpose and is a foundation of the grading process.	The district or building monitors on an ongoing, regular basis the pulse of efficacy for standards-based learning and grading from all stakeholder groups.

Source: © 2018 by Heartland Area Education Agency. Used with permission.

Figure 1.24: Consensus-building framework.

Analyze Existing Grading Practices and Beliefs

To begin preparing for new grading systems that are part of SBL implementation, it is important to seek first to understand (Covey, 2004). Instead of making assumptions about existing grading practices and beliefs, explore the lay of the land in your district or school. For school leaders, grading practices are often not on the radar until they happen to cause an issue. Understanding each teacher's current grading practices will provide an idea about the amount of change that will need to take place and specific aspects of training that will be necessary. This is especially important as more and more teachers are at least familiar with the concepts of SBL, and some might actually be implementing a few SBL ideas in their own practice. In our experience working with districts since 2010, we have seen the background knowledge of teachers improve in this area as well as the number of individual teachers experimenting with standards-based grading practices in some manner.

We suggest acquiring this information through two methods. First, ask teachers about their current grading protocols either during collaborative team meetings or through surveys. An example of questions for a grading survey is shown in figure 1.25. You may need to adjust some survey prompts to make the survey appropriate for your school and level. For instance, many elementary schools already separate behaviors from academics, so that question might be unnecessary.

Please respond to the following questions about grading. Candid responses are critical and honored as we work toward a common grading system.

What is the definition of a grade?

What should a grade represent?

What role should homework, attendance, behavior, and participation play in grading?

What role should reassessment play in grading?

Figure 1.25: Grading calibration survey example.

The second source of information is how teachers communicate with parents and students to explain current grading practices. Collecting copies of welcome-back letters, course syllabi, and so forth reveals current practices and what messages about grading teachers communicate to students and parents. In a district context, consider having principals collect these documents for their respective schools and reviewing them to develop a summary of themes that emerge.

Together, the survey results and a review of grading communication documents will tell a story about predominant grading beliefs and practices. This information will be useful in planning messaging and ideas for the transition to SBL. For example, if some teachers are already using rubrics for scoring and grading purposes on projects, this creates an easy bridge to the use of proficiency scales. Collecting some of the rubrics and visiting with the teachers about how they use them will provide an opportunity to make a connection and communicate that proficiency scales will be similar to the rubric approach they are already using. Conversely, a school leader might see that numerous teachers are heavily weighting homework completion in their calculations of final grades. This would provide some early knowledge that training about scoring learning rather than behavior and homework as a practice strategy instead of points-builder will be important. In our experience, leaders often find that there is a vast array of grading practices in their schools, and the few commonalities leave students confused as to how their grades are calculated. Clearly, common grading practices are necessary.

Establish Digital Storage for Standards and Scales

SBL requires common standards, common proficiency scales, common assessments, and so forth. Thus, it requires a method of storing and sharing these documents and resources. While it certainly is possible to keep a record of these documents and their development in hard-copy formats, it is more effective and efficient to work and store documents electronically. Therefore, it is critical that schools and districts establish systems for this early in the process. Schools might have a local server that can host curriculum documents, or they might elect to use cloud services such as Google Drive or Microsoft OneDrive. Some learning management systems include this function as well. Regardless of the platform chosen, schools and districts will typically use a system of nested folders to organize electronic documents. An elementary school might use grade-level folders with content-area folders inside each. A high school or departmentalized middle school might have content-area folders with folders for each specific course inside. Within each of the innermost folders in the structure is a folder for priority standards, proficiency scales, pacing guides, common assessments, and other relevant documents. The use of an organized system of folders ensures easy access to documents for all educators.

Figure 1.26 shows a second-grade curriculum folder, which would contain folders for each content area. Within each subject-area folder (in this example, ELA) are the priority standards, proficiency scales, relevant instructional resource documents, and team-developed common assessments.

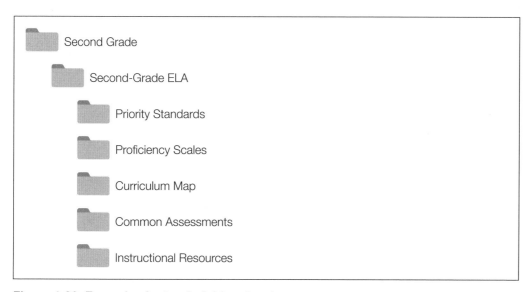

Figure 1.26: Example electronic folder structure.

In addition to establishing a folder structure, developing a common file-naming convention is helpful. For example, consider a third-grade team that develops a proficiency scale on the topic of the elements of a literary text. An appropriate naming convention might result in the document being saved as *ELA 3 Proficiency Scale Elements of Literary Text*. High school scales could follow a similar convention but use the name of the course instead of the content area and grade level. For example, a proficiency scale for biology might be saved as *Biology Proficiency Scale Thermal Energy*. While it might seem unnecessary to use the same naming convention for documents across teacher teams, this process keeps teams operating with the same protocols and makes it easy for leaders or teachers who want to look at another team's resources to navigate the files. These are important details that enhance the process and ensure everyone is on the same page.

Another way to electronically organize standards and proficiency scales might be within your electronic grading tool or learning management system. For example, the screen from Empower Learning in figure 1.27 displays a K–12 English language arts scope and sequence, the guaranteed and viable curriculum on which student growth is measured and the platform's gradebook and unit plans are built.

While figure 1.27 shows an overview of an entire content-area curriculum, figure 1.28 displays the standards for a specific class. The progress bars for each standard represent students' collective progress—how many students in the class have mastered the standard, how many are currently working on the standard, and how many have not yet started work on the standard.

Of course, there are multiple ways that this critical work can be stored. The important idea here is that leaders, technology support staff, and teacher teams plan to ensure that the products that result from collaboration are easily accessible so teacher teams can re-engage with previously accomplished work periodically over time.

Enlisting Consultants

Enlisting the support of outside consultants may be very useful as you design a guaranteed and viable curriculum and plan to transition to a standards-based system. Consider when an "outsider" can serve as a critical friend and trainer for content. Evaluate your own capacities for knowing, understanding, and delivering the various components involved in this phase. Some schools and districts bring in consultants to lead the phase 1 work; others use existing capacity to lead the work. Either can work very well. Consider the following list of ways consultants might help with phase 1.

- Providing an overview of SBL to leaders
- Guiding and supporting teacher teams in prioritizing standards and creating or customizing proficiency scales
- Helping leaders develop schoolwide or districtwide plans and communication documents
- Answering leaders' and teachers' questions through periodic webinars or in-person sessions

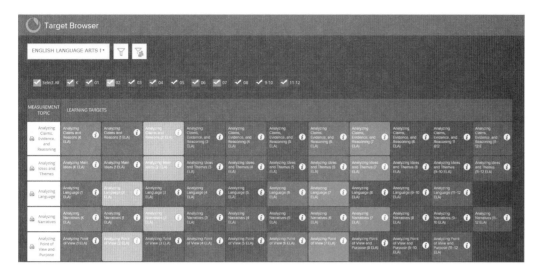

Source: © 2020 by Empower Learning. Used with permission.

Figure 1.27: Sample curriculum overview learning management system.

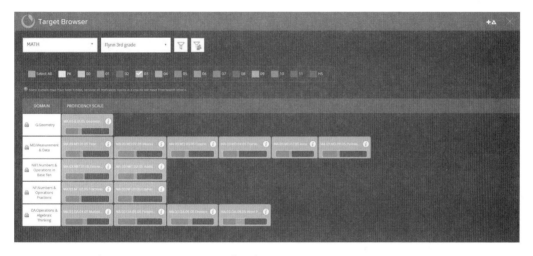

Source: © 2020 by Empower Learning. Used with permission.

Figure 1.28: Standards and class progress for third-grade mathematics.

Summary

In this chapter, we detailed phase 1, which includes the foundational work for SBL. Working through the components of this phase will set you up for success in the subsequent phases. You may find validation from some preliminary or existing efforts already underway. You may determine you have much more to do. At any rate, the key is to engage your building or district in the prioritization of standards, crafting proficiency scales, and building your communication and implementation plans.

Alignment and Capacity Building

In this chapter, we will describe the various processes and products in phase 2. This effort builds on the handiwork developed (or refined) in phase 1; it consists of the following leadership actions.

- Begin rolling out standards and scales for core content areas.

- Align instruction and assessment.

- Expand your efforts.

- Share information.

- Monitor implementation by school leaders.

Each of these main components has several associated activities. As in the previous phase, proceeding carefully through the components of this phase will set you up for greater success in the subsequent phases and ultimately in implementing SBL. You may again discover validation from initial endeavors underway and find you can expedite the efforts, or you may find more work to consider and initiate. Most leaders find this phase to take about a year to implement. Although there are many moving parts and some of them will happen simultaneously, rest assured. You have much underway, and the same processes will be used to expand products to other content areas. The descriptions and examples shared throughout this chapter will equip you well to handle any and all of the challenges.

Begin Rolling Out Standards and Scales for Core Content Areas

In order to validate the work of the design teams and develop further capacity within your system, you will want to obtain feedback about the work completed thus far. Seeking feedback from teachers who were not on the original design teams will begin to inform them of the ongoing work, as well as help them feel a part of the process.

Seek Feedback From Teachers

In phase 1, teacher teams worked together to determine the priority standards and to develop proficiency scales based on those standards. Prior to rolling these out in classrooms, it serves a school or district well to collect feedback, especially when the size of the school or district is such that not all teachers were part of the design processes. By offering teachers and other educators the opportunity to voice their thoughts about the priority standards and related proficiency scales, the potential increases for three positive outcomes.

1. The quality of the products increases as a result of additional expert opinions and ideas being considered. It will help clarify omissions or repetitions in the content or skills.

2. Educators not directly involved in the development processes become involved, therefore increasing the level of ownership of the priority standards and proficiency scales.

3. It will help in implementation. All teachers will see the products, be aware of the work, and know the timeline.

While soliciting feedback may add time and prompt multiple iterations of documents, it greatly increases staff buy-in. You may elect to request feedback at multiple stages of the curriculum-design process. The first round could occur after the initial identification of priority standards. This solicitation of feedback shares information throughout the building or system early in the process and demonstrates interest in others' opinions. This feedback opportunity also acts as a vetting checkpoint before getting too far along in the work. Proceeding without any input from other teachers who will be using the standards and scales may necessitate more revisions at a later point. A second round of feedback should occur after the design teams have drafted the proficiency scales.

In making the decision about how to go about collecting feedback, a leader must ensure that the information collected can be used effectively and efficiently. To solicit feedback, design team members can share priority standards and proficiency scales during collaborative team meetings or use surveys to collect input. Consider using an electronic survey instrument such as Google Forms (forms.google.com) or SurveyMonkey (www.survey monkey.com). Limit the survey to between three and five questions so it is easy for staff to complete. If the priority standards and proficiency scales are stored in a shared drive, it is quite easy to make these documents available as "view only," meaning no editing rights are granted. Along with the ability to view documents, participants in the feedback process are provided a means to offer comments, oftentimes through a document that can be electronically submitted. Figure 2.1 shows an example for obtaining feedback about prioritized standards.

However, some schools and districts elect to solicit feedback for prioritized standards and proficiency scales at the same time. It really depends on your timeframe, district size, and needs for involving other teachers (not on the design team) to increase cooperation and community. If you need to turn things around more quickly, then consider combining the feedback rounds into one. This may also be the best approach if you are a very large district and your teachers get many survey requests, so you want to limit the requests on teachers' time. A combined feedback form may also include some yes-or-no questions as well as some questions that ask respondents to give their opinions about the

The number of years I have been teaching this content at this grade level or course is _____.

I have read the draft version of the proposed priority standards shared by the curriculum-design team.

☐ Yes   ☐ No

Parts of the draft I agree with include:

I would propose the following specific formatting changes:

I would propose the following specific content changes:

I need more information about:

Figure 2.1: Survey for soliciting feedback on priority standards.

documents being reviewed. Figure 2.2 shows possible questions on a combined feedback form for both prioritized standards and proficiency scales together.

Priority Standards

1. Do you agree with most of the decisions made about which standards are priority and which are supporting?

   ☐ Yes

   ☐ No

2. What changes, if any, would you propose to the priority standards? Why do you propose the changes?

Proficiency Scales

1. Please rate your degree of agreement: The scale developers articulated a clear progression of knowledge from score 2.0 to score 4.0 on this scale.

   Strongly Disagree　　　**Disagree**　　　**Agree**　　　**Strongly Agree**

   ←——————————————————————————————————————→

2. What changes, if any, would you propose to this proficiency scale? Why do you propose the changes?

---

*Visit **MarzanoResources.com/reproducibles** for a free reproducible version of this figure.*

Figure 2.2: Sample feedback form on standards and proficiency scales.

Leaders will also need to determine the amount of time given for feedback collection. A two-week window is ample for obtaining meaningful feedback. Any longer and respondents forget about it, and much shorter may not provide sufficient time for thoughtful responses. Because this feedback is so helpful in ensuring the quality of decisions and products, those individuals leading the processes will want to communicate the invitation for feedback numerous times. Some online survey tools can send respondents a reminder if they do not fill out the survey during a certain window of time. After two requests for feedback, it is safe to assume anyone who has not responded does not have any specific input to share. In the end, some teachers will willingly offer their expertise as feedback, and others will not. Whatever feedback is gathered will be used to enhance the original decisions and documents. Most online survey tools will automatically collate responses to make them easier to analyze and incorporate.

It is important to keep in mind when making this decision that documents for explaining the prioritization and proficiency scale–development processes need to be included for the reviewers, as individuals not participating in the design processes may not have adequate understanding of standards and scales. Figure 2.3 is a sample document used by Jefferson County Public Schools to describe proficiency scales.

What is the point? How will this meet the needs of my students?

Proficiency scales define systemic and equitable high expectations for every student in Jefferson County (Jeffco). A proficiency scale takes the prioritized 2020 Colorado Academic Standards and breaks them down into four levels of knowledge and understanding. This information is organized in a visual chart that can be used as a tool for planning, teaching, assessing, and reflecting. The elements at the 2.0 level create a learning progression for both teachers and students to use as targets for instructional planning and student goal setting.

Considerations for Teachers

Jeffco proficiency scales are available for the prioritized 2020 Colorado Academic Standards in every content area from preschool through twelfth grade.

Jeffco proficiency scales will live in Bridge to Curriculum as a resource in the "Resource Library," below the unit overview, and also in Stage 2 Assessment Evidence in all curricular units of study.

Student-Friendly Scale Examples are now available! Look here for more information.

Overview

Proficiency scales provide teachers and students with clarity and the equitable calibration of 2020 Colorado Academic Standards. Proficiency scales are available for both academic and nonacademic high expectations for all Jeffco students and are organized by grade level, content area, and Jeffco Generations Skills.

Proficiency scales also provide a learning progression of the critical skills and knowledge that students must acquire and perform in order to be considered at or beyond proficiency.

Proficiency scales empower students as agents of their own learning and provide teachers with critical information to engage in the Jeffco Deeper Learning Model to plan, teach, assess, and reflect with clarity and precision.

Considerations for School Leaders

Proficiency scales are powerful tools for calibrating students' learning expectations both vertically and horizontally across grade levels and content areas.

Proficiency scales will provide support for collaborative decision-making/ accountability committees and families to better understand the progression of learning all students must master in order to be considered proficient or competent in one or more of the 2020 Colorado Academic Standards.

Proficiency scales can support back-to-school and curriculum nights at the beginning of the school year and middle and high school semester course transitions between the fall and spring semesters.

Proficiency scales help students better articulate their goals and how they will know when a goal is met or exceeded.

Links to Resources

The Pulse From Curriculum and Instruction blog

Deeper Learning Through Jeffco Proficiency Scales, May 2020

High Expectations for Deeper Learning FAQs

Family and community website support for understanding the Jeffco curriculum

Annotated sample of a Jeffco proficiency scale

Grading and Reporting on Student Learning and Achievement

Research

Butler, S. M., & McMunn, N. D. (2006). *A teacher's guide to classroom assessment: Understanding and using assessment to improve student learning*. San Francisco: Jossey-Bass.

Guskey, T. R. (2015). *On your mark: Challenging the conventions of grading and reporting*. Bloomington, IN: Solution Tree Press.

Heflebower, T., Hoegh, J., & Warrick P. (2014). *A school leader's guide to standards-based grading*. Bloomington, IN: Marzano Resources.

Jung, L. A. (2018, February). Scales of progress. *Educational Leadership*, 75(5), 22–27.

Lalor, A. D. M. (2017). *Ensuring high-quality curriculum: How to design, revise, or adopt curriculum aligned to student success*. Alexandria, VA: Association for Supervision and Curriculum Development.

Tomlinson, C. A. (2018, February). One to grow on / Measuring doesn't come first. *Educational Leadership*, 75(5), 90–91.

Tucker, C. (2018, February). The techy teacher. *Educational Leadership*, 75(5), 84–85.

Wiggins, G. P., & McTighe, J. (2008). *Understanding by Design*. Alexandria, VA: Association for Supervision and Curriculum Development.

Figure 2.3: Proficiency scales overview document.

Figure 2.4 is an example communication from a district to teachers regarding the collection of feedback on scales. This facilitator used a variation of the feedback process previously described. You will note the district facilitator seeking feedback about the prioritized (essential) standards as well as the essential vocabulary, and prerequisite knowledge and skills the team would use when reviewing proficiency scales at level 2.0.

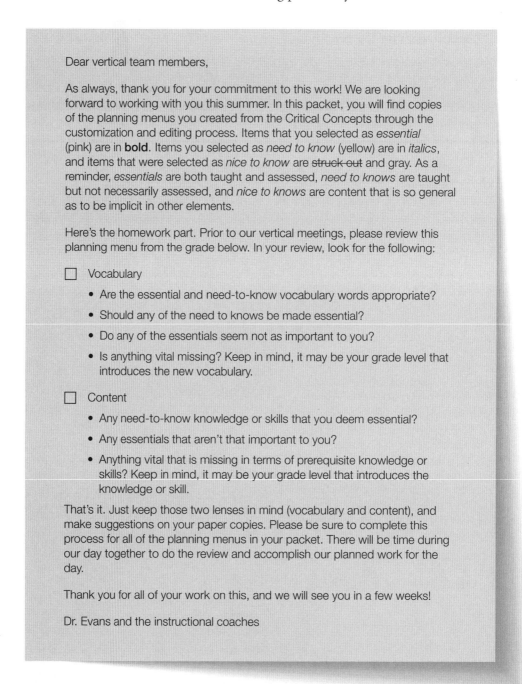

Dear vertical team members,

As always, thank you for your commitment to this work! We are looking forward to working with you this summer. In this packet, you will find copies of the planning menus you created from the Critical Concepts through the customization and editing process. Items that you selected as *essential* (pink) are in **bold**. Items you selected as *need to know* (yellow) are in *italics*, and items that were selected as *nice to know* are ~~struck out~~ and gray. As a reminder, *essentials* are both taught and assessed, *need to knows* are taught but not necessarily assessed, and *nice to knows* are content that is so general as to be implicit in other elements.

Here's the homework part. Prior to our vertical meetings, please review this planning menu from the grade below. In your review, look for the following:

- [ ] Vocabulary
  - Are the essential and need-to-know vocabulary words appropriate?
  - Should any of the need to knows be made essential?
  - Do any of the essentials seem not as important to you?
  - Is anything vital missing? Keep in mind, it may be your grade level that introduces the new vocabulary.

- [ ] Content
  - Any need-to-know knowledge or skills that you deem essential?
  - Any essentials that aren't that important to you?
  - Anything vital that is missing in terms of prerequisite knowledge or skills? Keep in mind, it may be your grade level that introduces the knowledge or skill.

That's it. Just keep those two lenses in mind (vocabulary and content), and make suggestions on your paper copies. Please be sure to complete this process for all of the planning menus in your packet. There will be time during our day together to do the review and accomplish our planned work for the day.

Thank you for all of your work on this, and we will see you in a few weeks!

Dr. Evans and the instructional coaches

Source: © 2020 by Michael Evans. Used with permission.

Figure 2.4: Letter soliciting feedback on draft curriculum documents.

The goal of this process is to receive valuable feedback from as many people outside the development processes as possible. Therefore, careful and strategic thought about the factors described in this section must occur prior to the feedback request to ensure optimum success.

Review and Incorporate Teacher Feedback

Once you have collected feedback, the design teams should review specific advice regarding their proficiency scales obtained from the electronic feedback process. It is essential for the design teams to read the feedback as constructive criticism and be willing to make improvements as warranted. However, it is also within the parameters of the design team to reject suggestions submitted. In so doing, require individual teams to keep track of any feedback they elected not to adopt by drafting a written rationale that would be shared back to teachers in the form of a question and answer. This process acknowledges both accepted and rejected feedback. This enables your non-design-team teachers to feel valued and their feedback respected. Simply put, your teachers feel heard.

In response to feedback, the teams modify the original draft where it makes sense to do so and keep track of suggestions with which they disagree and do not incorporate. Teams might even draft a summary of accepted and rejected suggestions and the corresponding rationales for each. This creates a record of revisions to the draft standards or scales and explanations for any feedback that was not adopted. Figure 2.5 (page 68) is an example of feedback provided to a team of mathematics teachers on a proficiency scale they had developed.

As another example, figure 2.6 (page 69) displays a third-grade ELA proficiency scale on which feedback has been recorded by educators not involved in its development. The development team would then review the comments and make decisions about necessary revisions to the proficiency scale. Through this process, the individuals offering feedback feel valued and included, and the revised version of the proficiency scale is a stronger tool.

Begin Field-Testing Standards and Scales

With proficiency scales created and revised, it is appropriate to encourage teachers to use these valuable tools with students. It is likely worthwhile to solicit volunteer teachers or teams to put the proficiency scales into practice. Building leaders should assure these teachers that there is no one right way to implement the priority standards and proficiency scales. As these volunteer teachers use the scales for the first time, they might experiment with developing and using a student version of the proficiency scale rather than the version created for teachers. The purpose of the student-friendly version is to ensure that students can understand what a proficiency scale is and actually use it while they learn the content. As part of the field test, teachers should also begin to provide students with feedback about their levels on the proficiency scale throughout a unit of instruction and help them set goals and next learning steps. Figure 2.7 (page 69) is an example of a student-friendly grade 2 ELA proficiency scale.

Scale Geometry: Logical Arguments and Constructions		Feedback
Priority Standard: (G.5A) Investigate patterns using constructions to make conjectures about geometric relationships, including angles formed by parallel lines cut by a transversal, criteria required for triangle congruence, special segments of triangles, diagonals of quadrilaterals, interior and exterior angles of polygons, and special segments and angles of circles choosing from a variety of tools.		I specifically looked for covariance, vocabulary, and breakdown of the specified skills. Overall, this looks solid. Good work!
Advanced	The student will: Create formal proofs of his or her conjectures based on investigations of parallel lines cut by a transversal, criteria required for triangle congruence, special segments of triangles, diagonals of quadrilaterals, interior and exterior angles of polygons, and special segments and angles of circles Find real-world models of his or her conjectures	These look reasonable. I like that you have a couple of options noted.
Proficient	The student will: (Vocabulary is underlined) Investigate patterns using constructions to make <u>conjectures</u> about geometric relationships, including angles formed by <u>parallel lines cut by a transversal</u> choosing from a variety of tools Investigate patterns using constructions to make <u>conjectures</u> about geometric relationships, including criteria required for <u>triangle congruence</u> choosing from a variety of tools Investigate patterns using constructions to make <u>conjectures</u> about geometric relationships, including <u>diagonals of quadrilaterals</u> choosing from a variety of tools Investigate patterns using constructions to make <u>conjectures</u> about geometric relationships, including <u>interior and exterior angles of polygons</u> choosing from a variety of tools Investigate patterns using constructions to make <u>conjectures</u> about geometric relationships, including <u>special segments and angles of circles</u> choosing from a variety of tools	Simplify the repeated language here? List vocabulary at Developing level—I added it below. Make sure students are required to explain their thinking. Good level of focus for a scale—skills are closely related and will covary.
Developing	The student will perform basic processes, such as: Identify congruent and supplementary angles Construct triangles with given specifications Identify diagonals of quadrilaterals Identify interior and exterior angles of polygons Identify and explain the differences between a radius, diameter, and chord	The student will recognize or recall specific vocabulary, such as: Conjectures, transversal, diagonals, interior and exterior angles, chord, radius, diameter, supplementary angles
Needs Improvement	With help, the student can perform developing and proficient expectations.	Combine the two levels below Developing in student-friendly version?
No Evidence	Even with help, the student cannot perform expectations.	

Figure 2.5: Sample feedback on a mathematics proficiency scale.

Reading Literature Topic: Describe the characters, setting, and events in a story. Essential Question: How might describing characters, setting, and events in a story help me understand what I can read in literature?		
	Scale	**Feedback From Reviewers**
Score 4.0	The student will create new events in the story using the same characters and setting.	Consider expanding this learning target to "The student will adapt the story by changing the characters, setting, or events." This would broaden the options for use in the classroom.
Score 3.0	The student will: • describe the events in a story using key details • describe the setting of a story using key details • describe the characters in a story using key details	Consider reordering the targets to align with the standard. Capitalize and use periods for each bullet as in level 2.0?
Score 2.0	The student will: • Name the setting of a story. • Name the characters of a story. • Identify an event in a story. • Recognize or recall specific terminology such as *character*, *setting*, *event*, *key details*, and *describe*.	You might use the verb "identify" instead of "name." Usually the vocabulary is listed first.

Source: © 2018 by Bismarck Public Schools. Used with permission.

Figure 2.6: Sample feedback on an ELA proficiency scale.

STANDARD
I can ask and answer questions based on the text and what I already know.

4	For example, I can . . . • Use multiple leveled readers and write literal and inferential questions and justify which leveled reader answers each question.
3	I can . . . • Answer literal questions using evidence from the text. • Answer inferential questions using evidence from the text. • Ask literal questions using evidence from the text.
2	I can . . . • Define *prediction* and *inference*. • Locate evidence within the text to answer literal questions.
1	With help from the teacher, I can . . . • Ask and answer literal questions based on the text.

Source: © 2018 by Columbus Public Schools. Used with permission.

Figure 2.7: A student-friendly version of a grade 2 ELA proficiency scale.

Another idea is to encourage teacher teams to use proficiency scales to draft a unit instructional plan (Heflebower et al., 2019; Marzano, 2017). Figure 2.8 is an example of a fourth-grade mathematics instructional unit that is based on a proficiency scale. You will see that the proficiency scale content is actually embedded within the unit plan.

Grade: Four	**Quarter Taught:** Third
Unit: Equivalent Fractions	**Duration of Unit:** Approximately two weeks

Grade-Level Priority Standards:

Standard: 4.NF.2—Compare two fractions with different numerators and different denominators, e.g., by creating common denominators or numerators, or by comparing to a benchmark fraction such as $\frac{1}{2}$. Recognize that comparisons are valid only when the two fractions refer to the same whole. Record the results of comparisons with symbols, and justify conclusions, e.g. by using a visual fraction model.

Supporting Standards:

4.NF.1—Explain why a fraction $\frac{a}{b}$ is equivalent to a fraction $(n \times a)/(n \times b)$ by using visual fraction models, with attention to how the number and size of the parts differ even though the two fractions themselves are the same size. Use this principle to recognize and generate equivalent fractions.

Essential Questions:

When and why is comparing fractions important?

Learning Progressions		
Previous Grade-Level Standards:	**Grade-Level Standards:**	**Next Grade-Level Standards:**
• 3.NF.3—Compare two fractions with the same numerator or the same denominator by reasoning about their size. Recognize that comparisons are valid only when the two fractions refer to the same whole. Record the results of comparisons with the symbols <, =, or >, and justify the conclusions.	• 4.NF.2—Compare two fractions with different numerators and different denominators, e.g., by creating common denominators or numerators, or by comparing to a benchmark fraction such as $\frac{1}{2}$. Recognize that comparisons are valid only when the two fractions refer to the same whole. Record the results of comparisons with symbols, and justify conclusions, e.g. by using a visual fraction model.	• 5.NF.1—Add and subtract fractions with unlike denominators by replacing given fractions with equivalent fractions in such a way as to produce an equivalent sum or difference of fractions with like denominators.

Essential Vocabulary
Key Academic Vocabulary: *common denominator, comparison, denominator, equivalent, fraction, generate, improper fraction, justify, numerator*

Assessment and Evidence	
District Common Assessments: • Equivalent Fractions	***Classroom Assessments:*** • *Equivalent fractions preassessment* • *Generating equivalent fractions activity* • *Vocabulary match* • *Score 2.0 check-in* • *Whiteboards activity* • *Score 3.0 check-in* • *Exit slips*

Proficiency Scale	
Score 4.0	In addition to score 3.0 performance, the student demonstrates in-depth inferences and applications that go beyond what was taught. For example, the student: • Explains why a set of fractions with unlike denominators is or is not ordered from least to greatest or greatest to least
Score 3.0	The student: • Explains that comparing fractions is valid only when they refer to the same whole • Compares two given fractions by generating equivalent fractions with common denominators • Compares two given fractions by reasoning about their size or their location on a number line, or comparing them to a benchmark fraction • Records the comparison using symbols and justifies each comparison
Score 2.0	**The student recognizes or recalls specific vocabulary, such as:** • *Common denominator, comparison, denominator, equivalent, fraction, generate, improper fraction, justify, numerator* **The student performs basic processes, such as:** • Compares two given fractions with different numerators • Compares fractions just using pictures and not number lines • Places a fraction on a number line

Source: © 2019 by Uinta County #1 School District. Used with permission.

Figure 2.8: Example of a fourth-grade mathematics instructional unit based on a proficiency scale.

As the unit of instruction proceeds, it is helpful for the volunteer teachers to jot down information about what worked well, whether revisions to the proficiency scale are needed and why, and other things that practicing teachers might have noticed. These things might include level of student ownership of the learning, the degree to which students understood the proficiency scales, and level of achievement at the end of the instructional unit. This is an opportune time for feedback from individual teachers or collaborative teams about commendations and recommendations for additional proficiency scale refinement and use. Leaders should seek and use this empirical evidence from the system by reconvening the original design team for a meeting to reflect on the proficiency scales after volunteer teachers or teams use them with students.

Align Instruction and Assessment

A key feature of SBL is that instruction and assessment must align. That is, assessments must cover topics that were actually taught in class. For example, a teacher may have external assessments, perhaps purchased from a curriculum provider by the school, which may not align with the proficiency scales. If the teacher uses an assessment that is not aligned to the basis of instruction, students will struggle, and may even fail on those assessment items. The following sections provide details on how to align instruction and assessment with proficiency scales.

Align Proficiency Scales With Instructional Activities and Resources

The first step in this activity is to plan instruction based on priority standards and proficiency scales. When transitioning to SBL, teachers realize that unit plans are the key to understanding the development of students' knowledge and skills as described in the standards. Teachers will still engage in lesson planning—instructional strategies operate at the lesson level—but the vision of student learning should start at the unit level. Traditionally, units have been the format in which teachers break down content into manageable chunks that they can teach and assess. In an SBL system, units function in the same way, but the purpose is to break down the development of knowledge and skills into the smaller components that the priority standards require. In other words, each individual item on a proficiency scale (often displayed as a bulleted list of targets) may become a classroom lesson or series of lessons. Those bulleted items are what is specified and taught within the entire unit. As summarized by Heflebower and colleagues (2019):

> Teachers new to standards-based learning may find a focus on the standards rather than content to be uncomfortable at first. Traditionally, the sequence of presenting content to students has been the guide for instructional planning. As teachers consider the planning process for standards-based learning, the content moves into a secondary position. That content will still be there, and likely in much the same sequence. But the starting place for planning instruction will be the priority standards and their associated proficiency scales. (p. 11)

Designing units essentially involves creating a sequence of standards. Some content areas, such as English language arts, contain standards that are very encompassing and are often applied throughout the entire school year. Other content areas have standards that are more sequential in nature. In this case, one standard forms the basis of another, so instructors teach them in that sequence. In an SBL environment, there will be a number of priority standards for the year, but only a few will be actively taught and addressed at a time. When students reach proficiency on a certain standard, the teacher removes it from direct instruction and replaces it with periodic review and then moves on to the next standard in the sequence.

Knowledge of the students and the standards will allow a teacher to accurately judge the proper sequence. Some schools, departments, or districts provide a suggested pacing guide or scope and sequence. We recommend pacing guides (see page 34), but teachers should use them as a suggestion only, and teach according to students' knowledge, rather than moving through a guide for the sake of getting through it in the allotted amount of time. As the sequencing process is complete, the teacher has a generalized plan for the year. The next step is to look at specific units of study and plan how to explore this journey with the students (Heflebower et al., 2019).

As teachers craft unit plans, they must provide students with a series of scaffolded learning opportunities based on the proficiency scale's progression of knowledge and skills. This process guides student growth. Early in the instructional unit, the focus is on establishing a solid foundation of prerequisite knowledge and skills for the priority standard or standards addressed within the unit. The focus will then shift to moving beyond those basics, identifying learning targets that represent the steps toward achieving proficiency on the standards. At some point in the unit, the teacher will present students with the opportunity to demonstrate knowledge and skill at and beyond the level of the standard. Again, teachers are gauging students' attainment of knowledge and skill levels identified in the proficiency scales. If students are not yet ready, the teacher slows the pace but continues to teach toward proficiency. As students obtain proficiency, the teacher pushes them toward the more advanced applications or depth in understanding of the topic at level 4.0.

As an example, teachers in Monett R-1 School District in Monett, Missouri, use the tool shown in figure 2.9 (page 74) to plan units based on proficiency scales. Note that the scale in this example has two learning targets, so the teacher has planned instructional strategies, resources, and assessments for each.

In linking the proficiency scale to a unit plan, teachers will sequence the type of lesson activities, resources, and assessments with their associated content to gradually move students up the proficiency scale. Obviously, instruction and learning activities will be different at varying levels of the proficiency scale. Early on in the unit, students will need to work at level 2.0 on the proficiency scale in order to understand and process new information. Eventually, the teacher moves them to level 3.0 activities and offers many of those ready the opportunity for them to work beyond level 3.0. Students require more direct instruction as they deal with basic knowledge and skills, and they can handle more independent learning opportunities as they achieve and exceed proficiency. This provides a logical sequence of activities connected to the learning progression found in the proficiency scale, and that means students are working toward, and possibly beyond, proficiency on a priority standard.

As leaders strive to ensure the alignment of instruction to proficiency scales, it is important to plan for how to support this process. A few suggestions for attaining success include the following.

- Provide templates and examples of how to align instruction to proficiency scales.

- Address this process with teachers in an ongoing manner during staff meetings and in one-on-one or small-group conversations. Share examples of practice through short videos and photos to build understanding among all teachers during these communication opportunities.

- Provide time for frequent collaborative instructional planning.

Unit: Speaking and Listening
(Standards: 9–10.SL.1.B, 9–10.RI.2.D)

		How will I teach this?	What resources will I need?	How will I assess this?
Score 4.0	Example activity: Students generate counterarguments and counterclaims based on a speech or presentation they select.			Student generated
	3.5	In addition to score 3.0 performance, partial success at 4.0 content			
Score 3.0	**The student will:** • SL1—Delineate a speaker's argument and claims • SL2—Evaluate a speaker's point of view, reasoning, and evidence	SL1—Practicing, deepening, and knowledge application (modeling, guided practice, varied practice) • Model identifying arguments and claims using an infomercial or TED Talk • Do one together, relying on students to delineate arguments and how they flow SL2—Practicing, deepening, and knowledge application • Using the work from SL1, help students evaluate the speakers' arguments and claims looking for examples of good and poor reasoning and evidence.	SL1—Wendy Troxel TED Talk, "Why School Should Start Later for Teens" ShamWow infomercial Other examples of persuasive speech SL2—Activities from element 11 of *The New Art and Science of Teaching* (Marzano, 2017)	SL1—ELA common formative assessment for analyzing claims and reasoning. Students will track a speaker's arguments, claims, reasons, and evidence by creating an informal outline while listening to a speaker. Students can create their own persuasive speech using valid arguments, claims, reasons, and evidence. SL2—Using the outline from SL1, students will evaluate the quality of the speaker's arguments, claims, reasons, and evidence by looking for solid logical arguments, reliable evidence, as well as exposing logical fallacies used by the speaker. Students can create their own infomercial using logical fallacies.
	2.5	No major errors or omissions regarding 2.0 content and partial knowledge of the 3.0 content			

Score 2.0	SL1—Recognizes or recalls specific terminology, such as *argument, claim, point of view, reasoning, evidence, formal logic, informal logic, deductive reasoning, inductive reasoning* Performs basic processes, such as: • Identify the speaker's main arguments or claims. • Identify the evidence used by the speaker to support his or her argument or claim. • Identify the reasoning or logic used by the speaker. SL2—Recognizes or recalls specific terminology, such as *dogmatism, overgeneralization, faulty analogy, circular reasoning, bandwagon* Performs basic processes, such as: • Identify faulty or flawed reasoning or logic and common logical fallacies, such as dogmatism, overgeneralization, faulty analogy, circular reasoning, and bandwagon.	SL1—Direct instruction (collaborative processing, think-pair-share, summaries, informal outlines) • Vocabulary • Use prior knowledge of main idea and supporting details to scaffold to claims and evidence. • Introduce logical arguments including formal, informal, deductive, and inductive reasoning. SL2—Direct instruction (collaborative processing, think-pair-share, summaries, informal outlines) • Vocabulary • Introduce common logical fallacies, linking them to the logical argument structure in SL1. • Model identifying logical fallacies using historical political propaganda examples.	SL1—Corresponding chapter in textbook Six-step vocabulary activities Slide deck for unit (remember to include slides from main idea and supporting details unit) Reasoning examples and activities Logical argument diagram SL2—Six-step vocabulary activities Examples of logical fallacies Political propaganda examples (World War II)	SL1—ELA common formative assessment for analyzing claims and reasoning ELA common summative assessment for analyzing claims and reasoning SL2—ELA common formative assessment for analyzing claims and reasoning ELA common summative assessment for analyzing claims and reasoning			
	1.5	With help, a partial knowledge of the 2.0 content, but major errors or omissions regarding the 3.0 content					
Score 1.0	With help, a partial understanding of some of the simpler details and processes and some of the more complex ideas and processes						
Score 0.0	Even with help, no understanding or skill demonstrated						

Source: © 2020 by Monett R-1 School District. Used with permission.

*Visit **MarzanoResources.com/reproducibles** for a blank reproducible version of this figure.*

Figure 2.9: Sample completed unit plan.

Share Methods for Using Scales for Feedback and Goal Setting

Specific feedback and goal setting are integral parts of a SBL classroom. These processes are useful to leaders as they help teachers focus students on individual needs related to specific learning targets stated on proficiency scales. The most important and influential instructional decisions are often made by learners themselves (Stiggins, 2008). When students know and understand the proficiency scales, they can take ownership of their learning. In other words, they can control their needs for additional support or extensions. Leaders know that feedback, goal setting, and tracking progress go together. As students obtain specific feedback, they can more easily set goals and track progress about those SBL targets. In turn, tracking progress provides students with information regarding their initial goals, and often will assist them in modifying the goal or creating a new one (Heflebower et al., 2019). Leaders will want to facilitate this understanding with teachers as part of the trainings on proficiency scales in the classroom.

It is a good idea to obtain examples of teachers sharing and using the proficiency scale with students, such as photos and videos of classroom use. Leaders may also want to provide guidance to teachers about how to use student work within their grade-level or other collaborative team meetings. When teachers present students with anonymous samples of student work at each level of the proficiency scale, it is very helpful in establishing clarity and consistency among teachers. Teachers can in turn help students obtain clarity about the learning they will undertake, and guide them into personal goal setting—an essential step in the SBL classroom. Student goal setting and tracking of progress on personal goals has been associated with as much as a 32-percentile-point gain in student achievement (Marzano, 2010). For this reason, leaders should ensure that teachers engage in the practice of goal setting with students on a regular basis. That means planning for the instructional time it will take to set goals, process feedback on the goals, discuss with students their progress on the goals, and celebrate success as students see gains toward their goals. For more details about these key ideas, see *A Teacher's Guide to Standards-Based Learning* (Heflebower et al., 2019). Leaders should also encourage teachers to reference the proficiency scales often during instruction as a method of reinforcing the importance of the learning progression during instruction, assessment, and feedback.

One way teachers can foster goal setting is to create digital or physical folders in which students can keep their goal-tracking forms and evidence of progress toward the goals. Evidence may come in the form of assessments and assignments, with scores providing feedback on students' progress. Having student-set goals and identifying and tracking progress toward those goals means that both student and teacher have the information available to make regular progress checks meaningful. These folders are also easy to share with parents and guardians.

Another strategy that leaders can encourage teachers to use in their classrooms is reflective prompts for student tracking and goal setting. Reflective prompts provide students with incomplete statements that the students must complete. These prompts require students to think critically about their own learning. Some teachers find that they can best stimulate critical thinking when reflection prompts align to goal setting. Students discuss what they did well and why and consider next steps for future work. Reflective prompts help students practice reflection, consider appropriate actions, and make use of those actions within the goal-setting process for increased achievement. Figure 2.10 exemplifies reflective questions that can be shared with teachers in order to help students use priority standards and proficiency scales for personalizing, reflecting on, and setting goals for their own learning. In this middle school science example, a student used the reflective prompts provided by his teacher to think back on his goals and process for the assignment.

As you reflect about what you wrote and the assignment expectations, what did you do well? How do you know? What is your evidence?
I did well. One thing was to include a lot of info that connects to the expectations. It states that we needed logical information, and to make my project logical, I included opinions along with the backing quotes from the text. That is evidence.
What are the next steps that you will focus on in your next project? Why? Remember to connect your ideas back to the expectations.
I worked hard, and still have some things I would do differently. For example, I would have added more points of view, like what the boys thought of the BTS group. That would have made my write-up more interesting and informative. I think I will take a bit more time to see that I have a piece of text evidence for each point I made. I will do that next time.

Source: Heflebower et al., 2019, p. 51.

Figure 2.10: Sample student response to reflective questions.

After proficiency scales have been in use for some time (perhaps a few weeks or a month), a leader may want to prompt teacher teams to discuss various ways in which to use the scales to provide students feedback. As teachers share such ideas, they will expand their repertoires of how to embed the scales in every aspect of teaching. Leaders may also consider taking video or pictures of positive examples they see during walk-through observations or other classroom experiences. Sharing these examples with staff provides reinforcement for the exemplified teachers, and also signifies the importance of proficiency scales.

Train Teacher Design Teams on Assessment Literacy

Assessment literacy is an essential component in an SBL system. This means building deeper understanding about the various facets of high-quality assessment practices (such as validity, reliability, common assessments, and so on), as well as solid assessment design, refinement, and use. It is important not only for teachers, who administer assessments, but also for leaders. Ensuring this explicit training and practice helps all educators within a building or district deepen knowledge and application of assessment principles and practices.

During a professional development day, a number of smaller districts in Missouri came together for sessions focused on validity, reliability, and fairness of classroom assessments. Table 2.1 showcases the session topics, which might serve as a model for training topics in your school or district.

TABLE 2.1: ASSESSMENT LITERACY TRAINING TOPICS

What and Why of SBL (Foundational Basics)	Understanding and Using Proficiency Scales	Creating High-Quality Assessments	Tracking and Reporting Student Progress	Personalizing Learning
• Foundational Basics • Getting Started With SBL	• Identifying Priority and Supporting Standards • Developing Proficiency Scales • Using Proficiency Scales to Plan Instruction	• Using Proficiency Scales to Build Assessments • Ensuring Validity, Reliability, and Fairness in Assessments • Auditing Assessments • Scoring Assessments	• Using Formative Assessment to Track Student Progress • Student Goal Setting • Student Self-Monitoring • Parent Communication	• What Is Personalized Learning? • How Do We Get Here?

Source: © 2020 by Michael Evans. Used with permission.

As you can see, there is a strong emphasis on learning to develop and refine classroom assessments. During the overview keynote, teachers learned about the three components of quality assessments—validity, fairness, and reliability—and examples of each. They learned teacher-friendly ideas for creating, refining, administering, and evaluating classroom assessments. Teachers were asked to bring a classroom assessment they use with students. After direct instruction about each of the three quality criteria, teachers applied their learning directly by revising the classroom assessment they brought to the training. For more information about quality assessment development, consider the following resources.

- *Teacher-Made Assessments: How to Connect Curriculum, Instruction, and Student Learning* by Christopher R. Gareis and Leslie W. Grant (2008)

- *The Principal as Assessment Leader* edited by Thomas R. Guskey (2009a)

- *Making Classroom Assessments Reliable and Valid* by Robert J. Marzano (2018)

- *Classroom Assessment: What Teachers Need to Know* (2nd ed.) by W. James Popham (1999)

- *The Truth About Testing: An Educator's Call to Action* by W. James Popham (2001)

- *Student-Involved Classroom Assessment* (3rd ed.) by Rick Stiggins (2001)

There are also many seminars and conferences devoted to quality classroom assessment development.

Align Quality Classroom Assessments

Building on the set of priority standards and proficiency scales created in phase 1, it is time to align classroom assessments to the finalized proficiency scales. This means that classroom assessments monitor progress against the knowledge and skills recorded on the proficiency scales. It is common for assessment development teams to be formed and come together for learning about high-quality classroom assessments based on proficiency scales. An assessment development team might be composed of three or four content experts. It is not necessary for this team to be the same group of educators who worked together on prioritizing standards or developing proficiency scales; however, it also may be that same group of teachers. Recall figure 1.6 (page 26), which showed proficiency scales' role as the hub of the standards-based system. Assessment is one of the spokes; this represents the idea that the items and tasks on any assessment connect to the learning targets on a particular proficiency scale.

There are multiple effective approaches to completing this alignment work. Some districts ask teachers to do the alignment at the building level, using their existing classroom assessments as the basis for the work. Others create districtwide assessments in order to track student progress on a common set of carefully crafted and aligned assessments. Regardless of the process used, this alignment—direct connections among the priority standards, proficiency scales, and assessments—is essential to a coherent and comprehensive system supporting further efforts toward standards-based learning and reporting.

The easiest method for this alignment is to begin with an already existing assessment. When teachers exercise this process, they typically have the proficiency scale being considered available and examine each item on the existing assessment to ensure it connects directly to a specific learning target on the scale. Some teams of teachers develop a system for labeling items, such as K = keep the item, R = revise the item, and E = eliminate the item. Once the examination of individual assessment items and tasks is completed, the existing assessment is revised to reflect the alignment process. This work often results in a common assessment (that is, an assessment that all teachers within a grade level or course use), or a tool that the team will use toward the end of a unit for the sake of making decisions about the current level of student learning. See *A School Leader's Guide to Standards-Based Grading* (Heflebower et al., 2014) for more details and step-by-step processes for leading the assessment alignment work.

An aligned assessment might cover an entire proficiency scale; assessments such as this are often called *leveled assessments*, as they include items from each level on the proficiency scale (scores 2.0, 3.0, and 4.0). Alternatively, a well-aligned assessment could address a single level on the scale, or even a single learning target. The key idea here is that the assessment items or tasks connect to the learning targets on the proficiency scale being assessed. Consider the proficiency scale in figure 2.11 (page 80) and aligned leveled assessment in figure 2.12 (page 80) for kindergarten English language arts. Note that the assessment developers even included the language from the proficiency scale in the left-hand column on the assessment to highlight the alignment to the scale. Additional examples of leveled assessments appear in appendix B (page 167).

4.0	The student will: • Write several sentences to explain important information about text
3.5	In addition to score 3.0 performance, partial success at score 4.0 content
3.0	The student will: • Explain how written words are organized on pages • Write sentences when told how to spell individual words
2.5	No major errors or omissions regarding score 2.0 content, and partial success at score 3.0 content
2.0	The student will recognize or recall specific vocabulary (for example, *back cover*, *bottom*, *front cover*, *left*, *page*, *right*, *top*) and perform basic processes such as: • State that pages in a book are read in order from the front cover to the back cover The student will recognize or recall specific vocabulary (for example, *alphabet*, *letter*, *lowercase*, *sentence*, *space*, *uppercase*, *word*) and perform basic processes such as: • State that words are made up of letters • State that words are separated by spaces when they are written down • Name the letters of the alphabet • Write the letters of the alphabet
1.5	Partial success at score 2.0 content, and major errors or omissions regarding score 3.0 content
1.0	With help, partial success at score 2.0 content and score 3.0 content
0.5	With help, partial success at score 2.0 content but not at score 3.0 content
0.0	Even with help, no success

Source: Adapted from Simms, 2016.

Figure 2.11: Kindergarten ELA scale on print concepts.

Learning Target	Page in Book	Teacher Directions	Student Responses
Score 2.0 • Vocabulary • State that pages in a book are read in order from the front cover to the back cover.	N/A	Hand the book with the spine down to the student. Ask the student the questions below. Record student responses in the column to the right. 1a and b) *"Where is the front cover? How about the back cover?"* 2) Open the book, point to a page, and then ask, *"What is this called?"* 3a, b, and c) *"Where is the top of the page? How about the bottom? When we read, do we start at the top of the page or the bottom?"* 4a, b, and c) *"If you were reading this book by yourself, where would you start reading? And where is the last page you would read? Why would you read it like that?"*	1a) 1b) 2) 3a) 3b) 3c) 4a) 4b) 4c)
Score 2.0 • State that words are made up of letters.	Page 2	5) Point to the word *kitten*. Then say, *"This is the word* kitten. *A book has many words. What makes up each word?"*	5)
Score 3.0 • Explain how written words are organized on pages.	Page 3	6) *"Look at page 3 in this book called* Kittens. *There are many words on this page. How are the words organized?"*	6)

Score 3.0 • Write sentences when told how to spell individual words.	Page 4	7) *"Look at the picture on page 4 in this story. What sentence would you like to write about this picture? Write your sentence on the lined paper that I provide for you."*	7)
Score 4.0 • Write several sentences to explain important information about text.	N/A	8) Give the student a bit of time to examine the book. Then say the following: *"What information would you like to write about this text for another reader? Write your ideas about the text on the lined paper that I provide."*	8)

Source: Adapted from Hoegh, 2020.

Figure 2.12: Assessment for kindergarten print concepts.

Train Teachers on Inter-Rater Reliability Processes

Fostering understanding of assessment reliability is paramount. Simply put, reliability is about consistency—consistency in how the assessment actually functions with students, as well as how consistent teachers are when evaluating constructed response and performance assessment items. Inter-rater reliability requires that different teachers who administer and score the same assessment exercise similar judgment as they score students' responses. Since common assessments will likely be a component of classroom assessment practices, it is important that teachers understand inter-rater reliability processes.

There will be frequent occasions when team-developed assessments, or common assessments, require the student to construct or produce something. This may be a written or verbal response, or in the case of performance assessment, a tangible product (such as a clay pot, an essay, or a wooden shelf) or even a demonstration of some sort (such as dribbling a basketball, playing the chromatic scale on an instrument, or making a presentation). When such circumstances arise, it is critical to consider the scoring of these assessments. Without careful thought and planning, one teacher's judgment about what constitutes mastery may be different from that of another teacher who gives the same assessment.

Of course, there are multiple ways to achieve that consistency. Table 2.2 (page 82) showcases some of the most common methods for attaining inter-rater reliability (consistency across scorers) with pros and cons for each. It is important to note that these processes need not be used to score every assessment. Instead, teacher teams might use them only for common assessments as these are typically considered to be the most important for making decisions about student achievement.

Besides collaborative scoring, an action step that can ensure calibration between teachers is to develop an administration and scoring document for each common assessment. This document requires teacher teams to plan and then record how they will ensure consistent scoring across all teachers who administer and score the assessment. Figure 2.13 (page 83) is the planning document related to the kindergarten ELA scale and assessment presented in the previous section (page 80). The scoring guidelines component of this document explains how this teacher team will ensure consistency across scorers.

TABLE 2.2: PROS AND CONS OF COMMON INTER-RATER RELIABILITY METHODS

Method	Pros	Cons
Scoring the assessment together as a team	• Ensures that all assessments are scored in a very similar manner • Builds knowledge of the assessment and students' level of understanding	• Time consuming, especially in the situation where each teacher has multiple sections of the same course
Scoring two or three assessments from each classroom together; teachers each score independently after this process	• Ensures high level of consistent scoring • Builds knowledge of the assessment and students' level of understanding	• Since most of the scoring is done independently, there is still the possibility of varying judgment being applied to the scoring process
Collecting student examples of work for comparison when scoring assessment items or tasks	• Ensures high level of consistency when scoring • Provides examples of varying levels of mastery, which serve as anchors for the scoring process	• Since the scoring is done independently, there is still the possibility of varying judgment being applied to the scoring process
Using video or other technology to provide scorers with anchors (assessments that have been team-scored) on which to base scoring processes	• Ensures high level of consistency when scoring • Provides examples of varying levels of mastery, which serve as anchors for the scoring process	• Potentially a time-consuming endeavor • Since the scoring is done independently, there is still the possibility of varying judgment being applied to the scoring process

Source: © 2019 by Jan Hoegh.

If scoring consistency and reliability are new concepts in your school or district, consider introducing them to teachers through thirty to sixty minutes of direct instruction about the concept of reliability and strategies for inter-rater reliability and intra-rater reliability (see the following section). Share a definition of reliability, why it is important, and how to go about determining it. Consider a time when issues of reliability brought to the surface questionable interpretations—umpires in a baseball game, referees in football or basketball game, a faulty scale, for a few examples. Next, introduce the concept of reliability. Then teach about inter-rater reliability first, because most teachers are somewhat familiar with this concept, and may even refer to it as *calibration*. Provide a few strategies to improving it, including the following.

- Use exemplars of student work.

- Conduct inter-rater reliability with two pieces of student work—one you feel confident in scoring and one you don't. Score them prior to attending a collaborative team or department meeting. Seek agreement about the scores.

- Conduct inter-rater reliability with a random sample (purely chance) and a stratified random sample (sort into categories of beginning, proficient, and advanced, then randomly select from each stratum) of student work.

Either in the same training session or a separate one, introduce intra-rater reliability next.

Course or Grade: Kindergarten	Unit: **Foundational Skills** Quarter: First	Assessment Title: PRINT CONCEPTS			
Measurement Topic	Learning Target(s):	2.0 Number and Item Types	3.0 Number and Item Types	4.0 Number and Item Types	Total
Print Concepts	• PC1—Explain how written words are organized on pages. • PC2—Write sentences when told how to spell individual words.	5 personal communication	1 personal communication 1 short answer	1 extended response	8
Assessment Administration (important information for teachers who give the assessment)	• Use the book *Kittens* for this assessment. It is not necessary for the student to read the book independently or for the teacher to read the book in its entirety to the student. • The assessment will be administered by the teacher or a paraeducator to one student at a time. • The teacher will read the italicized text as directions (see figure 2.12, page 80) for the student. Every effort should be made to keep administration directions consistent across all students. • The teacher may reread the question if needed in order for the student to understand what is being asked. • Students should be given adequate time to complete all parts of the assessment as long as the student is actively working.				
Scoring Guidelines (important information for teachers who score the assessment)	• Record the student responses in the designated space on the assessment. • Teachers will score one assessment from each classroom to calibrate their own scoring processes. • A score 2.0 performance requires that the student responds correctly to eight of ten score 2.0 questions. It is important to note that some items have more than one question. • A score 3.0 performance requires the student to meet the score 2.0 requirements *and* to respond correctly to items 6 and 7. • A score 4.0 performance requires the student to meet the requirements for score 3.0 and to respond correctly to item 8.				
Other Information	• Use the lined paper included in this assessment for items 7 and 8.				

Source: © 2019 by Jan Hoegh.

Figure 2.13: Assessment administration and scoring document.

Share Strategies for Intra-Rater Reliability

In addition to inter-rater reliability, we also recommend that leaders train teachers on *intra-rater reliability*—that is, strategies for an individual teacher to maintain consistency when scoring different students' work. When explaining this concept to teachers, discuss how time of day, feelings about certain students, fatigue, and unclear criteria can affect how teachers score student work. Such factors can inadvertently cause teachers to assign different scores to identical responses by two different students. When a teacher isn't internally consistent, it can greatly affect how students perform in the class. Suggest the following strategies to increase teacher intra-rater reliability.

- Having students place names on the back of tests or papers so as to not influence how a teacher feels about a student, thereby heightening impartiality.

- Grading one type of constructed-response item (short-answer or extended-response item) all the way through the stack of papers being graded. Doing so increases how dependably a teacher will recall and apply the criteria for proficient responses.

- Shuffling the test papers or other assessment artifacts. When grading each assessment item all the way through the stack, shuffle the papers randomly before moving to the next item. This ensures that a teacher's reliability doesn't increase or decrease throughout the process of grading. Sometimes one's grading trends easier or tougher as the evaluation process progresses.

- Re-norming criteria expectations as teachers encounter new constructed responses by reviewing the predetermined scoring guidance, such as a rubric. For instance, if a teacher grades test question five all the way through the stack, he or she should review the criteria for proficiency prior to assessing the question six responses, and for each subsequent response.

Figure 2.14 is a handout we have used to explain inter-rater reliability, intra-rater reliability, and strategies for increasing teachers' reliability in scoring assessment items.

Expand Your Efforts

While new work in phase 2 primarily concerns the rollout of standards and scales for core content areas and the initiation of alignment work around instruction and assessment, this phase also includes the continuation and expansion of several activities from phase 1. We detail these in the following sections.

Continue Revising Proficiency Scales for Core Content Areas

As assessment development and alignment begins, it is important that district or building leaders give collaborative teams permission to refine proficiency scales as part of this work. Typically, attention to assessment uncovers necessary additions or revisions to scales. This often results from deep conversations among teachers about what students need to know and be able to do and how they will learn about this through the assessment. Although changes to a proficiency scale are not always necessary during assessment work, there will be occasions when teams need to make significant changes to a scale to ensure that the scale clearly articulates the knowledge and skill students must acquire to demonstrate mastery. The goal of this process is making the proficiency scale the basis for the assessment, such that every item or task aligns clearly to a learning target on the proficiency scale.

Reliability Considerations

- Does the assessment provide enough opportunities for students to demonstrate what they know about the intended learning?
    - Number of items
    - Test blueprint
- Two Types of Reliability
    1. Inter-rater reliability
        - What is it?
            - Consistency between or among various raters
        - How do you enhance it?
            - Use examples.
            - Review student work collaboratively and conduct inter-rater conversations.
            - Randomly sample.
            - Stratify a randomized sample.
    2. Intra-rater reliability
        - What is it?
            - Consistency within the rater
        - How do you enhance it?
            - Ask students to put their names on the backs of assessment items.
            - Grade one constructed-response item all the way through the stack of assessments.
            - Shuffle papers between each step of the evaluation.
            - Re-norm your expectations with the criteria when you go to a new constructed-response item.

 Key question about any assessment:
Can we make a confident inference about the learning that has occurred as a result of the instructional unit?

Source: © 2017 by Jan Hoegh and Tammy Heflebower.

*Visit **MarzanoResources.com/reproducibles** for a free reproducible version of this figure.*

Figure 2.14: Reliability considerations.

Prioritize Standards and Draft Proficiency Scales for All Other Content Areas

As you begin implementation in core content areas, you should also begin foundational standards and scales work in all other content areas. In some schools and districts, initial standards and proficiency scale development occurs for one or just a few content areas. It is very common to begin this important work with English language arts and mathematics. At this point it is appropriate to determine the next content areas for proficiency scale development. If ELA and mathematics are addressed first, it may be that science and social studies scale development occurs next. If leaders in the district or school feel that all teachers have adequate understanding of proficiency scales, your team might decide to address all remaining content areas at this point. Selecting content areas for phase 2 standards and scale development is a local decision.

When prioritizing standards and drafting scales in phase 2, refer to the guidance in phase 1 for prioritizing standards (chapter 1, page 14) and developing proficiency scales (chapter 1, page 25), but learn from your own experience with phase 1 as well. Replicate what worked well and plan differently for what did not. New design teams for new content areas will need training similar to that provided for the initial scale developers. If possible, include some of the team who worked on the prior scale development in this new cycle of scale work.

Continue Working With Technology for Storage and Access

At this point in time, teacher teams will likely have created documents related to their priority standards and proficiency scales. These documents might include instructional resources, unit plans, and common assessments. Therefore, leaders must monitor the digital storage system to ensure it is being utilized in the manner intended. Shared folder systems can become disorganized and almost unmanageable, as many people are potentially saving documents to the folders as work is completed. The individuals responsible for managing the electronic repository should monitor it periodically and make every effort to ensure that the prescribed folder structure and naming conventions are being followed. They should also maintain backups of the files in case users inadvertently delete or replace important resources. This action step is also a means for monitoring the product-development process and helps to identify teams that are behind in the development of scales, assessments, or other related resource documents. When leaders keep an eye on the work, it is possible to support individual teams in an ongoing manner. This support may include providing additional time beyond what is planned for, one-on-one coaching or additional learning, or even just help with the electronic storage of the documents. For example, consider a team that works collaboratively to develop proficiency scales. On examination of the scales stored in the appropriate folder, a building leader notices the only content at score 2.0 on each scale is the related vocabulary. This circumstance requires for additional learning to be provided for the team, as the teachers clearly are missing some necessary understanding of what score 2.0 on a scale includes—specifically, basic knowledge and skills, in addition to vocabulary.

Another consideration at this point in the process is the school or district gradebook platform. Schools and districts must examine their current gradebook software and determine its capacity for reporting student performance relative to standards, rather than averaged percentage or letter grades. This is in preparation for later phases, but also serves to reassure staff that a completely standards-based system is the goal and the transition will be smooth. Once teachers begin using proficiency scales and aligned assessments in the classroom, it will become obvious to them that traditional grading practices do not align to the standards-based classroom practices they are implementing. They will begin to ask about what "grade" a score 3.0 earns and other questions specifically related to the gradebook. It will be paramount to assure teachers that leaders are critically examining the gradebook so that when standards-referenced grading is phased in, there will be tools in place to support that work.

Share Information

Another activity that continues in phase 2 is sharing information. This includes both developing expertise among staff and communicating plans to stakeholders. As the implementation process continues, there will be a natural expansion of the number of people involved and in need of more information. This will require consistency of information while also differentiating for the specific needs and actions required of specific groups, such as campus-level administrators and content-area lead teachers.

Engage in Learning Opportunities for Additional Learning Leaders

Traditionally, district and school administrators have not gotten deeply involved with grading. That cannot be the case if a district or school is going to make a successful change in its grading and learning practices. While the movement to standards-based grading must be a collaborative effort, and facilitating teacher development is critical, staff involvement does not eliminate the principal's obligation to stay well informed. In fact, it requires principals to be informed and involved. In an article in *Educational Leadership*, Joanne Rooney (2008) reinforced this point:

> Principals expect teachers and students to take ownership of their own learning. They must expect no less of themselves as they continually seek to improve their professional knowledge and skills. [Leaders should] become informed about any programs your school is considering adopting or has initiated. Research them thoroughly and insist that teachers do the same. Avoid the pitfall of adopting silver bullets of education reform. Easily accessible online resources provide extensive information about any creditable program. (p. 82)

To support the implementation of SBL, principals must be one of the lead learners in the concept. Knowledge is key, and principals should develop a well-rounded understanding of grading practices. We suggest several vehicles for this purpose. First, read the literature and begin to develop an understanding of the concepts. *Formative Assessment and Standards-Based Grading* (Marzano, 2010) and *A School Leader's Guide to Standards-Based Grading* (Heflebower et al., 2014) are good beginning resources for this purpose. In our experiences, administrator book studies have served this purpose well and allow school leaders to collaboratively explore the topic. Second, attend workshops and trainings with teachers early in the transition. This can give principals additional perspectives as teachers learn about and pilot practices ahead of their colleagues. Third, actively participate in staff trainings when teachers are learning about SBL practices and processes.

Communicate the Initial Implementation Plan to Key Leaders

Clarifying the process and plans for implementation provides transparency and establishes a clear understanding across the leadership structures regarding what specifically needs to be done. In phase 1, we recommend drafting an initial implementation plan; here, leaders of the transition to SBL should share the implementation plan with other leaders in their systems. As part of this process, a school should consider developing a system for monitoring the implementation to assist administrators and teacher leaders in planning for and managing the process step by step.

An excellent example of this can be seen in the work of the Austin, Texas, charter elementary school known as Not Your Ordinary School (NYOS) as it planned for the transition from a standards-referenced system to a standards-based system. Recall that a standards-referenced system reports a student's status on each of the priority standards, while in NYOS's standards-based approach, students move on to the next grade level once they have demonstrated proficiency in each of the priority standards. For this transition, NYOS developed an implementation guide. Knowing they had specific aspects of practice that all teachers at every grade level needed to account for in the transition, the school leaders planned and implemented a system that included each of those critical aspects. They also were able to use this system for teachers to clearly see and track their own progress on each of the critical aspects. The first page of this document is shown in figure 2.15, with additional pages in appendix B (page 172). The content elements in the left-hand column indicate the various aspects of practice that need to be addressed and completed as part of the transition. The other three columns allow school leaders an easy and efficient monitoring system for each aspect as individual teachers or teacher teams are addressing them. The Not Yet column indicates no action has been taken at this point to address that aspect. If school leaders see this column as the predominant reporting category for a teacher or team, it signals a need for direct involvement to assist and support in the process. The In Progress column shows that the teacher or team is currently working on this aspect, and school leaders should be able to see clear evidence of their work and progress in these aspects. The All Set! category indicates this aspect is finished and ready for a critical review.

This type of systemic planning and tracking is important within each phase of the implementation and should reflect the specific aspects of progress that need to be accomplished within a phase. At the school level, this type of matrix provides principals the ability to monitor the progress of the entire staff in each of the vital aspects within each phase. It can be set up easily in a digital format so teachers can track their own progress and embed links directly to other digital documents, artifacts, and examples of work they are working on or have completed. This type of process can also be used at the district level. Principals could track the progress of their entire school using the same categories, which would then align the progress tracking throughout the entire system. In this case, once all teachers in a school have indicated they are All Set! in an aspect and the principal has confirmed that fact, she or he would mark the school as All Set! on a similar reporting form, which is monitored by district leadership.

IMPLEMENTATION GUIDE			
Content Elements	**Stages of Progress**		
Identify topic for unit of study. • *What larger topic will this unit address?*	All Set!	In Progress	Not Yet
Review and sequence learning goals within the topic. • *In what order should students work on each learning goal?*	All Set!	In Progress	Not Yet
Identify and gather resources that will help students master each learning goal. • *What will I use to help students practice and deepen their knowledge?* • *Examples: small groups, online games or videos, center activities, practice pages*	All Set!	In Progress	Not Yet
Create pretest to determine students' prior knowledge. • *What evidence do I have of the students' current knowledge?*	All Set!	In Progress	Not Yet
Create formative assessments that will give students and teachers feedback about progress on each individual learning goal. • *How can students demonstrate they are making progress?* • *Examples: exit ticket, short quiz, conversation with teacher, demonstration of skill, correctly completed practice page, video of student explaining concept or showing how to do the skill*	All Set!	In Progress	Not Yet
Create summative assessment that will confirm student proficiency on all goals within the unit of study. • *How do I know students have retained all of the unit's learning goals?*	All Set!	In Progress	Not Yet

Source: © 2019 by NYOS. Used with permission.

Figure 2.15: Sample implementation guide.

Establish Core Beliefs With Teacher and Leader Teams

Core beliefs are the guiding principles that inform decision making in an SBL system. By establishing them, you uncover values, attitudes, and practices within your system. Through the process for surfacing and establishing beliefs, leaders will also determine areas where teachers and other leaders need more information or professional development.

Crafting some initial belief statements about SBL will be important when providing guidelines and practices within your system. Some of these beliefs will convey teachers' mindsets around reteaching and reassessment, use of zeros, how to deal with student behaviors and academics, and what is thought about homework. The process of establishing core beliefs should include leaders sharing what they learned through their review of current grading communications from their teachers (see chapter 1, page 56) as well as their own beliefs about SBL. By discerning current beliefs and practices, you will better understand where to validate or modify practices. After discovering current beliefs and practices, school and district leaders are ready to establish a set of core beliefs that will drive the implementation. The following process is useful with leadership teams at the school and district levels, as well as teacher teams such as departments or collaborative teams.

The first step is to select a few topics related to SBL, such as reteaching and reassessment, assigning effective homework, separating student behaviors from academics, relating standards-based practices to existing collaborative structures, and so on. Place three topics on chart paper around the room. Ask participants to first consider their own beliefs about each topic, writing such beliefs on sticky notes. After each participant silently records his or her own thinking about the topics, ask the group to read various print resources, such as sample belief statements from other schools or research summaries on the topics. After that, provide time for participants to refine or revise their initial thinking. Then split your team into groups of three to four. The small groups then rotate to each chart discussing their thinking and placing belief statements on the charts. As teams rotate to the next chart, they read, reflect on, and add to the statements. Repeat this process until every group has visited each topic. At the conclusion, seek areas of agreement and summarize the groups' beliefs on each topic. Use these agreements to draft belief statements about SBL practices. Where disagreements surface, capture them for review and further exploration, to be addressed during future meetings. These initial belief statements are drafts, and they should be reviewed and possibly revised at later points during the implementation, such as in phases 3 and 4, when further establishing practices for SBL.

Send Scouts to Learn From Other Schools and Districts

While the guiding team coordinates and leads the implementation of SBL, another critical group investigates and experiences standards-based learning and grading concepts and work firsthand ahead of other staff. We refer to this group as your *scouts*. Scouts are teachers who are willing to be in the advance group that will explore the challenges ahead and investigate what is to come. Scouts need to be carefully selected to represent various teacher groups in a school, including teachers who are ready for the change and those who are still on the fence. Some scouts can be part of the guiding team, but more often they are educators outside the guiding team who are respected early adopters. The size of the school and district will determine the number of scouts needed. In small schools we have seen as few as two teachers work in advance as scouts while larger schools have identified ten to fifteen teachers as scouts. Scouts can be individual teachers in different grade levels or content areas who are already tinkering with SBL practices on their own and were discovered to be doing so through the surveys of current grading practices conducted in phase 1. Scouts may also consist of an entire collaborative team or content-area department that collaborates well and successfully engage with new ideas. In fact, leaders may build more capacity in the initial stages by recruiting existing teacher teams as scout teams so the members can support one another through the early experimentation phases. Selecting the scouts might also involve the use of a simple application process that offers the opportunity to an entire staff. The key to selecting the scouts is to identify the people who will invest themselves in truly exploring ahead and learning about the concept. It is critical that the district or school empower and support the scouts. In other words, give them the resources they need to learn, understand, and actually implement different aspects of SBL in their own classrooms so they can begin to become embedded experts in the process.

At this point in the implementation process, we recommend that scouts visit schools that are practicing SBL to see and hear the system in action firsthand. As standards-based practices continue to become more common, it is easier to find example schools to visit, and with the ease of virtual communication, scouts can connect with schools in nearly any area to learn about their processes. Districts often describe their standards-based systems on their websites, making online searches a viable way to find example schools. There are also numerous standards-based grading blogs that can help school leaders identify possible model sites for their scout teachers.

In our experiences, some schools have their scouts visit two or three different schools and others perform a single visit. The key is to give the scouts enough opportunity to construct their own mental models of what SBL might look like in their own practice and eventually in the school as a whole. During a visit, scouts should look for the following.

- How teachers communicate with students using proficiency scales
- How students use the scale to identify where they are in their learning
- How classroom assessment practice is informed by the proficiency scale
- How students track their own progress
- How teachers track student learning using scale scores

Scout teachers can also attend trainings or workshops to explore SBL together. On returning from school visits and trainings, the scouts will often debrief with the guiding team, report to the staff as a whole, and if appropriate, present their thoughts and ideas to the board of education as part of the ongoing communication with the board.

Continue to Educate the Board of Education

In each phase of implementation, the guiding team should consider the question, What will the board of education need to know and understand at this point? As mentioned in chapter 1 (page 48), portfolios of resources for board members can be very effective in helping keep specific concepts organized and in order of implementation. At this point in the process, board members who have attended trainings might also update the whole board regarding the information they gleaned and the ideas they received at the training.

In order to provide a realistic look at the work of SBL, consider showing short videos of training activities and processes so the whole board can get a sense of what is occurring. For example, a video of teacher teams discussing and identifying priority standards can provide some additional context to understand the process. Or, a video of teachers talking about some of the most important concepts they learned during a training and how they can see these concepts enhancing student learning can indicate the thought processes behind important decisions. Another consideration would be the inclusion of videos or artifacts of practice that the scout teachers have collected during their visits to other schools.

These updates, ongoing communication, and continued trainings are important because at some point, board members will have to discuss SBL with stakeholders. Disgruntled parents or resistant staff might bring complaints about new grading practices.

Perhaps a community member is simply curious about the changes. Whatever the case, board members will eventually have to explain or defend SBL. By continually updating the board and providing members with an ongoing understanding of the new systems, you enhance their understanding of the initiative and the processes being used to cultivate it.

Educate Parents

Parents are a critical audience to communicate with when it comes to implementing SBL. For some parents, the concept of SBL is completely different from their paradigm of learning and grading, which was built through their own experience with school and is really all they know about the topic. For this reason, communication with parents should be designed to teach the concept—not just inform them about a change. It is also important to make fundamental information available in ways that parents can refer to throughout the implementation process—for example, a link on the school's website that offers information about the use of proficiency scales, how standards-based grades are figured, or an example of how to read a standards-based report card. A toolkit listing many modes of communication appears in appendix B (page 173). This information can also be useful in an ongoing manner, as a way of educating new families who have come to the district and are not familiar with the concept of SBL, which will be addressed in phase 5 (page 143).

Consider beginning by communicating within existing parent structures such as site-based teams that consist of parents and educators for strategic planning purposes (for example, parent-teacher organizations or parent steering committees). Within groups that meet regularly, providing an update on the most pertinent topics throughout the SBL implementation process can become a standing agenda item. Some of the early messages that administrators and teacher leaders provide to the board of education are the same messages that need to be provided to parents. For example, district leadership partnering with school-level leadership should educate parents on the concept of why this change makes sense, what it can do for student learning and transparency for parents in understanding student progress, and how laws such as No Child Left Behind (NCLB, 2002) and Every Student Succeeds Act (ESSA, 2015) have refocused U.S. education on a criterion-referenced approach to learning. Similar to having a few board members attend trainings and inform the other board members, you might even solicit a few supportive parents to receive more extensive training and serve as a resource for other parents.

As an example, consider the communication documents that Deer Creek Public Schools in Oklahoma created to teach parents the fundamental concepts of their standards-referenced reporting system. The first piece of communication (figure 2.16) is a glossary of important terms for parents to understand relating to the concept of SBL. The second piece of communication the Deer Creek team developed is a parent FAQ document (figure 2.17, page 94) that serves as a continuous source of information for parents and works in conjunction with the glossary document. A third piece of communication the Deer Creek district team developed is a handout for parents that describes key concepts and background information on standards-referenced reporting (figure 2.18, page 95).

Glossary

Standards-Referenced Reporting

Alignment—The directness of the link among standards, district curriculum, instructional practices, assessments, and student performance.

Differentiation—Through standards-referenced reporting, teachers are able to design multiple instructional strategies to provide varied learning opportunities based on students' individual performance level, including remediation and enrichment.

Evidence—Demonstrations of learning, which may include teacher- and student-generated assessments, teacher observation, student projects, and other means of evaluating student performance.

Growth Mindset—Students' belief that they can learn anything through practice and effort and that their intelligence is not fixed but can grow over time. Students with a growth mindset are those who persevere when work is hard; they are persistent.

Multiple Assessment Opportunities—Evaluation of student learning by providing enough opportunities for the student to demonstrate mastery of a standard and avoiding reliance on one assessment alone to measure learning.

Process Skills—Factors and habits of work that support student learning, such as responsibility, time management, and respectfulness. These are portable skills that students can take with them to the next level of learning, including college and career.

Proficiency—Having or demonstrating an expected degree of knowledge or skill.

Proficiency Scale—Proficiency scales are standardized at the district level for each course to allow teachers and students to track progress toward mastery of a standard. It is a document that organizes the progression of learning for students to move from the foundational skills to proficiency and possibly beyond adopted standards.

Source: © 2019 by Deer Creek Public Schools. Used with permission.

Figure 2.16: Glossary of important standards-referenced reporting terms.

While the messages may be similar, different districts use many different vehicles to communicate with parents about SBL. Jaci Lenz and Sarah Burger served as scout teachers in the SBL initiative for Northwood Public School in North Dakota. One of the practices they initiated was an SBL newsletter for parents to facilitate ongoing communication about SBL and help parents understand how the two of them were implementing it in their classrooms for the first time. Figure 2.19 (page 96) shows an example of one of these newsletters.

Communication with parents in Northwood Public School also involves a comprehensive parent handbook on SBL (see appendix C, page 181). The handbook covers the rationale for the district's move to SBL, the concept of proficiency scales, how proficiency scale scores will be translated into traditional grades for reporting, and how student eligibility for school activities will be addressed in the standards-based system.

Another common method of communication takes the form of presentation slide decks that contain all the consistent messaging for SBL. A district can distribute the slides, and individual schools can efficiently adjust the language and add examples appropriate for their specific student age groups. In preparing for the pilot of standards-referenced reporting at its intermediate school, members of the Deer Creek Public Schools' curriculum team customized their presentation slides to be used with parents of learners of different age groups. Visit **MarzanoResources.com/reproducibles** to view examples of these slides.

Parent FAQ

Standards-Referenced Reporting

What are the advantages of standards-referenced reporting?

- Allows students, teachers, and parents or guardians to track each student's progress per standard

- More accurately represents students' knowledge and skills related to a specific standard

- Provides multiple opportunities for students to show what they know

- Offers students opportunities to learn from mistakes made during the learning process and correct their understanding

- Increases consistency in grading policies and criteria across teachers and schools

- Ensures that every student has a chance to meet the standard, knowing that it may take longer for some students

- Provides accurate and specific information to all partners in student learning

What are the main differences from traditional grading?

- Standards-referenced reporting focuses on a student's progress toward meeting grade-level standards rather than a simple accumulation of points.

- It uses a number scale (4, 3, 2, 1) rather than a percentage or average.

- Nonacademic behaviors are reported separately.

- Grades are determined by each student's ability to meet the priority standards, not on how he or she compares to other students in the class. All students are given a chance to meet or exceed (if appropriate) the standard.

What does my child need to do to achieve a 4?

- A score of 3 is the expectation and represents mastery of the standard on the proficiency scale.

- To earn a score of 4, students need to demonstrate they have a deeper understanding by elaborating on their answers, solving more challenging problems, or showing connections between varying concepts that they have made on their own.

- Not all standards qualify for a level 4 (for example, "Demonstrate multiplication fluency through 12 × 12" does not allow for elaboration beyond mastery of the standard).

Source: © 2019 by Deer Creek Public Schools. Used with permission.

Figure 2.17: Frequently asked questions document for parents.

Standards-Referenced Reporting

Information for You

The No Child Left Behind Act (NCLB), which was signed into law on January 8, 2002, ushered in a new criterion-referenced era of education in the United States.

Criterion-referenced teaching and learning measures an individual student's performance against a set of criteria established as academic standards and indicates an individual student's level of proficiency in relation to specific standards.

Following the NCLB Act, the Every Student Succeeds Act (ESSA) was passed in 2015. According to the U.S. Department of Education, ESSA "requires—for the first time—that all students in America be taught to high academic standards that will prepare them to succeed in college and careers."

To meet ESSA requirements, states must define high levels of performance in academic standards and implement systems that clearly track students' performance. A systematic way for schools to meet these requirements is to implement standards-referenced reporting.

STUDENT CENTERED	PROGRESS BASED
Scores should reflect the proficiency of each individual student in relation to the priority standards for each grade level. Standards-referenced reporting provides information about a student's level of performance in reference to each of those priority standards.	Students work through a progression of knowledge to master each grade-level standard throughout the year. The focus is on achieving mastery in all standards over a period of time. Students are able to track their growth and describe their current status within the proficiency scale.
TARGETED INFORMATION	**DATA DRIVEN**
A standards-referenced report card shows a student's progress on each standard rather than a general number that may or may not accurately represent where that student is in a course. It also separates academic achievement from habits, efforts, and behaviors, and provides specific student progress as it relates to the standards.	Student progress, instruction, and data are analyzed regularly through various forms of evidence, such as classroom assessments, projects, teacher-student conversations, and other methods of evaluating student progress. Data are used to drive instruction and provide teachers with information for enrichment or remediation, as necessary.

Source: © 2019 by Deer Creek Public Schools.

Figure 2.18: Parent handout on standards-referenced reporting.

In addition to educating parents about SBL in general, we recommend emphasizing proficiency scales in parent communication. Since proficiency scales form the backbone for standards-based learning, grading, and reporting practices, parents must understand the concept well. One of the most effective methods of communicating the role of scales in learning and grading to parents is to ensure students understand proficiency scales and how they work in standards-based learning and grading. It has been our experience that students who clearly understand proficiency scales can help educate their parents on the concept. This is an additional reason student-friendly scales are important—they enhance students' ability to speak about scales as users or when they are explaining how they use them to their parents.

Standards-Based Grading Newsletter

Miss Lenz, High School Mathematics ~ Mrs. Burger, High School English

Friday, September 15, 2017

Tracking Progress

In both English and math, students are tracking their own progress toward their goals. We have folders with the scales, and at the bottom there is a place to record assessment scores. Though we do not have a lot of scores in yet (we've been practicing a lot, though!), students will soon see their scores grow.

Tutors

Tutors are available for students in any subject area during common learning time (CLT). If and when students are struggling to get to the next level of a scale, we will use the tutors to help the students practice skills. This a great opportunity for the students!

Reassessment

Once we move on from a concept in class, students are still able to learn more about it and take more assessments to reach a higher score. They will need to meet with the teacher or tutor to get further practice first.

English 9 News

We started off the year focusing on developing a reading life. We're reading a little bit every day, and we've set some goals that we want to accomplish by the end of the semester. In terms of scales, we are working on the Analyzing Narratives Scale. This scale deals mostly with character analysis. We're read a few short stories, and the students have also been applying these skills to their free-choice novel. The novel *A Long Walk to Water* will be our next shared text, and we are moving on to Generating Narratives (writing stories) and Analyzing Narrative Structure.

Algebra I News

Algebra I started the year off with the Real Number System. We have been learning about different sets of numbers and their properties. We are wrapping that unit up and moving into Components of an Expression. As we have been moving through these scales, the student have been tracking their own progress in their folders during class. Please ask them how they are doing in these areas.

Source: © 2017 by Northwood School District. Used with permission.

Figure 2.19: Sample parent newsletter.

One strategy that serves this purpose is to have students create their own personal proficiency scales that demonstrate the progression of learning for something they have learned in their lives, academic or not. This activity gives students a personally relevant example of how they moved through a progression of learning to acquire a specific talent or skill. Students then share their personal scales with their parents, which creates a valuable connection to what a proficiency scale is and how it relates to development within a content area. To introduce such an activity to students, a teacher might say the following.

> Everything we learn involves going through steps until we learn that thing. These steps are called *learning progressions.* They begin with the basic information or skills we learn first and then progress to or beyond what we want to learn. To show these steps to other people, so they can get an idea about how to learn the same thing, we can use a proficiency scale. We have talked about the different levels of a proficiency scale and what they represent. Now you are going to make a proficiency scale that describes the steps you would use to help someone else learn an idea or skill that you have already learned.

Figure 2.20 shows a sample scale from this activity about how to learn to dribble a basketball.

Advanced Score 4.0	I can • Dribble with either hand while moving forward or backward at full speed during a game or scrimmage.
Proficient Score 3.0	I can • Dribble with either hand while moving forward or backward. • Dribble alternating hands while moving forward or backward.
Score 2.0	I can • Dribble a basketball with either hand standing still. • Dribble a basketball with my left hand while walking. • Dribble back and forth between my right and left hands while walking.

Source: Adapted from Heflebower et al., 2019.

Figure 2.20: Student-created scale activity example.

It is also important to help parents understand what scales can communicate to them about and during the learning process. First, using scales offers parents a window into the standards that are being taught. Second, scales help parents see the concept of learning progression that is built into each instructional unit. Third, scales provide specific information regarding areas where students are having success and areas where they need more development. Considering the importance of proficiency scales to the entire process, schools and districts should consider developing a scale explanation document that can be posted on a website and offered in hard-copy communications for any grade level. Figure 2.21 (page 98) shows a scale explanation document developed by Deer Creek Public Schools.

As proficiency scales are developed and begin to be used in classroom practice, consider making proficiency scales the basis for conversation in parent-teacher conferences. This provides a direct connection for parents to see how scales relate to student learning and progressions of knowledge. Schools that conduct student-led conferences can use the scales as the basis for conversations to help students communicate their current level on the scale, see what they are doing well, and understand where they need to grow. When appropriate, having students share samples of their own self-tracking can enrich these conversations.

Proficiency Scales

Explanation

Definition: Proficiency scales are district curriculum documents that identify clear learning progressions for each of the priority standards. The most important consumer of the information in the scale is the student.

Level 4 (Exceeding Standard):

Students are able to independently *extend* their knowledge through transference of learning to more complex content and thinking, including deeper conceptual understanding and application.

Level 3.5: The student has mastered all the level 3 criteria and demonstrates progress toward exceeding the standard.

Level 3 (Meeting Standard):

Students who meet the standards are able to *independently* use the content, details, concepts, academic vocabulary, processes, procedures, and skills that relate to the standards. These students not only understand the *what* but can correctly explain or demonstrate the *how* and *why*, as directly expressed with the language of the standard.

Level 2.5: The student has mastered all the level 2 criteria and demonstrates progress toward meeting the standard.

Level 2 (Approaching Standard):

Students have the foundational understanding of the content and concepts. At level 2, students *understand* or can use the foundational concepts, academic vocabulary, skills, procedures, and details.

Level 1.5: The student has demonstrated progress toward foundational understanding.

Level 1 (Attempting Standard):

Students consistently require help and support to understand foundational content. At level 1, students are beginning to understand simple concepts, academic vocabulary, skills, procedures, and details.

Source: © 2019 by Deer Creek Public Schools. Used with permission.

Figure 2.21: Sample scale explanation.

As mentioned previously, parents new to a district or school who are not familiar with the concept of SBL will need some type of orientation to the concept. As communication materials are developed for parents throughout the implementation, the district should collect these pieces into a portfolio of resources for new parents. Additionally, a district can archive videos of presentations that allow new parents to study the concept and some of the individual aspects of SBL, such as the use of proficiency scales and examples of what a report card will include.

A common parent question districts need to address during the implementation process is, Will this type of grading and reporting be accepted by colleges? It is a fair question that provides districts with a great opportunity to clarify and strengthen the move to standards-based or standards-referenced grading and reporting. Many districts are reaching out to colleges both in their areas and across the nation to get statements that reaffirm they accept transcripts from all types of grading approaches when they consider students for admission. These statements provide a powerful message when included in parent handouts and on school and district websites. Appendix B (page 175) shows an example of such a statement from Harvard College.

Monitor Implementation

School leaders must actively monitor specific aspects of the implementation throughout the entire process. This can be done through the use of specific checkpoints indicating where their school currently stands in the process. In the book *Leading a High Reliability School*, authors Robert J. Marzano, Philip B. Warrick, Cameron L. Rains, and Richard DuFour (2018) spoke about the concept of leadership accountability—"leaders having an accountability for a school's status" (p. 47). For this purpose they provide leadership accountability scales. Throughout the implementation of SBL practices, school leaders can use two leadership accountability scales. Each of these scales represents the implementation of a *leading indicator*, or condition of practice that must be in place. School leaders should track their school's progress using *lagging indicators*, or evidence that effective practices are in place and functioning as intended. The two leadership accountability scales for SBL provide a consistent metric for principals to monitor where their schools are in the implementation and what the next steps in the implementation should involve. The first leadership accountability scale is represented in figure 2.22. This scale addresses a school establishing specific protocols and practices for identifying clear and measurable academic goals for each individual student. For leaders, this means ensuring their school establishes priority standards, develops proficiency scales for those priority standards, and creates assessments that specifically measure levels of proficiency on each priority standard.

The school establishes clear and measurable goals focused on critical needs regarding improving achievement of individual students.				
Sustaining	**Applying**	**Developing**	**Beginning**	**Not Attempting**
The school has protocols and practices in place to ensure that clear and measurable goals are established and focused on critical needs regarding improving achievement of individual students, and it takes proper actions to intervene when quick data indicate a potential problem.	The school has protocols and practices in place to ensure that clear and measurable goals are established and focused on critical needs regarding improving achievement of individual students, and it can produce lagging indicators to show the desired effects of these actions.	The school has protocols and practices in place to ensure that clear and measurable goals are established and focused on critical needs regarding improving achievement of individual students.	The school is in the beginning, yet incomplete, stages of drafting protocols and practices to ensure that clear and measurable goals are established and focused on critical needs regarding improving achievement of individual students.	The school has not attempted to ensure that clear and measurable goals are established and focused on critical needs regarding improving achievement of individual students.

Source: Marzano et al., 2018, p. 144.

Figure 2.22: Scale for clear and measurable goals.

The second leadership accountability scale (see figure 2.23) deals with a school establishing protocols and practices to ensure that data are analyzed in order to monitor individual student progress toward proficiency in each of the priority standards. This scale refers to the development of student tracking systems for each priority standard as well as establishing standard-referenced or standards-based report cards that show each student's progress on priority standards in different content areas.

The school analyzes, interprets, and uses data to regularly monitor progress toward achievement goals for individual students.				
Sustaining	**Applying**	**Developing**	**Beginning**	**Not Attempting**
The school has protocols and practices in place to ensure that data are analyzed and used to regularly monitor progress toward achievement goals for individual students, and it takes proper actions to intervene when quick data indicate a potential problem.	The school has protocols and practices in place to ensure that data are analyzed and used to regularly monitor progress toward achievement goals for individual students, and it can produce lagging indicators to show the desired effects of these actions.	The school has protocols and practices in place to ensure that data are analyzed and used to regularly monitor progress toward achievement goals for individual students.	The school is in the beginning, yet incomplete, stages of drafting protocols and practices to ensure that data are analyzed and used to regularly monitor progress toward achievement goals for individual students.	The school has not attempted to draft protocols and practices to ensure that data are analyzed and used to regularly monitor progress toward achievement goals for individual students.

Source: Marzano et al., 2018, p. 149.

Figure 2.23: Scale for analyzing data.

Please take note that in both of the leadership accountability scales the highest level of implementation is *sustaining* the initiative. School leaders must engage in monitoring for sustained practice, especially within critical aspects of SBL as represented in the accountability scales. This level of monitoring involves leaders periodically gathering quick data. Marzano and colleagues (2018) defined *quick data* as easy-to-collect data that can come in one of three forms.

1. Quick conversations (asking staff deliberate questions about specific aspects of practice)

2. Quick observations (observing specific aspects of practice in operation to assess progress or effectiveness)

3. Easy-to-collect quantitative data (collecting information quickly through short surveys, checklists, or written responses)

The term *quick data* indicates that a data-driven approach to leadership does not have to involve reams of information. In fact, just the opposite. Consider the following examples. Early in the implementation process, a principal wants to know how her staff is understanding the initial training concepts regarding standards-based grading. She decides to use a quick conversations approach and crafts two questions that she will ask ten different teachers to gauge the level of their early understanding. As each teacher answers the two questions, the principal records his or her answers so she can quickly determine where teachers are in their early understanding of the concept. In a similar manner, a principal whose school is moving through the implementation process wants to determine the progress of each content department in developing proficiency scales. He decides to use easy-to-collect quantitative data as his quick data source. The principal sends a digital survey to all department chairs asking them to identify how many proficiency scales they have developed and what percentage of the total scales that number represents. These approaches allow the principal to make leadership decisions regarding the allocation of resources such as time that might be needed to complete the task. Conversely, if the principal is seeing effective and successful implementation, he or she should use this as a point of celebration to reaffirm the work schoolwide.

Active monitoring by school-level leaders is critical for any initiative but especially important for an initiative such as SBL. The leadership accountability scales provide the metric necessary for principals to determine where their schools reside in the implementation process and to monitor whether the system is being sustained and functioning correctly.

Enlisting Consultants

Enlisting the support of outside consultants may be very useful as you align instruction and assessment and begin enacting elements of SBL. Consider when an "outsider" can serve as a critical friend and trainer for content. Evaluate your own capacities for knowing, understanding, and delivering the various components involved in this phase. Consider the following list of ways consultants might help with phase 2.

- Working with your leadership team in planning and implementation

- Training leaders on specific components of SBL—for instance, the *what*, *why*, and *how* of proficiency scales—or using proficiency scales with teachers and students

- Creating webinars for subgroups of teachers (early adopters, later adopters) or specific to each component of SBL (prioritization, creating units of instruction, designing quality classroom assessments, using scales for tracking progress, feedback, and goal setting)

Summary

By the end of phase 2, the process is well underway. You have drafted proficiency scales for many content areas and grade levels, obtained feedback, and begun field-testing the scales. You are seeing evidence of alignment with instructional units and quality classroom assessments—all the while developing deeper understanding about the essence of the standards taught, foundations of quality classroom assessments, and the uncovering of existing grading beliefs and practices that exist in your building or district. You and your teammates have also systematized all of this into an initial implementation plan, and you are beginning to share it. This is tremendous work! In phase 3, you will build on this in other content areas or grade levels and formalize your plan across your system.

Universal Implementation, Communication, and Reporting Systems

In phase 3, you are deeply into implementation. Many teachers are using proficiency scales with students and aligning their instruction and assessments accordingly. You are aware of the prevailing attitudes and practices that surround grading and evaluation, and you are working closely with your technology team to ready your informational system for this new work. Continue to feed pertinent information into the system, including updates with your board of education. In this phase, you will expand your proficiency scales and assessments into other content areas and other grade levels not yet directly involved, as well as address your exceptional learner needs. In phase 3, your activities fall into these main categories.

- Expand work in non-core content areas
- Continue to train staff on assessment literacy
- Align scales for core content areas
- Include teachers of exceptional learners
- Plan and initiate the rollout
- Prepare for reporting systems

The following sections address each topic and associated activities. This phase will likely take six months to a year, depending on local groundwork and conditions.

Expand Work in Non-Core Content Areas

The work described thus far in phases 1 and 2 involves the core content areas of English language arts, mathematics, science, and social studies. It is now time to expand SBL work into non-core content areas, such as physical education, career and technical education, family consumer science, music, art, and so on. SBL is for all content areas. Therefore, learning and productivity opportunities must be planned for and provided to all educators.

Align Quality Classroom Assessments With Standards and Scales

In this phase, you should begin to train teachers of non-core content areas in high-quality classroom assessment practices, as well as the development of assessments based on proficiency scales. Form design teams for this stage, similar to those for core content areas—ideally three or four teachers per grade level or course. The process and considerations for aligning assessments are described in phase 2 (page 71). The same information provided to the initial assessment development team for core content areas will need to be shared with this broader group of teachers prior to any actual assessment development work for non-core content areas. It is helpful to provide examples of assessments that are based on proficiency scales for content areas that are the focus of this stage. See appendix B (page 167) for examples of leveled assessments.

As discussed in phase 2, the assessment alignment process works best when teachers from across the district come together to discuss their priority standards and proficiency scales, and use these to determine how to assess the learning described on the scales. Leaders should schedule work days to give teachers the opportunity to collaborate. This productivity time often occurs on district-level professional development days, but there are also times when leaders choose to hire substitute teachers in order to have teacher teams come together to work. There is no perfect number of days for this; however, as stands true in most circumstances, the more time made available, the greater the productivity. One day per month might be viewed as ideal.

In advance of the days planned for this assessment work, request that participants plan to bring existing classroom assessments to the work session. Existing assessments may indeed work well for the learning targets on proficiency scales. Or, it may be that an existing assessment can be modified to better align with standards and scales. Sometimes teams of teachers doing alignment work decide to develop brand-new assessments, but typically only when they aren't satisfied with what they have used in the past to assess learning. The most important reminder to offer assessment developers is that this work will evolve over time and that every assessment is truly a work in progress. In the end, teachers acquire valuable knowledge, and teacher teams produce proficiency scale–based assessments. See appendix C (page 177) for additional vertical alignment tools.

Request That Design Teams Field-Test Standards and Scales

Just as core content–area teachers engaged in field-testing their priority standards and proficiency scales, teachers of non-core courses will do the same for the sake of improving the quality of their tools. Refer back to phase 2 (page 67) for details about this field-test process. As suggested in phase 2, there are typically two approaches to this process.

1. Invite all teachers to begin using the scales in their classrooms with their students in the manner of their choosing.

2. Solicit specific classrooms to participate in a formal field-test process.

Either can work effectively and will result in teachers gaining knowledge and improving proficiency scales.

If you select the first approach of inviting all teachers to begin using scales in the classroom, advise existing teacher teams (such as content-area or grade-level teams) to use collaborative team time to plan for how this will take place. This will engender consistency in how the scales are used during instruction. It is also important that these teacher teams commit to capturing information about how the scales can be improved, which is a positive side effect of this field-test process.

When a narrower field-test process occurs, as in the second approach, it is common to select a certain grade level or content area to participate in the process. For example, it might be that the teachers who participate in the field test consist of representatives from physical education, music, theater, family and consumer science, career and technical education, and any other elective course. These teachers are provided ongoing learning opportunities in which they share the results of their process and are able to ask questions about how to approach a specific challenge. These additional learning opportunities can be provided by district or building leaders along with core content–area teachers who are ahead of the non-core teachers in the process. The goal is for teachers to gather information about the scales in an ongoing manner for the sake of scale revision at a later point in time. Proficiency scales become better tools through this initial use.

As part of the field-testing process, it is important to gather feedback to enhance the quality of the proficiency scales. Teachers should keep a running record of thoughts about scales as they engage in their use. We have found it effective to keep notes electronically to facilitate sharing and revising. Regardless of the method used, it is solid practice to bring teacher teams together at the end of the time period in which scales are field-tested for the purpose of using the feedback collected to revise proficiency scales. Ultimately, a school or district will want to reserve proficiency scale revision for a single point in time during an academic year. This often takes place at the end of the year or just prior to a new year getting underway. This process typically requires a full day or two of collaboration among representative teachers; we suggest about three teachers per grade level or course.

Solicit Feedback From Teachers Not on Design Teams and Revise

In addition to the revision process with design teams, solicit feedback from other teachers to refine scales. Use the same feedback process described in phase 2 (page 61). In this round of feedback, obtain input from additional content areas and grade levels not represented in the first round of the work. Be sure to provide direction to teachers before asking for feedback: they should look for consistency in format and the breakdown of content. For example, the score 2.0 level should always include vocabulary, multiple learning targets within one scale must covary (that is, increased understanding of one causes increased understanding of the other), and so on. Remember, although the process may be well understood by those leading it, it is new for those teachers just coming on board through the new content areas and grade levels. As we stated in phase 2, it is very common for teams to continue to revise scales when assessment development gets underway. As classroom assessment efforts begin, it is important to offer teachers the opportunity to determine additional edits to the scales.

Continue to Train Staff on Assessment Literacy

To prepare teachers in non-core content areas for standards-based assessment practices, use the same or similar training process described in phase 2 (page 79) regarding quality assessment practices and ensuring validity, reliability, and fairness. These teachers will also need to learn inter-rater and intra-rater reliability strategies (pages 81 and 83). Begin by training your non-core design team members, then build in additional training for these concepts across your system. You may elect to have design team members lead some of this, or provide specific professional development for all teachers about these important assessment concepts. As you think about new content-area and grade-level teams and teachers who need training, also consider new teachers to your building or district, as well as teachers moving grade levels or courses.

Assessments in non-core subject areas will have more performance-based prompts and assignments, typically. Addressing this and modifying the inter-rater reliability processes for the needs of non-core teachers will be especially important. Additionally, be sure to validate non-core teachers' practices by including the various types of assessments (obtrusive, unobtrusive, and student-generated; Marzano, 2010). Subject areas such as physical education, career and technical education, and visual and performing arts often benefit from additional training on how to incorporate more obtrusive assessment items, as they often rely heavily on unobtrusive approaches (that is, simply observing students).

Align Scales for Core Content Areas

This stage is also a time when it makes sense to facilitate a vertical alignment process related to the proficiency scales for the core content areas. The purpose for this process is to ensure that there is progression from one grade level to the next across a set of scales related to the same topic. Since the scales have been used over the course of an academic year, teachers have strong familiarity with them, which makes the vertical alignment process more meaningful at this point in time.

As an example, Columbus Public Schools in Nebraska developed proficiency scales and used them in the classroom across the district for a year. Then, selected teachers from core content areas worked with a consultant to conduct a vertical alignment process for English language arts scales to alleviate any concerns about appropriate level of rigor in a particular grade level or course. The alignment process included three phases and required one grade-level representative from kindergarten through high school. A full day of collaboration was allocated for the participants to learn the process well enough that it could be replicated at a later point in time by leaders of the district.

The first phase of the vertical alignment process involves individual teachers examining their respective grade-level proficiency scale for a standard that crosses a span of grade levels—sometimes even the entirety of the K–12 continuum. For example, the ELA topic of main idea and supporting details is one that appears in the standards for many grade levels. In this phase, a first-grade teacher would examine the grade 1 scale for main idea and supporting details, the second-grade teacher examines the grade 2 scale on the same topic, the eighth-grade teacher the grade 8 scale, and so on. The goal of this step is for individual teachers to identify aspects of their scales requiring discussion with other teachers. This stage should take about ten minutes.

The second phase requires the scales to be examined by teachers of adjacent grade levels. To illustrate this phase, envision teachers from grades K, 1, and 2 sitting together looking at their three respective scales for main idea and supporting details to ensure vertical alignment. The group makes certain that the kindergarten content is foundational to the first-grade content, which is foundational to the second-grade content. The end goal of this phase is for a progression to exist across all three grade levels for scores 2.0, 3.0, and 4.0.

Finally, the third phase of this process requires addressing any gaps that exist between grade bands. For example, in the second phase, grades K, 1, and 2 worked together, and grades 3, 4, and 5 collaborated. In this phase, grades 2 and 3 meet to ensure alignment, and so on. The end result of this entire process is that participating teachers propose changes to proficiency scales and take them back to their respective grade-level teams. Additionally, all educators involved gain a higher level of confidence in the quality of the scales. The vertical alignment process is described in more detail in appendix C (page 177). As an example of what this process might look like, see figure 3.1 (page 108). The scale has been transcribed onto chart paper, and teachers from adjacent grade levels have placed sticky notes with suggestions for revisions to improve alignment.

Include Teachers of Exceptional Learners

As more teachers learn about and start to use proficiency scales in the classroom, new questions will continue to arise. One common question relates to how proficiency scales are to be used with *exceptional learners*, which includes three categories of students: "students with disabilities, English learners, and gifted and talented students" (Heflebower et al., 2014, p. 71). Because of the word *help* at score 1.0 on a proficiency scale, some people initially believe that students with special learning needs and English learners can only earn a score 1.0 on the scale, due to the instructional help they may receive. In truth, score 1.0 can apply to any student in the classroom, including an exceptional learner. However, there are considerations that classroom teachers must know and understand for students with disabilities and English learners. Sometimes staff also have questions related to students who consistently perform at very high levels or who have been formally identified as gifted and talented. Leaders must be prepared to build understanding among all educators about using scales with these groups of exceptional learners.

The first idea to communicate is that teachers will use the grade-level or course proficiency scales with the vast majority of students. As a reminder, score 3.0 communicates the target content, or the learning expectations for *all* students. While the target content is for all learners, the way the content is taught can vary greatly based on individual student needs. In some schools, teacher teams work collaboratively to identify instructional

Student will make inferences in a work of fictional prose.

4 - Can utilize knowledge of author, genre, and time period to extend and support inferences

- Can compare and contrast alternate inferences and determine best inference based on context

3 - Can draw conclusions from prose where things are not explicitly stated

- Can explain and support inferences using textual evidence

2 - Can define *inference, explicit, evidence, authorial intent, tone*

- Can differentiate between showing and telling

- Can make inferences from specific texts that feature easy-to-interpret dialogue or actions

Source: © 2018 by Tammy Heflebower.

Figure 3.1: Scale revision example.

supports that scaffold the learning but do not change the level of learning on the scale. These supports—also called *accommodations*—are sometimes recorded as part of the proficiency scale. These teams of educators directly responsible for supporting a specific student are made up of grade-level representatives and specialists, such as special education, English learner, and gifted and talented teachers. Including the specialists in the scale-development work helps to ensure that all exceptional learner groups are considered during the work session.

Figure 3.2 displays the score 3.0 learning target on a proficiency scale for third-grade mathematics. It also shows the instructional supports that the teacher team determined to address the third-grade mathematics scales. The right-hand column presents ideas for instructional supports (accommodations) that do not change the level of learning; they can be provided for any student the teacher determines will benefit from the support.

The process of identifying instructional supports for each proficiency scale can be a time-consuming process. For that reason, some schools or districts begin this endeavor by identifying supports that are applicable to numerous proficiency scales. In other words, they identify a set of ten to twelve instructional supports that can be helpful regardless of the content area or grade level. To illustrate, teachers in Columbia Public Schools in

Grade 3 Mathematics Solving Two-Step Word Problems		
	Learning Targets	**Instructional Supports**
Score 3.0	• Solve two-step word problems using the four operations. • Represent two-step word problems using equations with a letter standing for the unknown quantity. • Assess the reasonableness of answers using mental computation and estimation strategies including rounding.	Educators will provide students with the following supports, as needed. • A graphic organizer for solving two-step word problems • Completed examples to follow when representing two-step word problems using equations with a letter standard for the unknown quantity • Probing questions and feedback when assessing the reasonableness of answers • Support when reading word problems independently

Source: Adapted from Hoegh, 2020.

Figure 3.2: Sample proficiency scale with instructional supports.

Missouri were very concerned about their exceptional learner populations in relation to how they would perform on their newly developed proficiency scales, especially their English learners. In an effort to provide an instructional support document to teachers in a very timely manner, an expert group of special education and English learner teachers developed a single document that provides a set of research-based, high-quality instructional strategies that teachers can use in the classroom to support all students, but especially English learners, striving to learn the content on proficiency scales. These are not the only resources teachers can use to support exceptional learners, but this set of strategies supplies useful information to classroom teachers as they provide students the opportunity to master the target content on proficiency scales. Figure 3.3 displays a few of the strategies in the instructional support document.

General Instructional Supports for English Language Learners
These instructional supports do not change the rigor or expectation of the standard. Appropriate instructional supports for English language learners may include, but are not limited to, the following.
Reading directions or text aloud to student Providing picture or drawing support to explain concepts and processes Highlighting key words Simplifying language while still maintaining academic vocabulary essential to content Giving single-step directions Simplifying complex directions Providing an example or model Providing a graphic organizer for specified task Increasing wait time

Source: © 2019 by Columbia Public Schools. Used with permission.

Figure 3.3: Sample general instructional supports.

While teachers might provide accommodations to any student, some students will have individual learning plans (for example, IEP, 504 plan) that require teachers to provide modifications to the learning expectations. *Modification* refers to adjusting the learning expectations themselves, as opposed to providing extra support. Depending on the degree of modification required, this may be a simple process that involves moving the score 3.0 content up to 4.0 and the score 2.0 content up to 3.0 (or the reverse for increasing expectations on the scale). Figure 3.4 illustrates this idea.

	General Education Scale	Decreased Expectations	Increased Expectations
Score 4.0	The student will: • Solve a multistep word problem involving dollars, quarters, dimes, nickels, and pennies	The student will: • Solve word problems involving dollars, quarters, dimes, nickels, and pennies	The student will: • Use mental computation and estimation strategies to assess the reasonableness of an answer at different stages of solving a multistep word problem involving money • Design scenarios in which solving word problems with money is an essential skill
Score 3.0	The student will: • Solve word problems involving dollars, quarters, dimes, nickels, and pennies	The student will: • Identify coin values (quarter, dime, nickel, penny) • Add or subtract different coins to determine a total amount of money collected or money remaining	The student will: • Solve a multistep word problem involving dollars, quarters, dimes, nickels, and pennies
Score 2.0	The student will: • Recognize or recall specific terminology, such as *$, ¢, value, coin, penny, nickel, dime, quarter, dollar, all together, remaining, decimal* • Use *$* and *¢* symbols appropriately • Identify coin values (quarter, dime, nickel, penny) • Add or subtract different coins to determine a total amount of money collected or money remaining	The student will: • Recognize or recall specific terminology, such as *$, ¢, value, coin, penny, nickel, dime, quarter, dollar, all together, remaining, decimal* • Use *$* and *¢* symbols appropriately	The student will: • Solve word problems involving dollars, quarters, dimes, nickels, and pennies

Source: Adapted from Hoegh, 2020.

Figure 3.4: Sample scale with modifications.

There may also be instances when the suggested modification is inadequate for a particular student. When this is the case, the teacher team may need to identify a related scale from a lower or higher grade level that aligns to the student's current ability level. Or, the team may even need to craft a new scale for the student. It is important to emphasize that this last statement represents a very rare occasion—for example, when there is no related proficiency scale at a lower or higher grade level. For additional information about using scales with exceptional learners, please refer to *A School Leader's Guide to Standards-Based Grading* (Heflebower et al., 2014), *A Teacher's Guide to Standards-Based Learning* (Heflebower et al., 2019), or *A Handbook for Developing and Using Proficiency Scales in the Classroom* (Hoegh, 2020).

Figure 3.5 delineates Jefferson County's timeline of comprehensive work related to SBL. Portions of the plan related to modifications, accommodations, and other methods of including exceptional leaders are circled. You will notice that English language arts and mathematics content-area teams were further along and ready to insert instructional accommodations into their proficiency scales and begin working on the assessment alignment. Social studies and science teams followed, replicating efforts of instructional accommodations and assessment alignment. You may notice that this thoughtful leadership team also infused presenter skills training for all their TOSAs to augment their work with on-site follow-up.

Dates	Content
September 11	ELA and Mathematics: Accommodations and Modifications
	• Work with special education and some general education teachers to draft accommodations or instructional supports and modifications for the drafted proficiency scales.
September 12	ELA and Mathematics: High-Quality Assessments
	• Continue and complete any accommodation and modified instructional supports.
	• Review quality criteria for district interim assessments and develop assessment literacy.
	• Apply validity and curate quality, aligned assessment items from local curriculum resources.
October 4	ELA and Mathematics: Assessment Development
	• Review items for elements of fairness.
	• Teach about inter- and intra-rater reliability, with application to subjective items.
November 5	Leadership Considerations for Standards-Referenced Reporting (use *A Teacher's Guide to Standards-Based Learning* and *A School Leader's Guide to Standards-Based Grading*)
	• Provide overview and present common language; share glossary of terms.
	• Set the context for curricular connections in units of study.
	• Discuss the *what*, *why*, and *how* of SBL. Address the process of prioritizing Essential Outcomes in the 2020 Colorado Academic Standards and the *why* of doing so.
	• Come to an understanding that targets are a minimum expectation: the floor rather than the ceiling.
	• Create unified improvement goal (School Improvement)—all schools.
	• Engage in action planning.
November 19–20	Social Studies and Science: Accommodations and Modifications; High-Quality Assessments
	• Work with special education and some general education teachers to draft accommodations or instructional supports and modifications for the drafted proficiency scales.
	• Review quality criteria for district interim assessments.
	• Apply validity and curate quality, aligned assessment items from local curriculum resources.
	• Review items for elements of fairness.
	• Teach about inter- and intra-rater reliability, with application to subjective items.

Figure 3.5: SBL implementation plan, Jefferson County.

continued →

December 3	Leadership Training
	• Train leaders on the *what*, *why*, and *how* of proficiency scale refinement.
	• Train leaders on how to infuse and integrate scales in practice within buildings.
	• Train leaders in action planning.
	• Follow up with the *who* and the *how* of the scale refinement process for Professional Learning Networks for leaders, module 3.
December 5–6	Facilitator Learning Days With TOSAs and Instructional Assistance Team
	Presentations Skills (Use *Crafting Your Message*)
	• Plan the message.
	• Deliver a dynamic message.
	• Facilitate and troubleshoot.
December 17	ELA and Mathematics: Assessment Development
	• Draft table of specifications for quality interim assessments.
February 4	• Go over the *what*, *why*, and *how* of quality assessment.
	• Address feedback, tracking, scoring, and goal setting with students.
	• Look at action planning from PLC perspective.
	• Follow up with teacher videos for evidence of use and unit planning labs.
March 9–10	ELA and Mathematics: Student-Friendly Proficiency Scales; Unit Design
	• Work as teacher teams to generate student-friendly scales for units.
	• Plan curricular units.
	• Learn ways to use scales with students.
March 11–12	Social Studies and Science: Student-Friendly Proficiency Scales; Unit Design
	• Work as teacher teams to generate student-friendly scales for units.
	• Learn ways to use scales with students.

Source: Heflebower et al., 2019.

Plan and Initiate the Rollout

This phase involves rolling out the initial implementation plan drafted in phase 1. Leaders have examined the plan and made any needed modifications; now it is time to formalize the implementation plan and share it with all staff. Doing so brings the document to life, in a sense. Leaders see the need to continually address and embed efforts at the local level. Teachers see the natural progression from topics and grade levels. The entire district is involved, and by sharing the written plan, individuals can contextualize their local efforts.

Decide the Progression of the Rollout

The rollout of the implementation plan consists of enacting proficiency scales and other components in the classroom with students. As mentioned previously, you may decide to implement in all content areas and grade levels at once, or you may elect to phase in SBL a few grade levels at a time. Ultimately, this decision is based on your school and district size, as well as the amount of preliminary work completed, and the knowledge and understanding of those leading the work.

As you contemplate the rollout for standards-based teaching and learning, be mindful that secondary teachers may be able to move through the implementation of priority standards and proficiency scales at a bit more expedited rate. The rationale is because they do not teach all content areas as elementary teachers often do. Figure 3.6 is a product from a facilitated process where Anoka-Hennepin School District in Minnesota planned its rollout on a whiteboard. This figure only shows a portion—a few months of a multiyear process—but provides a helpful look at a real-life artifact. This district planned separately by level (early elementary, upper elementary, middle school, and high school). You will see each team brainstormed key components of SBL implementation onto sticky notes, for ease in moving them around. The teams then arranged them into a draft timeline.

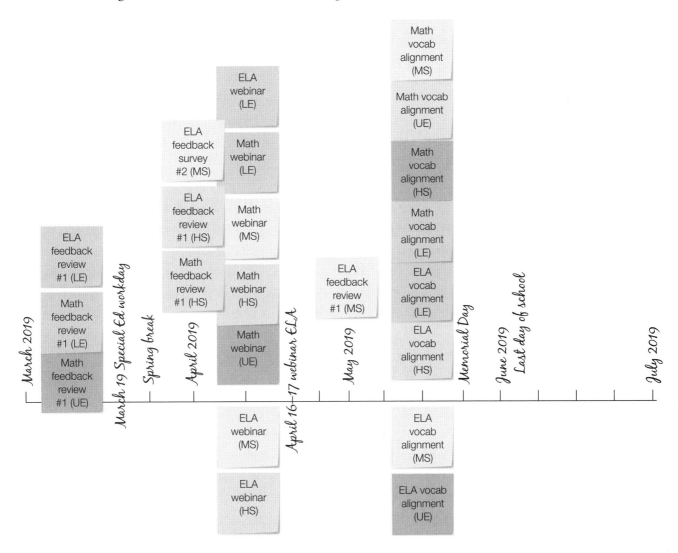

Source: © 2020 by Anoka-Hennepin School District. Used with permission.

Figure 3.6: Sample rollout process.

Figure 3.7 shows an additional implementation sample. This sample implementation plan was drafted by one of the authors for a district. It indicates that mathematics was first to roll out standards-based systems, science second, and so forth. You may also notice that one summer was devoted to planning for electives. A large district summit was held that included bouts of whole-group direct instruction interspersed with content-area team work time. District curriculum, instruction, and assessment staff facilitated the electives work sessions to expedite the work.

An additional, more detailed plan (see figure 3.8, page 116) was used for mathematics teams who were first to implement SBL.

Announce the Implementation Plan

Shifting to SBL is transformational change, so you must not simply hope the work is implemented as you intend. You must ensure it is. You cannot, nor would you want to, rely on informal networks or rumors to share the details of your implementation plan. Remember, without information, people will naturally make things up. Do not allow all of this magnificent work to be derailed by misinformation. You will want to carefully craft the implementation plan message for each respective audience. For example, what do elementary teachers need to know about, and when? What about middle school and high school? Think, too, about the various modes of your communication. Will you use print, email, video, brochures, websites, or a variety of each?

Require Teachers to Use Proficiency Scales in Core Content Areas

It is time for the first formal step of the rollout: require that all teachers of core content areas begin using their proficiency scales in the classroom on a frequent (if not daily) basis. Planning, instruction, assessment, and feedback all revolve around the proficiency scales. As a teacher or team of teachers initially uses the scales, it is important that they record potential revisions about each proficiency scale to be made later. It is common in schools that proficiency scale revision occurs at the end of an academic year. In fact, some schools or districts plan for scale revision to occur at the end of each year. This scale revision is the result of feedback provided by those teachers who implemented the proficiency scales over the course of the year. Regardless of the scheduling for proficiency scale revision, it is important that scale users collect information about the scales in an ongoing manner to ensure that the quality of scales is enhanced gradually. For example, after using a proficiency scale, teams may realize they are missing a critical learning target at score 2.0—a foundational skill needed to attain mastery of score 3.0. This information is recorded so that educators involved in the scale revision process can consider its inclusion.

Continue to Educate and Update the Board of Education

As the implementation progresses, the guiding team should offer updates to the board of education and be available to expand on the information and artifacts being added to

	System Feedback	Prioritized Standards Drafts Completion Date	Systemwide Prioritized Standards Implementation	PD on Quality Instruction	Interim Assessment Development	Interim Assessment Field Test	Interim Assessment Implementation
Mathematics		February 2007	2007–2008		2007–2008	2007–2008 Algebra I 2008–2009 Others	2008–2009 Algebra I 2009–2010 Others
Science		December 2007	2008–2009 Grades K–8 2009–2010 Grades 9–12	Summer 2008	2008–2009	2008–2009 Study team only	• Finalized in March 2009, after CDE revision process • 2009–2010 middle school, high school, and selected elementary—likely fourth grade • 2010–2011 Systemwide
Language Arts		• December 2008 • In tandem with Colorado Department of Education model content standards revision process	TBA		2008–2009	2009–2010	• In tandem with CDE model content standards revision process
Social Studies		• December 2008 • In tandem with CDE model content standards revision process	TBA		2008–2009	2009–2010	• In tandem with CDE model content standards revision process
World Languages		December 2007	2008–2009		2008–2009	2009–2010	TBA 2010–2011
Information Literacy		December 2007	TBA	2008–2009	TBA Eighth-grade tech 2008–2009		
Health		June 2008	2008–2009 Grades 7–12 2009–2010 Grades K–6		2008–2010	2009–2010	2010–2011
PE		June 2008	2008–2009		2008–2010	2009–2010	2010–2011
Theater		June 2008	2008–2009		2008–2010	2009–2010	2010–2011
Music		June 2008	2008–2009		2008–2010	2009–2010	2010–2011
Art		June 2008	2008–2009		2008–2010	2009–2010	2010–2011
Practical Arts		May 2008					
School to Career (7–12)		April 2008	2008–2009				
Middle School Family and Consumer Science		April 2008	2008–2009				
Elementary Progress Report Revisions	Study team review 2008–2009	February 2009	2010–2011				

Source: © 2008 by Tammy Heflebower.

Figure 3.7: Curriculum, instruction, and assessment implementation sample.

Implementation Plan for Mathematics Prioritized Standards

- *Release mathematics prioritized standards with implementation plan.*
  - *Timeline—March 2007*
  - *Who—administrators and building resource teachers*
  - *Materials—overview; prioritized standards question and answer form; prioritized standards document (all grade levels); example of curriculum, instruction, and assessment (CIA) guide completed for mathematics*
  - *To do—review, contact curriculum and instruction office for any questions, plan for release to staff, building resource teachers and staff members attend training in order to lead the curriculum planning process, plan with curriculum and instruction office contact person*
- *Introduce mathematics prioritized standards to staff.*
  - *Timeline—spring 2007 during staff meetings*
  - *Who—all staff*
  - *Materials—overview, prioritized standards question and answer form, prioritized standards document (all grade levels), example of CIA guide completed for mathematics*
  - *To do—review prioritized standards document (all grade levels) for clarity regarding building of big mathematical ideas and relationship to standards, plan for team meeting*
- *Engage in further discussion around mathematics prioritized standards.*
  - *Timeline—spring 2007 during team meetings*
  - *Who—grade-level team or department team, members from instructional support systems (ISS) who work with students in special education, gifted and talented, and ESL*
  - *Materials—prioritized standards document (all grade levels), example of CIA guide completed for math*
  - *To do—review grade-level expectations for clarity regarding mathematics and connections between mathematics concepts*
- *Complete the CIA guide at each grade level or course.*
  - *Timeline—summer or beginning of school year 2007 during PLC or team meetings*
  - *Who—grade-level team or department team, building resource teachers, CIA contact person (if needed), members from ISS who work with students in special education, gifted and talented, and ESL*
  - *Materials—example of CIA guide completed for math, grade-level or course-level CIA guides from first class to implement SBL*
  - *To do—start where you are comfortable; discuss the instruction, assessment, interventions and extensions, and timelines for the learning of the essential learning; record the conversations on the guides; use the guides to inform long-range planning for students*
- *Review the CIA guides at the site level.*
  - *Timeline—fall 2007 during site curriculum team meetings*
  - *Who—site curriculum team, building resource teachers, administrator, and CIA contact person (if needed)*
  - *Materials—completed grade-level or course-level CIA guides for mathematics*
  - *To do—review CIA guides; discuss any gaps or overlays in instruction or assessment; ensure students will have a coherent path for mathematics that focuses on important mathematics ideas; if gaps or overlays arise, bring information back to the staff for possible revisions*

- *Grade-level or course-level teams use the guides.*
  - *Timeline—2007–2008 school year, team meetings or PLC time*
  - *Who—grade-level team or department team, members from ISS who work with students in special education, gifted and talented, and ESL*
  - *Materials—completed grade-level or course-level CIA guides for mathematics*
  - *To do—use the guides to structure conversations around the* what, how, *and* how well; *make notes about possible revisions throughout the year*
- *Review the CIA guides at the feeder level (lower-level schools that feed into yours).*
  - *Timeline—fall and winter 2007–2008 during meeting with feeder schools*
  - *Who—feeder curriculum team, CIA contact person, director of schools (overseeing a set of feeder schools)*
  - *Materials—site-completed grade-level or course-level CIA guides for mathematics*
  - *To do—review CIA guides; discuss any gaps or overlays in instruction or assessment; ensure students will have a coherent path for mathematics that focuses on important mathematics ideas; if gaps or overlays arise, bring information back to the site for possible revisions*

Source: © 2008 by Tammy Heflebower.

Figure 3.8: Implementation for mathematics teams.

the board's SBL portfolios. At this point you might consider having students share their early experiences with the board. For example, students might explain their use of proficiency scales and how they engage with them as learners. These updates can also include scout teachers sharing their early experiences with the board as they forge ahead in the SBL initiative.

Prepare for Reporting Systems

Standards-based learning requires standards-based reporting systems. Preparing these will involve the development of a new report card and the use of a gradebook system designed or modified to work for standards-based grading and reporting practices.

Develop New Report Cards

The report card will be the most noticeable and public change in this implementation. The design of the report card format must reflect that a student's progress is monitored and reported based on the priority standards identified by the district. A student's level of mastery is reported in reference to each priority standard that has been taught and assessed. We suggest a district begin by examining sample report cards from different districts that are engaged in SBL. In our experience, schools use some common approaches but also develop interesting and unique ideas for the report card as the SBL concept continues to grow.

The report card should be a valid representation of a student's progress and inform students and parents of strengths and areas for continued growth on the prioritized standards. We suggest three considerations for the report card.

1. Consider how the report card can explain the prioritized standards that are important for each grade level or content area.

2. Think about how the report card can incorporate the proficiency scale levels used to gauge student progress. For this aspect the report card might have an online link to the corresponding proficiency scales.

3. Examine how the report card can separately report students' academic scores and scores for life skills such as work completion and class participation.

The report card must also be easy for students and parents to interpret. See appendix C (page 181) for sample parent resources. Sometimes, a district will elect to shorten prioritized standards into topic statements. This approach is often easier for parents to understand and saves space. Standards-based report cards also enable schools to report growth as well as final status. Figure 3.9 shows a report card section for priority topics taught and assessed in ELA. The dark bars represent a student's initial status for each prioritized standard written as a topic. The lighter bars show a student's growth and final status. This system allows students and parents to see how much students have improved in addition to their current level of mastery in coordination with the proficiency scale levels.

Language Arts		0.0	0.5	1.0	1.5	2.0	2.5	3.0	3.5	4.0
Reading										
Word Recognition and Vocabulary	3.5									
Reading for Main Idea	2.5									
Literary Analysis	3.0									
Writing										
Language Conventions	4.0									
Organization and Focus	2.0									
Research and Technology	1.5									
Evaluation and Revision	2.5									
Writing Applications	1.0									
Speaking and Listening										
Comprehension	3.0									
Organization and Delivery	3.5									
Analysis and Evaluation of Media	2.0									
Speaking Applications	2.0									

Source: Adapted from Marzano, 2010.

Figure 3.9: Example ELA report card section.

Figure 3.10 shows an example of how life skills and behavior can be reported separately from academic scores. In traditional reporting formats, this information is usually camouflaged inside a traditional percentage or letter grade. In an SBL system, this information can be purposely separated for better transparency.

Life Skills		0.0	0.5	1.0	1.5	2.0	2.5	3.0	3.5	4.0
Participation	4.0									
Work Completion	3.0									
Behavior	4.0									
Working in Groups	2.5									

Source: Adapted from Marzano, 2010.

Figure 3.10: Life skills reporting section.

Some schools elect to translate proficiency scale scores into traditional A–F grades or report both. An example of this is shown in figure 3.11. Here, a student's overall academic scores are reported for ELA, mathematics, science, social studies, and art on the left. On the right, life skills scores are reported for participation, work completion, behavior, and working in groups. For both sets of scores, the report card includes a letter grade and a proficiency scale score.

Language Arts	C (2.46)	Participation	A (3.40)
Mathematics	B (2.50)	Work Completion	B (2.90)
Science	C (2.20)	Behavior	A (3.40)
Social Studies	A (3.10)	Working in Groups	B (2.70)
Art	A (3.00)		

Source: Heflebower et al., 2014, p. 68.

Figure 3.11: Report card with dual scores.

As you develop new report cards and explore grading technology choices, it will be important to consider how these components interact. More and more, learning management system companies adapt their gradebooks to allow for SBL and embed report card options into their systems. Electronic gradebooks and report cards are potential land mines in the SBL implementation process if they do not function well for teachers, parents, and students.

Finalize Technology for Digital Storage

By this point in time, teacher teams are very familiar with the electronic system for storing the documents they generate (see page 57). The work of leaders is that of monitoring, which includes keeping aware of product development and revision, as well as ensuring that the prescribed folder and document naming conventions are being followed. It is important that all educators who access this repository are committed to ensuring that it doesn't become a disorganized collection of everything possible. Instead, it should only house the most current version of priority standards, proficiency scales, assessments, and so on. Individual teachers and teacher teams may certainly store previous versions in a folder system of their own, as there are occasions when it may behoove the team to look back at previous versions of documents.

As an example, building leaders in the Columbus Public Schools district are responsible for monitoring the development of resources, including proficiency scales, instructional units, and common assessments. The district director of curriculum designed a monitoring document (see figure 3.12). The principal in each school keeps track of progress via this document. Besides keeping the district-defined structure intact, this monitoring process helps to ensure that the building leaders are savvy about the critical components of SBL because their monitoring work means that they examine many teacher-developed documents.

Unit or Cycle / Document Links / Document Links	Scale Number & Topic / Proficiency Scale Template	CA Plan Fully Completed / Tradition CA Plan / Performance-Based CA Plan	CA Completed •Traditional Test •Rubric/Check list	CA Key Completed	CA Checklist Completed (Review) / Traditional CA Checklist / Based CA Checklist	Notes	Follow-Up Meeting Date/Time	2nd Grade PS/CA Folder Link
Ex: Topic 2A	2. Analyze/Solve Linear Equations	yes	yes	yes	no	Checklist not yet completed	1/30/2020 at 2:30	
Unit 2	Making Predictions and Inferences	yes	yes	yes	yes	Completed	Begin working on Keys and Checklists in Jan 2 or 3 2020 at District PLC	
Unit 3	Ask and Answer Questions	yes	yes	yes	yes	Completed		
After Unit 3	Context Clues / Text Features	yes	yes	no	no	Need to complete keys and checklist		
After Unit 4	Compare and Contrast	yes	yes	yes	yes	Completed		
Unit 4	Retell	yes	yes	yes	yes	Completed		
After Unit 4 and 5	Synonym/ Antonyms/ Multi-Meaing	yes	yes	yes	yes	Completed		
Unit 4 and 5	Word Parts	yes	yes	yes	yes	Completed		
Unit 5	Main Idea Details	yes	yes	yes	yes	Completed		

Source: © 2019 by Columbus Public Schools. Used with permission.

Figure 3.12: Progress-monitoring document.

Field-Test the Gradebook

Just as it is important to field-test the proficiency scales and common assessments, it is paramount that the gradebook be tested to find and resolve any issues. Most standards-based schools and districts will use gradebook software to keep track of students' scores on each priority standard. Some gradebooks include reporting features that generate report cards automatically. The field-test process can occur quite easily by asking for volunteer teachers to use the gradebook for a period of time, perhaps even the entirety of an academic year or the duration of a course. Provide these teachers with at least a draft of guidance instructions they can use and monitor throughout the field-testing process. As the field test transpires, it is critical that the team of educators responsible for the field test meet with participating teachers periodically in order for them to report on how it is working. As a result of these reports, adjustments may be necessary, as the goal is for the gradebook to be ready for all teachers in the first year of full implementation.

Figure 3.13 shows an example gradebook from Empower Learning, specifically developed for standards-based grading practices. This view is sorted by activities, which are aligned to multiple standards. For example, "4H Essay" is aligned to two standards, "Allegory" is aligned to three standards, and so on.

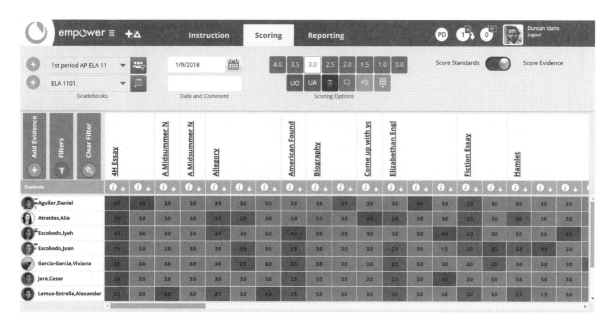

Source: © 2020 by Empower Learning. Used with permission.

Figure 3.13: Electronic gradebook for activities.

An additional screen (see figure 3.14) depicts student scores on standards rather than sorted by activities—a key component of moving toward SBL. The standards for this class appear in the bar across the top, with students' current scores in these standards represented in the cells.

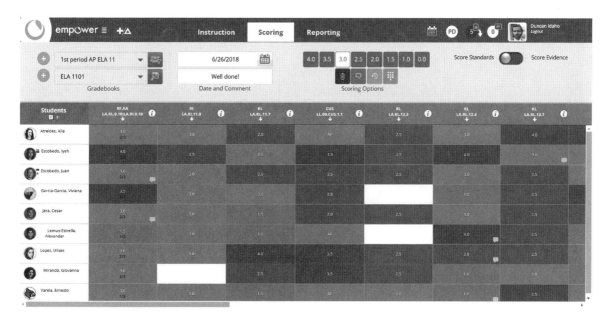

Source: © 2020 by Empower Learning. Used with permission.

Figure 3.14: Electronic gradebook for standards.

It is also important to understand how the gradebook calculates a final score. In traditional grading practices, teachers usually average students' scores on various assignments from throughout the grading period to determine a final grade. This is a simple method, but it does not reflect a student's learning over time—scores at the beginning of the grading period, before students receive instruction, practice, and so on, are just as important in the final grade as scores from the end of the grading period, when students know more. Luckily, gradebook software can perform more complex calculations to generate scores that more accurately reflect a student's true level of understanding. Figure 3.15 exemplifies how the Empower Learning gradebook calculates scores for each student. The Marzano True Score Estimator (a built-in part of the gradebook) analyzes scores entered over time, calculates three different trend lines, and recommends the final score that best fits the student's pattern of evidence.

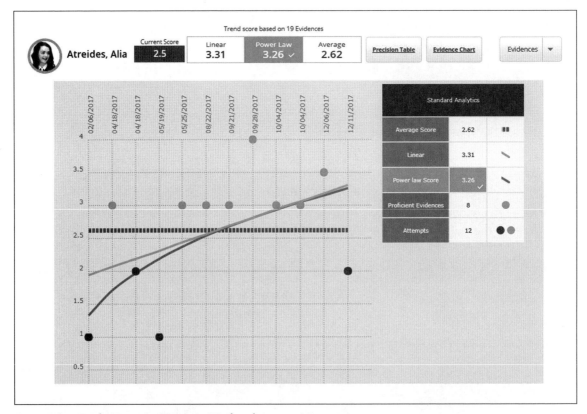

Source: © 2020 by Empower Learning. Used with permission.

Figure 3.15: Gradebook score calculator.

Getting the gradebook technology working correctly is absolutely critical. Parents want easy access to monitor their students' progress, and teachers need an efficient way to enter scores and monitor student progress as well. Overlooking or insufficiently addressing the technology aspect of the implementation process is a mistake. Even with all the good work being done in curriculum, assessment, and other aspects of this change, a failure in gradebook technology can derail the entire initiative. Conversely, when gradebook technology works and teachers can make a fairly easy transition to using the technology, it can serve as a catalyst for implementation.

Enlisting Consultants

Enlisting the support of outside consultants may be very useful as you begin to implement SBL. Consider when an "outsider" can serve as a critical friend and trainer for content. Evaluate your own capacities for knowing, understanding, and delivering the various components involved in this phase. Consider the following list of ways consultants might help with phase 3.

- Training teachers at different levels (elementary, middle, and high school) according to their specific needs on feedback, tracking progress, and goal setting

- Leading informational and question-and-answer sessions with your board of education

- Assisting with planning how parents will obtain initial information about proficiency scales

- Preparing and training leaders for phase 4 so they are ready to lead the next steps

- Selecting and setting up electronic gradebook programs

Summary

Phase 3 requires the monitoring of previous work and the development of new components. Here you ensure that all grade levels and content areas have completed the prioritization of standards and the creation of proficiency scales. You are seeing those tools used with students. Additionally, you are seeing direct alignment with instruction and classroom assessments, as well as specifically addressing the needs of exceptional learners. This phase provides the true foundation of a guaranteed and viable curriculum. In the next phases your work will lead to stakeholders seeing the fruits of this labor, and systems for monitoring the impact of SBL on student achievement.

PHASE 4

Continuation, Revision, and Expansion

Phase 4 continues implementation and making needed modifications. During this phase, you must monitor the programs put in place in the earlier phases while initiating the later phases of your plan. Therefore, this phase will take as long as you need to monitor the work so far. In most cases, six months to one year is ample time. You might think of this phase as the check-up phase: What will you need to modify? What is working well? Who needs more information? Specific activities include the following.

- Seek feedback from teachers about classroom assessments in core content areas.
- Continue the implementation rollout.
- Continue work in non-core content areas.
- Communicate with stakeholders.
- Implement new reporting systems for selected grades.

The following sections detail each one of these activities.

Seek Feedback From Teachers About Classroom Assessments in Core Content Areas

It is important to obtain feedback throughout the development and refinement of the classroom assessments to continually improve their quality through revision. When teachers not on the original design teams have opportunities to read the draft assessments and provide feedback, not only does this feedback create better products, but it also increases buy-in from your staff. Ensure you schedule time to draft feedback surveys, disseminate them, collect and collate the information, and share the feedback with the original design team.

Columbus Middle School, in Nebraska, used a feedback protocol (shown in figure 4.1, page 126) to ensure that all content-area teachers could provide feedback on a common assessment the design team developed. This process involved teachers exchanging common assessments with one another and receiving feedback based on an assessment criteria checklist.

Common Assessments—Getting Feedback

Team Roles

Within your group for today, select:

One person to be the facilitator (responsible for keeping everyone on track)

One person to be the timekeeper (responsible for setting time limits)

One person to be the recorder (responsible for writing official feedback)

Protocol

1. Trade assessments to be reviewed with members of your assigned group.

2. Silently read through and annotate the materials provided for five minutes.

3. Begin with the common assessment plan (fifteen minutes):

   a. Read the administration guidelines for the assessment. What is helpful? What is missing? What would you need to know if you were giving this assessment?

   b. Read the scoring guidelines. Do you know how to grade the test? Do you know how a student achieves a performance level?

4. Look at the assessment criteria checklist (fifteen minutes):

   a. Examine questions for bias. Make a note of questions in need of possible revision.

   b. Look at the directions. Do they follow good direction guidelines? Make suggestions for improvement.

5. Pull together feedback (five minutes):

   a. Go back and clarify your feedback, if needed.

   b. Add feedback about other areas, as appropriate.

Reflection and Feedback in Small Groups

You have five minutes per group to share feedback with another group. This is a time to *listen* to feedback. You then have five minutes per group to *ask questions* for clarification (total time: twenty minutes).

Make your feedback constructive and positive.

You then have ten minutes to reflect as a team about what you will change or improve based on this feedback.

Source: © 2019 by Amy Mancini, Columbus Public Schools. Used with permission.

Figure 4.1: Common assessment feedback protocol.

The primary purpose for the protocol was to ensure that all teachers receive constructive feedback for how to enhance their tools and hear some positive comments as well. While there are certainly numerous ways feedback can be gathered, this collaborative and interactive activity resulted in enhanced knowledge and better common assessments.

Continue the Implementation Rollout

Your plan is underway, and you are continuing to monitor, communicate, and expand it. At this point you will require that teachers use proficiency scales in all content areas and with all students, as opposed to only in core areas. Here you will also ensure that aligned instructional practices and classroom assessments are embedded into daily practices.

Announce and Share Written Plans With All Staff

One of the most important things a leadership team can offer to other educators in a building or across a district is clarity about the transition to standards-based grading. A well-articulated implementation plan accomplishes this. Sharing this plan is not the sole responsibility of a single leader; instead it should be tackled by a small group of leaders and representative teachers. Sometimes schools and districts enlist the support of an outside consultant for the refinement of the implementation plan. Of course, implementation plans can look very different. However, there are certain components that are typically included on any plan that will be used to guide the transition to standards-based grading. To illustrate, consider the example implementation plan for Converse County School District #2 in Glenrock, Wyoming, in figure 4.2 (page 128).

Sharing the implementation plan with the entire staff is critical. In some schools, the building principal is the primary person responsible for communicating the plan. Sometimes a school superintendent or district curriculum director shares the plan, especially when SBL is a districtwide initiative. Shared responsibility might also be the best means for communicating this plan. Regardless of the method, it is very important that all parties understand that the plan is a flexible document and that it will provide guidance for the transition to standards-based grading or to another desired end point. Visit **MarzanoResources.com/reproducibles** to view sample presentation slides used to share a district's implementation plan with staff.

Implement Proficiency Scales in Non-Core Content Areas or Selected Grade Levels

Depending on the district implementation plan for SBL, it may be time to implement proficiency scales for non-core content areas or a new band of grade levels or courses. There is no one right way for this implementation to occur, as long as everyone is on the same page. Since implementation of scales has already occurred in previous phases, the same scale-development process (previously described, see page 25) can be used. Be certain you provide teachers new to using scales with the *what*, *why*, and *how* of proficiency scales during the initial implementation. You may elect to provide this support through a large-group meeting, webinars, or collaborative team meetings. Be certain you provide multiple opportunities for learning about proficiency scales and provide examples of how to begin using them. It is also possible that teachers already using proficiency scales in the classroom can offer information and support during the learning opportunities. Remember that it is important for school leaders to monitor this implementation within their buildings. Collaborative team agendas may serve as one source of evidence of implementation.

Implement Common Classroom Assessments in Selected Grade Levels

Along with the implementation of proficiency scales comes the rollout of the aligned classroom assessments. Depending on your plan, the assessment rollout could occur in tandem with the scales, or you may elect to have a semester of proficiency scale

CONVERSE COUNTY SCHOOL DISTRICT #2 SBL ACTION PLAN					
	2018–2019	**2019–2020**	**2020–2021**	**2021–2022**	**2022–2023**
Prioritized Standards and Proficiency Scales	• ELA and mathematics experts learn about components of an SBL environment. • Learn about and work collaboratively to customize the Critical Concepts proficiency scales for ELA and mathematics.	• Complete the customization of proficiency scales for ELA and mathematics. • Plan for other content areas to learn about the components of an SBL environment. • Develop pacing guides or curriculum maps to guide instruction of the content on proficiency scales for ELA and mathematics.	• Additional content-area teachers learn about components of an SBL environment. • Begin using proficiency scales with students in ELA and mathematics classrooms. • Begin writing proficiency scales for all grade levels, content areas, and courses. • Continue to revise proficiency scales for ELA and mathematics based on their use.	• Fully implement proficiency scales in ELA and mathematics classrooms. • Begin using proficiency scales in classrooms of other grade levels and content areas. • Develop pacing guides or curriculum maps to guide instruction of the content on proficiency scales for other grade levels or content areas.	• Fully implement proficiency scales in the classroom for all grade levels and content areas. • Continue to revise proficiency scales for all content areas based on their use.
Aligned Classroom Assessments		• Learn about classroom assessment practices that align to the Critical Concepts proficiency scales for ELA and mathematics.	• Select or develop assessments (common assessments where appropriate) for ELA and mathematics. • Plan for other content areas to learn about high-quality assessment practices that align to proficiency scales.	• Finish selecting or developing assessments that align to proficiency scales for ELA and mathematics. • Continue assessment work in all other grade levels and content areas.	• Continue developing and revising classroom assessments based on using them in the classrooms of all content areas.
Effective Grading Practices		• Leaders and teacher representatives begin learning about effective grading practices.	• All teachers learn about effective grading practices in an SBL environment. • Research examples of standards-referenced report cards used in other school settings. • Determine a plan for secondary levels regarding a standards-referenced report card.	• Revise elementary report card to be piloted in 2022–2023. • Ensure gradebook platform supports standards-referenced reporting.	• Implement standards-referenced report card in elementary school. • Collect feedback about new elementary report card from teachers, parents, and students.
Other Considerations	• Develop new teacher training to ensure all new staff are informed about critical concepts, proficiency scales, high-quality classroom assessments, and effective grading practices. • Provide frequent collaboration time for teams to accomplish the work related to proficiency scales and assessment development, review, and data analysis. • Develop a communication plan so that all stakeholders understand what proficiency scales are and their purpose.				

Source: © 2019 by Converse County School District #2. Used with permission.

Figure 4.2: Implementation plan.

implementation followed the next semester by the aligned classroom assessments to match. Either approach is appropriate. Simply monitor the workload and needs of your staff. Some will want the assessments available at the same time, while others may want to try out the scales first, then move toward the assessments. Teachers are encouraged to use the drafted assessments as they are first developed and field-tested. After the revisions, they are then required to be used by teachers, and results are monitored for addressing any student learning deficits or accelerations. At any rate, set a soft deadline for the carrying out of assessment use: expect it, monitor it, provide support, and seek evidence for it. Remember—what gets monitored gets done. If leaders fail to follow the expectations of building-level implementation, it sends the message that this work is not essential and other expectations will fill the agendas instead.

Continue Work in Non-Core Content Areas

Non-core content area teachers are now in full swing of using proficiency scales with students and field-testing the assessments created. What the core content–area teachers did in phase 3 is now what you will expect of non-core areas in phase 4. As mentioned previously, monitor and adjust to your specific situation. You may have non-core areas ready to move faster than your core counterparts. By all means, move faster if you can, and slower if you need.

Revise Proficiency Scales as Needed

Proficiency scale revision will continue in an ongoing manner over time for all content areas. It is necessary to inform all teachers of the process for submitting and collecting suggestions for revision for each scale. The process described previously (see page 61) can be replicated for all content areas. This information will be used during a time when teachers come together for the purpose of scale revision. It is important to restate that by this point in your process, proficiency scale revision is typically part of a yearly cycle. When this is the case, the new content areas can simply become part of the yearly proficiency scale review.

Align Quality Classroom Assessments With Standards and Scales for Non-Core Content Areas

With a reviewed and finalized set of priority standards and proficiency scales in place, it is time for non-core content area teams to align their classroom assessments. Just as with your core content teams, this process can be done in multiple ways. Some districts ask teachers to do the alignment at the building level using their existing classroom assessments. Others use districtwide common assessments. Be mindful that many non-core teachers primarily use performance assessments for their skill-based fine and practical arts courses, including physical education, music, art, career and technical education, and so on. These assessments require a performance or a product, rather than traditional item types, such as multiple-choice, fill-in-the-blank, or constructed-response items. Therefore, they may also include rubrics, checklists, or other components specific to the scoring process. As a result, a leader must ensure that learning opportunities are designed to verse teachers on the specific type of assessments they will use to monitor progress to their scales. See *A School Leader's Guide to Standards-Based Grading* (Heflebower et al., 2014) for more details on defining, outlining, and step-by-step processes for leading the assessment alignment work.

Train Non-Core Teachers on Inter-Rater Reliability Processes

As teachers for non-core classes develop and begin using common assessments based on proficiency scales, it is important that they are trained on the scoring of these assessments. Because they are *common* assessments, teachers must understand and use processes that ensure the consistency of scoring. Begin with existing assessments used by the various non-core content area teachers. Review them through the lenses of quality (validity and fairness). Then, move into modeling the process of inter-rater reliability. Teachers may start by selecting two samples of student work. Each teacher initially scores each student (using consistent criteria). Each teacher then brings the two samples of work—one for which he or she is confident of the evaluation, and another about which he or she may be unsure. During a collaborative team or grade-level team meeting, teachers then exchange the samples and independently score the student samples. The teachers then discuss their areas of agreement and disagreement. They often need time to clarify, ask questions, and provide explanation. At the end of the meeting (or another, as needed), they leave all in agreement as to how they would score the samples of student work. This process replicated over and over is a profound way to develop and increase inter-rater reliability. Refer to page 81 for additional methods for ensuring this consistency.

Share Intra-Rater Reliability Strategies

Use the same or similar process for training intra-rater reliability processes as described in phase 2 (page 83). As you think about new content-area teams and grade-level teachers who need training, also consider new teachers to your building or district, as well as teachers moving grade levels or courses. Recall that intra-rater reliability involves the rater (teacher) carefully controlling for situations that may cause inconsistency. For example, teachers who begin to grade some student work samples, and then stop and come back to it a day or two later, might grade differently in the two sessions. Therefore, teachers should carefully reset themselves by reviewing evaluation criteria and doing all they can to ensure objectivity. It might mean they review previously evaluated samples prior to assessing new ones. A teacher could even reassess one or two samples from the previous set without first seeing his original evaluation comments or scoring—and check that he gave the same score the second time. Teachers should always reference their grading criteria prior to assessing student work.

An additional idea would be for teachers to shuffle papers in between evaluating various assessment items or sections. This way, the same students' papers don't always remain at the beginning or the end of the grading session. Natural fatigue can set in for teachers, and shuffling the papers between sections will lessen the effect of such fatigue on a few specific students.

A final strategy is to have students place their names in inconspicuous places, like on the back of physical papers, so that teachers don't see student names prior to assessing them. This simply helps teachers remain more objective—not allowing any personal feelings to inadvertently influence their neutrality. Teachers are human, and sometimes past situations with students or student behavior may influence their judgment.

Communicate With Stakeholders

Communicating with all stakeholders—staff, parents, students, the board of education, and so on—is essential throughout the SBL implementation process. This continues in phase 4.

Organize Learning Opportunities for All Staff

The key to planning and providing continued learning opportunities is to consider the needs of your educators. What will they need, and when? How is the training most efficiently and effectively done? How will you consider new hires every year? What will you do to provide updates and deeper information? Learning opportunities need thoughtful consideration. You will want to differentiate training for novice and experienced educators. You may want some training specifically targeted to leaders and instructional coaches, different training for classroom teachers, different training for specialists, and even different training for those working with exceptional learners. For instance, school leaders and instructional coaches need training to assist them in understanding upcoming phases of implementation so they can lead this work at local sites. Even within this group, you may want to consider multiple options for delivering the training. For instance, district leaders might record a series of webinars that can be distributed throughout their systems. Topics could include the major components of SBL, such as how prioritization occurred; what proficiency scales are, how they are developed, and how they are used; quality components of classroom assessments; ways to track progress, align instruction, provide students feedback, and set goals; and ways to more consistently grade students. Teachers will need to see examples of each of the components and how to implement them in the classroom. Allowing teachers to self-select according to their professional development needs may be an effective way to differentiate. On the other hand, board of education members don't need classroom details; rather, they need to understand the rationale for increasing consistency and coherence within the system, as well as student achievement results.

If in doubt, ask your constituents what they need to know. Use your existing staff teams, professional development days, and virtual options to design a myriad of options and ensure support for all levels of needs. As you consider learning opportunities, be mindful of various formats, which might include full-day sessions, shorter sessions lasting an hour or so, book studies, and podcasts. Using existing collaborative structures may also be an effective and efficient means for disseminating information and conducting mini-training sessions. Consider working with your district and site leadership teams to plan professional development opportunities.

Figure 4.3 is a sample chart to assist you in your discussions and planning of learning opportunities. It highlights various modes of professional development with the corresponding level of impact, immediacy, time and effort, and interactivity. In other words, it helps you consider the type of communication and training mode and also weigh the characteristics of each. For example, attending a conference tends to have significant impact on practice and is highly interactive, leading to better learning, but it also requires a lot of time and effort in terms of travel, coordinating schedules, and so forth.

Learning Formats	Impact	Immediacy	Time and Effort	Interactivity
Face to Face	High	Variable	High	High
Book Study	Moderate	Limited	Moderate	Moderate
Podcasts and Webinars	Moderate	Variable	Low	Moderate
Printed Materials for Collaborative Team Conversations	Limited	Variable	Low	Limited
Conference Attendance	High	Variable	High	High

Source: Adapted from Heflebower et al., 2014.

Figure 4.3: Communication matrix example.

Share Belief Statements

The belief statements drafted during phase 2 (page 89) need to be disseminated first among your leadership team, whether that be principals or district-level leaders. By beginning with your leaders, you help build knowledge, foster common expectations, and model a process to be used with site staff. Consider the following questions for planning the dissemination.

- Will these beliefs simply be distributed, or do you want to seek input?
- Will you want buildings within the district to customize the drafted set of beliefs?
- Will teams create documents for sharing the belief statements formally? Will such guidance be inserted into staff and student handbooks?

To share the beliefs, you may want to reference them on your website. You may want to ask teachers to post them, as well as provide them in your staff and student handbooks, share them on course syllabi, and make them available in other locations used for students and parents to obtain clarity about the workings of your school or district.

Whatever you decide, you need to be sure the belief statements are not only dispersed but lived. How will these core beliefs guide practice? In an effort to provide teachers with adequate guidance for enacting the core beliefs, some districts develop a grading practice handbook for teachers. This document often includes information about the components discussed in this book, such as grading beliefs; priority standards; the *what*, *why*, and *how* of proficiency scales; assessment; and the basics of grading. This teacher resource is a valuable tool to ensure that teachers feel supported and confident that they can be successful with the grading practices required of them. As an example, Rutland High School in Rutland, Vermont, uses the following belief statements (Rutland High School, 2020b).

- What do grades mean at RHS? Grades communicate individual student academic achievement in relation to course expectations to our students, their families, employers, and postsecondary institutions.

- We believe:
    - Grades reflect student academic achievement.
    - Grading will not be used for disciplinary purposes.
    - At the start of a course, students and parents will be provided with information regarding grading practices and expectations.
    - Summative evidence will constitute the majority of a student's grade.

Conduct Focus Groups With Students and Parents

Focus groups are a useful way to gauge more qualitative information from constituent groups like students and parents. Using a specific protocol for conducting effective focus groups (Krueger, 1994) will help you in setting up focus groups, formulating effective questions, coding the responses, and extracting a meaningful sense of how standards-based learning is permeating the beliefs and practices of various populations. Following are the phases of a focus group protocol. For the complete process, see appendix D (page 187).

1. Planning the focus group
2. Conducting the focus group interviews
3. Interpreting and reporting results

In this case, using focus groups to access opinions and attitudes from students and parents can be an authentic means for gathering implementation information. To plan a focus group, select a topic about which you want to gauge understanding or opinion. Then, formulate a set of questions for the specific audience. For example, you might use the following prompts during a student focus group about assessment.

- Tell me about assessment at your school.
- Tell me about reteaching and reassessment. Have you heard these terms? Have you experienced these? Please describe.
- What would you like your teachers to know about assessment from a student's perspective?
- What is one thing you would compliment about how your teachers use assessment?
- Is there anything you would modify? If so, be specific.

For a parent focus group on assessment, you might use these prompts.

- Tell me about assessment at your children's school.

- Tell me about reteaching and reassessment. Have you heard these terms? Have you heard your children discuss these? Please describe.

- What would you like teachers to know about assessment from a parent's perspective?

- What is one thing you would compliment about how teachers use assessment with your children?

- Is there anything you would modify? If so, be specific.

By asking similar yet differentiated questions for each group, you can obtain a great deal of information. Focus groups also allow you to capture quotes (anonymously) to help deepen the responses and tell the story.

The other aspect of planning a focus group is selecting the participants. We would suggest between six and ten participants for each focus group. Be sure to invite a varied group to gain widespread perspectives that include a mix of grade levels, families of various ethnicities, newcomers to the district, struggling learners and their families, and highly involved students and parents, as well as those who do not usually participate much. Most often, focus groups are held in a central location (your school conference room could work perfectly). Focus groups are held during the day for students, and at times most convenient for parents.

While you will have other ways of discerning staff mindsets, you may consider conducting focus groups with teachers as well. Used thoughtfully, focus groups can provide valuable information as to the implementation strengths and challenges of SBL.

Provide Board Members Opportunities to Observe New Systems in Action

As mentioned in phase 1 (page 48), training and informing the board of education is essential throughout the entire process of implementation. That training and information is not always best delivered at formal board meetings. In this phase, consider organizing tours of schools for board members to see firsthand how standards-based practices are used with students. This approach shows board members that the entire process was far more than a change in grading. In fact, the message to the board should be focused on learning for every student and how the criterion-referenced approach meets the needs of all students. As part of these tours, consider having students, teachers, or parents share positive changes they have noticed from the implementation.

For example, Jaci Lenz is a secondary mathematics teacher in Northwood, North Dakota, who made specific adjustments to her professional practices as a result of implementing SBL. As part of her classroom practice, Lenz communicated SBL norms to students by providing each student with a document showing those norms and reviewing them for clarity. A copy of Lenz's standards-based grading norms is shown in figure 4.4.

Standards-Based Grading

Miss Lenz

2019–2020

1. Work habits will not be figured into your final grade. Your scale scores are going to be worth 100 percent of your final grade.

2. Work habits scores are still going to be reported; they just will not be included in your grade.

3. In order to reassess, you must have all your practice turned in for that scale.

4. You must take at least three assessments for each scale.

5. You must try all questions at a level in order to get a score at that level.

6. After the last assessment is taken in class on a particular scale, you will have two weeks to practice and reassess before the scale will be locked. Reassessment will be offered on the last day of the week, and you must attend a majority of the reteaching sessions in order to earn the opportunity of reassessment.

Source: © 2019 by Jaci Lenz. Used with permission.

Figure 4.4: Sample standards-based grading norms.

As part of her standards-based grading norms, Lenz set specific expectations and guidelines for key aspects of standards-based grading, which include relearning, reassessment, and a timeline during which that reassessment must occur. To further support that norm, she developed reteaching and reassessment schedules based on her priority standards and topics. She additionally identified student tutors who are available for peer tutoring opportunities as part of the relearning options for students seeking reassessment. By doing this, Lenz clearly communicated that the focus will be on learning the content rather than cobbling together points that are actually meaningless in what they represent. She also sent a strong message about her expectations for all learners and how she is making the opportunity to learn available to them as long as they are willing to make the choice to engage in the opportunity within the prescribed timeline. Figure 4.5 (page 136) shows an example of her reteach, reassess, and tutoring schedule, including how Lenz identified students who can serve as tutors for specific topics other students might need help with during this time.

Having teachers share specific practices and artifacts such as Lenz's norms and reassessment and tutoring schedule provides board members with a classroom-level look at how the standards-based process positively impacts learning daily in a classroom.

Additionally, schools can demonstrate to board members how the implementation of SBL practices connects to collaborative structures such as collaborative teams and content departments by reviewing meeting minutes, watching short videos of meetings, or visiting meetings where SBL is being discussed.

RETEACH AND REASSESS SCHEDULE
February 25 to March 1

Time	Monday, February 25	Tuesday, February 26	Wednesday, February 27	Thursday, February 28	Friday, March 1
Before School		Algebra II Reassess Functions	Pre-Algebra Reassess Algebraic Expressions	Algebra I Reassess Solving Quadratic Equations	
CLT	Algebra II Reteach Functions **Geometry Reteach** Parallel or Perpendicular Lines (Tutors)	Algebra I Reteach Solving Quadratic Equations **Pre-Algebra Reteach** Algebraic Expressions (Tutors)	ACT Exam Prep Juniors	Geometry Reteach Parallel or Perpendicular Lines (Tutors) **Pre-Algebra Reteach** Solving Linear Equations (Tutors)	Geometry Reassess Parallel or Perpendicular Lines **Pre-Algebra Reassess** Solving Linear Equations
Tutors	Caleb Avery Logan Lexi	Teddy Isaiah Alex Arwyn		Alex Carter Reese	Cassie Brennen Emma

Source: © 2019 by Jaci Lenz. Used with permission.

Figure 4.5: Sample reteach, reassess, and tutoring schedule.

Implement New Reporting Systems for Selected Grades

Developing new report cards was addressed in phase 3 (page 117). By this phase there should be an initial version that can be implemented at selected grade levels (see examples in appendix D, page 190). You are done piloting report card formats, and you've also reviewed and decided on the best technological option for your district. Now you are ready to use the report card for its intended purpose. A common approach is to implement the new report card in the primary grades first as these families have fewer attachments to traditional report cards and may therefore be more accepting of the adjustment. A district might also select various grade levels throughout the K–12 span so that initial implementation includes interaction across elementary and secondary grades and courses. Often the grade levels that are the first to implement are selected based on key teacher leadership or strong collaborative teams in those grade levels.

As the report card is implemented and used in conjunction with the gradebook program, continue to gather feedback from teachers, parents, and students to check on the effectiveness of the report card design. As the report card is rolled out in the initial grade levels, you will continue to train additional teachers on the technology use needed for this change, which they will be involved with in the near future. As part of this training you will want to ensure you have tutorials developed for use at the beginning of the year, and also during the times you expect grades to be configured and reported. Often these tutorials can include video examples or suggestions from teachers who are the initial implementers of the new reporting system.

Ensure Students and Families Understand New Reporting Practices

Be sure to continue developing the understanding of reporting practices with your students and their families. Invest the time necessary for students to understand how this will be similar to and different from any past experiences. A parent FAQ document appears in appendix D (page 194). Figure 4.6 shows a communication excerpt. It includes guidance and links for viewing final grades.

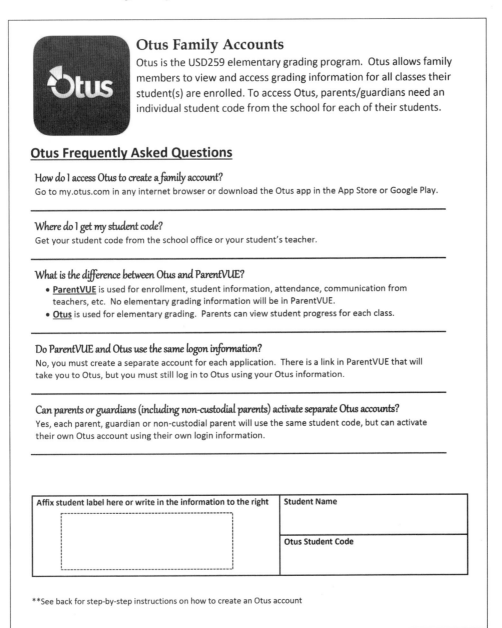

Source: © 2020 Wichita Public Schools. Used with permission.

Figure 4.6: Viewing final grades in Otus.

Figure 4.7 shows another communication excerpt for parents. It includes guidance and links for viewing final grades.

 Viewing Student Grades in Synergy

Parents and/or guardians with a Synergy ParentVUE account can follow the directions below to see student performance in each class/subject

1. Go to parentvue.usd259.net (or the app on your device) and log in with your Synergy username and email

- If you have forgotten your username, please contact your child's school for assistance
- If you have forgotten your password, click Forgot Password?
- If you do not have a ParentVue account, please contact your child's school for assistance

2. Choose Your Student (if you have more than one)

- Use the drop-down arrows at the top to select your student (if you have more than one) and then click on the student name/photo.

3. View Current Report Card

- Click the Report Card option on the left side menu
- When the screen opens, click the correct grading period at the top (currently for the 19/20 school year, this would **MAR Rpt Card**).
- Each class with the posted grades now shows with the grade legend at the bottom
- Users can see previous progress reports by switching the reporting periods at the top

**To see grade book grades (grades on individual assignments), click Grade Book on the left side and navigate through the classes and assignments.

4. HELP/FAQ

- <u>Need help with login</u>? Contact your child's school
- <u>Forgot Password</u>? Click Forgot Password
- <u>Have questions about a student's grade on report card or in grade book</u>? Please contact the classroom teacher

Source: © 2020 Wichita Public Schools. Used with permission.

Figure 4.7: Viewing student grades in Synergy.

If you are beginning with your primary or elementary families, they may not have a lot of past history to unlearn, and they will work with this type of grading and reporting for their entire school experience. When students clearly understand what their grades represent, opportunities for reassessment, proficiency scales, and so forth, their parents will be far more at ease in transitioning to SBL. If grades are reported as proficiency scale scores for a specific standard or topic, students can show their parents the progression of scores and explain the meaning in relationship to their current knowledge. Informing students is usually done at the classroom level, but it should be coordinated to a large degree by school leaders and especially key teacher leaders. This coordinated approach could be done in several ways. Two that are predominant are the use of common presentation slide decks give to all teachers or a recorded video introduction that all teachers use with their students. It would also be advisable to provide a basic script for teachers to use for initial introductions so there is a clear and consistent message being provided. To further facilitate these conversations throughout the year, schools can provide clear descriptions for students and parents to use as they view student scores. Figure 4.8 is an example of a scale score translation document that can help communicate the meaning of scale scores as they relate to student performance.

Scores and Descriptors	Progressions of Learning
4.0 Advanced	Evidence clearly demonstrates knowledge and skills above the level identified in the standards.
3.5	Evidence indicates growth in student knowledge and skills beyond proficiency.
3.0 Proficient	Evidence clearly demonstrates knowledge and skills that meet the standards.
2.5	Evidence indicates knowledge and skills beyond the foundations and moving toward proficiency.
2.0 Progressing	Evidence indicates knowledge and skills of the foundational concepts for the standards.
1.5	Evidence indicates growth in student knowledge and skills beyond beginning.
1.0 Beginning	Evidence indicates beginning stages of knowledge and skills with assistance from the teacher.

Source: Adapted from Heflebower et al., 2019.

Figure 4.8: Scale score translation guide.

You may pair a document such as this with the student and family information and training discussed previously in this section, or make this an information-sharing opportunity used in combination with the new reporting format each time a reporting period arrives. To provide an ongoing source of information, consider establishing a specific page on the school or district website that provides explanation and examples of the reporting systems. An excellent example of this is *A Parents' Guide to Proficiency Based Learning* created by Rutland High School (2020a) in Rutland, Vermont.

Continue to Fine-Tune Technology Needs

By now you will have decided on which technological systems will best support your work. As described in phase 1 (page 57), be sure to include technology staff early in the process. It is important that those individuals supporting the use of technology understand the components of SBL, especially the features that relate most closely to the learning management and gradebook platforms. The long-term desire is for technology to support classroom practices. Often schools and districts find that simple modifications within their existing student information and learning management systems are sufficient. These modifications might be as simple as changing the weighting of grading categories or using a different algorithm for determining the end-of-grading-period score. Other times, they select a new gradebook platform. In either case, remember to plan for any refinement needs and train the users accordingly. Consider piloting these modifications in a few grades before a systemwide rollout. It will allow opportunities to correct any issues and have a smoother comprehensive enactment later.

Track Correlations Among Scales, Common Assessments, and State Assessments

You will want to put systems in place to track your student achievement data. Not only will this help you see your efforts come to fruition among your various student achievement measures, but it will also help you provide support and information for any areas of concern. Over time, you should see student learning improve, with the goal that all students reach proficiency. As more students reach proficiency on the priority standards, inequities in achievement between student subgroups should decrease.

We also recommend comparing students' proficiency scale scores or other classroom learning data to external data such as statewide and national exam scores. One purpose for classroom assessment is to gain knowledge of how students will perform on state or national exams. For example, if fourth-grade students perform consistently well on classroom assessments based on proficiency scales, that should indicate that the collective group is prepared for the state test covering those same standards. A correlational study can help to affirm that the existing classroom assessments are indicative of performance on a state or national test. If such a study results in low correlations, it may be an indication that classroom assessments are not adequately rigorous, which may result in false indications of mastery of standards. Figure 4.9 is an example of how the results of a correlational study can be displayed. This example relates to MAP, or the Measure of Academic Progress, which is a computerized adaptive test administered by many schools and districts across the country. It is important to note that the majority of correlations fall within the Strong to Very Strong range, meaning that strong performance on classroom assessments has prepared students well for the MAP assessment opportunity.

Ensuring that staff, board of education members, and parents see results builds confidence in the SBL processes that have been and will continue to be implemented. This massive change must be monitored and tracked for effectiveness by those educators leading the implementation process.

Enlisting Consultants

Enlisting the support of outside consultants may be very useful as you continue implementing SBL. Consider when an "outsider" can serve as a critical friend and trainer for content. Evaluate your own capacities for knowing, understanding, and delivering the various components involved in this phase. Consider the following list of ways consultants might help with phase 4.

- Determining what technology resources exist and which work with your existing systems

- Training on how the new grading technology supports the work underway

- Working with teachers willing to pilot new components and having them share their experiences

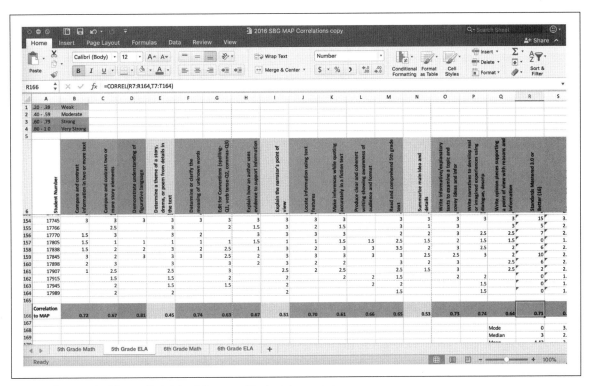

Figure 4.9: Student learning data correlation study.

Summary

Phase 4 contains a great deal about the continued implementation of SBL components. For example, proficiency scales are now being used with all content areas and grade levels. Teachers have given feedback about the aligned assessments and modified them accordingly. Parents have learned about SBL from training sessions and informational resources. Families have given feedback through focus groups, keeping you aware of the successes and challenges of implementation. You are implementing reporting systems for specified grade levels. Remember to share specific examples of implementation with your board of education, and begin tracking correlations between your common assessments and statewide assessments.

Monitoring, Tracking Student Achievement, and Celebrating

In phase 5, you will continue implementation and monitor ongoing systems and practices, considering all the facets of training, feedback, support, and problem solving. Some districts will take years to reach full implementation of SBL, particularly those that begin with grades K–2, then add grades 3–5, and so on. Others who implement in all grades at once or in larger bands (like elementary in one phase, middle school the next, and high school thereafter) will reach full implementation more quickly and move toward monitoring and maintenance. As mentioned, your school or district size, existing knowledge and application of key components, and willingness to change will affect your pacing. All in all, you are monitoring from here on out, but more closely for the next six months to a year. Whatever your situation, remember that such a transformational change will require constant maintenance. Check in with staff, students, and parents and ensure they have the resources and knowledge they need. Monitor how well students are prepared for their next levels of schooling or next steps in life, whether they are entering college, the world of work, or military service. Plan for next steps and the needs of your school or district. And don't forget to pat yourself on the back—this has been difficult, arduous work!

To support monitoring and sustaining SBL, this chapter covers the following activities.

- Expand implementation to additional content areas or grade levels.
- Continue tracking student achievement data.
- Train incoming stakeholders.
- Celebrate success.

As you have full implementation of most components (prioritized standards, proficiency scales, and common assessments) well underway, this phase will culminate with ensuring the final components (such as report cards) are in place throughout all grade levels and new staff are brought on board. The following sections detail these activities.

Expand Implementation to Additional Content Areas or Grade Levels

By now, SBL is well underway in your school or district. The topics discussed in this chapter are not new topics for the most part. Instead, they are expansions to additional groups within your system, including teachers, students, and parents. Therefore, it is important to treat everything addressed in this phase with as much care and concern as if it was the initial implementation. It is likely that momentum is in your favor, and you want to ensure this continues. While proficiency scales, common assessments, and other SBL processes and practices exist, groups of educators have differing degrees of understanding and are at varying places with implementation. This phase helps to ensure that all stakeholders gain deeper understanding and continue making progress.

Proficiency Scales

It is now time to implement proficiency scales in the next determined content areas or grade levels according to your local plan. The process is similar to the enactment of scales in phase 4 (see page 127). As you implement proficiency scales in the next content area or grade level, be mindful of your communication plan and ensure as thoughtful a rollout as you did with the initial scale implementation. Proficiency scales will be the first standards-based experience for these new content areas or grade levels. However, there are other content areas or grade levels that have already been using scales in the classroom. These local experts can provide support to those new to the implementation of proficiency scales. It will serve everyone well if a leader ensures that teachers with experience using scales share strategies and other helpful information with the new-to-the-process teachers. Proficiency scales will also be new to some students and parents. Consequently, it is better to overcommunicate rather than undercommunicate.

Common Classroom Assessments

Throughout the first four phases, teams planned for and developed common assessments. All teachers should now be using these tools as an integral part of their classroom practice, regardless of whether the school or district phases them in by content areas or grade levels. You are at a place in the implementation plan where all educators have been provided learning opportunities, time, and resources for developing common classroom assessments. It is important, however, that ongoing learning and sharing opportunities occur. The topics of these opportunities can vary, but may include the following.

1. Providing feedback on a specific common assessment for the sake of enhancing its quality

2. Learning the results of a particular common assessment and offering ideas for next steps

3. Sharing ideas for score 4.0 assessment opportunities

4. Examining common assessment data displays

5. Brainstorming different ways to achieve consistent scoring of common assessments

6. Active progress monitoring (see appendix E, page 199)

Leaders might include such learning opportunities in staff meetings, in part- or full-day professional development, and especially in the frequent collaborative team time scheduled for teams.

Most important is that teacher teams *use* the results of their common assessments to determine how to support all students in their learning journey. It is during this phase that the idea of a common assessment protocol might be introduced to teacher teams. A protocol is simply a set of questions a collaborative team answers following the administration and scoring of any common assessment. By answering this set of questions, the team attains clarity for next steps in supporting all students. The following is a set of questions that may be part of a common assessment protocol.

1. On which parts of the assessment did students perform well? Why do we believe this occurred?

2. On which parts of the assessment did students struggle? Why do we believe this occurred?

3. Do any items on the assessment need revising or to be eliminated? Why is this the case?

4. Which students are in need of additional support? What does this support entail?

New Reporting Systems

At this point in time, some content areas and grade levels are practicing standards-referenced reporting (see phase 3, page 117, and phase 4, page 136). Therefore, additional grade levels just beginning the new system of reporting have the benefit of many students and parents already understanding this process. That is not to say communication about the new reporting isn't necessary. It is critical that teachers take the time to communicate with students and parents in a variety of ways, including email, SBL brochures, and face-to-face conversations, to name a few. The success of standards-referenced reporting is often a direct reflection of the degree of effective communication that occurs as the process unfolds. This stems from the understanding of SBL that is fostered as a result of the communication.

Continue to Conduct Focus Groups With Students and Parents

At this stage, you may want to expand your focus groups to include new students and new parent groups. As mentioned previously, ascertaining your students' and parents' perspectives on SBL is vital. If students lack clarity and understanding, parents certainly do as well. Ramifications may include frustrated and angry responses from students and parents, lack of clear expectations, and the like. In addition to surveys and other methods of collecting brief written feedback, the use of focus groups allows students and parents to share more detailed input. Use the focus group protocol previously shared (phase 4, page 133; appendix D, page 187) with your new and expanded student groups, new parent groups, and perhaps some colleges or community employers. As with any feedback process, be certain you carefully examine the results and share the pertinent parts of such results with key constituents. You can compile the general results—for example, how many responses to each question were positive, and how many negative?—and substantiate them with quotes from respondents. These compiled responses and anonymized comments are appropriate to share with leaders, teachers, and board of education members. These focus groups allow you to collect information for your system, address any glaring needs, and provide support for the work.

Continue Tracking Student Achievement Data

Continue tracking and monitoring your student achievement data. The strongest support you can provide for the effectiveness of standards-based learning and grading systems is a correlation between how students perform on your proficiency scales and how they perform on common assessments, district benchmark assessments, statewide exams, and national results. One way to do this is to correlate student proficiency on classroom and district assessments developed based on proficiency scales with student proficiency in those same standards on state assessments (see phase 4, page 140). One example is figure 5.1, which shows Lincoln Elementary School (St. Charles, Missouri) students' scores on the Missouri Assessment of Progress. Here, you will notice, in third and fourth grade for both communication arts and mathematics, a steady increase in student achievement resulted as the school implemented SBL. The only exception is 2015, when the statewide assessment was re-normed.

	Grade 3 Communication Arts	Grade 3 Mathematics	Grade 4 Communication Arts	Grade 4 Mathematics
2009	31	33.3	50	52.5
2010	40.5	35.7	51.3	46.2
2011	65.9	73.2	61	58.5
2012	59.3	66.7	70.6	64.7
2013	65.6	75	73.9	78.3
2014	79.3	75.9	69	69
2015	69.7	73.6	85.2	75

Source: © 2015 by St. Charles School District. Used with permission.

Figure 5.1: Increasing state assessment scores.

Another data point to track is graduation rates. Dackri Davis, former principal of Gateway High School in Aurora, Colorado, shared the following results from SBL practices.

- A 16 percent increase in graduation rate occurred from 2014–2015 (66 percent) to 2015–2016 (82 percent).

- An additional 3 percent increase in graduation rate occurred in 2016–2017.

- Average SAT scores increased nineteen points from 2015 to 2016.

- Students never before proficient have demonstrated proficiency.

Finally, Bill Barnes, former principal, shared that Charlotte High School in Charlotte, Michigan, tracked PSAT and SAT scores, as well as dual enrollment trends for students obtaining dual credit from both high school and college. Figures 5.2 and 5.3 (page 148) show significant increases in both.

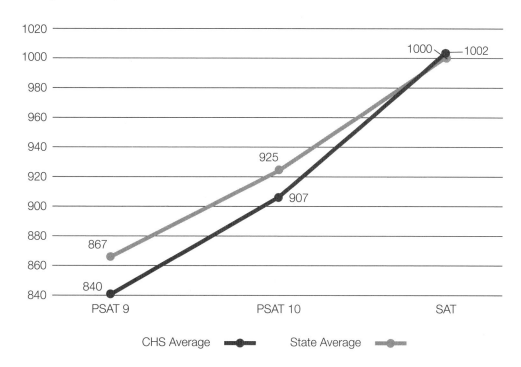

Source: © 2019 by Charlotte High School. Used with permission.

Figure 5.2: Class of 2019 PSAT 9, PSAT 10, and SAT data.

These are but a few examples of how schools and districts may want to monitor achievement connected with SBL. The important consideration is to start that monitoring early (as suggested in phase 2, page 99) and continue with it. By the time you reach phase 5, you will have results to review—and often they provide support needed for continued backing for SBL.

Train Incoming Stakeholders

Sustaining a districtwide approach to standards-based learning and grading will require entry-level training for new teaching staff, new administrators, and new families. Teachers and administrators who have not worked in a standard-based learning and grading system before will need to be trained in the concept and processes the district has adopted. This is a new venture for school districts because for years very little if any specific training has focused on grading practices. Likewise, families new to a district will need to be introduced to the specific grading and reporting practices the district is using to measure and report learning.

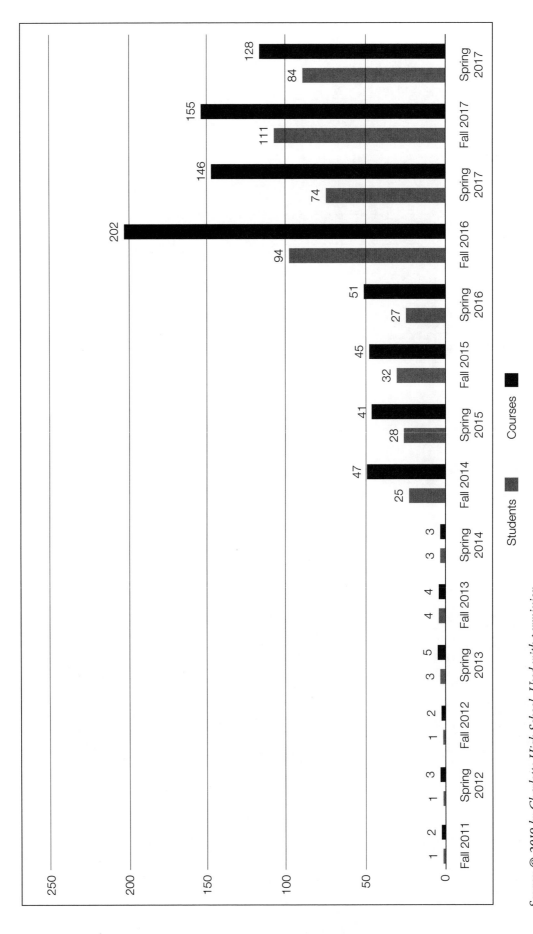

Source: © 2019 by Charlotte High School. Used with permission.

Figure 5.3: Dual enrollment trends.

New Staff

One ongoing need in a standards-based system is a systemic approach to help new teachers enhance their knowledge in SBL practices. New staff will need specific training as they transition to your SBL systems. This also provides an opportunity to provide refreshers for existing staff. Even when implementation is well underway, new questions, struggles, support, and ideas will emerge.

For example, one of the daily touchpoints for every teacher is the gradebook. So, it stands to reason that one area in which teachers new to a school or district need training is the use of gradebook technology. For this purpose, schools often create gradebook tutorials that can introduce new staff to and provide existing staff reminders on how to use the gradebook. This is especially important to consider in the first few years of the implementation, when grading technology has changed and all teachers are still developing knowledge about how to use it. Leaders at NYOS charter school created this type of training resource for their teachers to provide help in adding evidence scores to their gradebook. School administrators, working with an instructional coach, created documents showing the step-by-step process for entering scores, figuring summative grades, and submitting grades in their system. The tutorial documents contained a series of screen captures of their grading system and short how-to videos created by their instructional coach. These training documents are able to guide a teacher through each step of the grade entry process and are available to teachers at any time through a staff-only access link on the school's website.

Another way to build the capacity of new and existing staff is to embed specific SBL practices and information into new-teacher mentoring programs. For example, teachers often get very little formal training in classroom assessment. This is a critical aspect of the SBL process and could be a recurring topic throughout the year as part of the new-teacher mentoring process. For example, a district could identify topic sessions for new teachers as part of the mentoring program and have a recurring session (perhaps once each quarter) dealing with developing quality classroom assessment practices. These can also present a great opportunity for existing teachers to attend the mentoring sessions. In doing so they will help new teachers learn by sharing their current knowledge and continue their own development in the topic as well.

For an example of an SBL training document, see appendix E (page 199). This document was developed by school leader Carrie Swanson and instructional coach Vanessa Valencia in Aurora Public Schools in Colorado, for the purpose of helping teachers better understand how to connect proficiency scales to daily formative assessment practices, which in turn inform instructional planning.

Last but not least, a district needs to be mindful that leading an SBL school requires a deep understanding of SBL rationale, practices, and systems. This knowledge is imperative for new school-level leaders to successfully monitor and sustain the practice within their respective schools. Training for new administrators looks similar to training for new teachers. New administrator training will often be conducted by district-level leadership or through a principal mentoring approach similar to the teacher mentoring approach. Of course, the level of training a new administrator will need will be dependent on his or her experiences in the concept. New-administrator training can be combined with refresher opportunities for existing administrators and should be embedded as a recurring topic for leadership meetings and principal mentorship programs.

New Parents

As a school or district moves forward in the use of SBL, one of the challenges is to train new families as they arrive in the system. During the different phases of the SBL implementation, scout teachers, the guiding coalition, teachers, and administrators created multiple training sessions, artifacts of practice, and pieces of communication. Many if not all of these can be used to train parents in standards-based concepts. A school should strategically identify specific communications and archive them in ways that new parents can easily access, perhaps on the school website. As the implementation continues, schools can strategically add to this collection with video testimonials from teachers, parents, and students who have experienced SBL firsthand. For example, as part of their ongoing communication plan, NYOS elementary charter school leaders developed a video in which students and teachers talk about the use of proficiency scales, the meaning of grades, and the system for standards-referenced reporting in place at the school. The school uses the video to introduce the concept to new parents and prospective parents.

New Board Members

In phase 1, as part of training the board of education, we suggested developing a portfolio of artifacts, articles, and videos (page 48). When new board members get elected, these portfolios can educate the new board members and provide them with a record of the entire process of implementing SBL. Just as new staff and administrators need to be trained, so do new board members. It is important for them to understand the entire development process so they have a sense of the overall commitment the district had made in different aspects of the implementation. Likewise, if videos of presentations to the board by guiding team members and scout teachers are archived, new board members also have access to these. The portfolios and any archived videos will be especially important for the first few years of full implementation as the SBL concept is still new and just taking hold. These resources may not be as necessary, say, five years into the implementation once SBL has become the normal way the district does business. However, having these educational materials available for one or two cycles of potential board turnover will be extremely helpful.

Celebrate Success

As you consider the necessary components of this colossal change, remember to celebrate the small successes and the products from each phase of implementation. Celebrating successes is an important part of the implementation process. Seek examples from teachers, students, and parents where the added clarity of SBL proved helpful. You may find numerous instances where you can obtain student examples or quotes about their appreciation of teachers' providing clear expectations for learning. When you see or hear of it, capture it. This might be in quotes, on video, or in pictures of student success. Examples of entire classes mastering their prioritized standards, in a chart or other visual form, can prove a celebration to the system. Students demonstrating success after a reteaching opportunity is another great artifact to share in celebration. Remember the ultimate goal—all students mastering prioritized standards at proficient levels.

Because you are tracking student achievement (see phase 4, page 140, and phase 5, page 146), you will have plenty of milestones to celebrate. Celebrate the increased numbers of students demonstrating proficiency on internal and external assessments. Share results on statewide exams and any correlations you have noted. Highlight trends such as increased dual enrollment or other advanced coursework. Increased graduation rates are certainly worth celebrating. You might even conduct graduate surveys to showcase preparedness for the next levels of education or experience.

Whenever possible, personalize success and celebrations. For parents, share specific examples of how their child succeeded in learning after an additional learning opportunity. This can be especially powerful for students who may have struggled in the past. Give parents the opportunity to share examples of their children obtaining proficiency and the motivation that ensued. Go beyond achievement data and share stories of how SBL affects students beyond grades. For example, if your school employs student-led conferences, perspectives from all parties involved (students, parents, and teachers) can provide excellent evidence of how SBL lets students take ownership of their learning. Share these examples with your system. Help everyone see how your system is working for students.

Enlisting Consultants

Enlisting the support of outside consultants may be very useful as you monitor and sustain your standards-based system. Consider when an "outsider" can serve as a critical friend and trainer for content. Evaluate your own capacities for knowing, understanding, and delivering the various components involved in this phase. Consider the following list of ways consultants might help with phase 5.

- Providing perspectives of other schools and districts near your implementation level

- Sharing successes to provide external validation

- Working with board of education members during meetings or retreats

Summary

During this phase you completed your implementation of standards-based learning and grading in all grade levels, including new reporting documents, in most cases. You also monitored your progress with various constituents by tracking student achievement and conducting focus group interviews with students, parents, and teachers. You are ensuring training of new staff, new parents, and new board of education members, and you are celebrating your success. Your system is better: Teachers provide clarity about what they are teaching and what proficiency entails. They are using common assessments and consistent, trustworthy grading practices. Students know how to be successful with embedded opportunities for reteaching and reassessment. For perhaps the first time, your system is no longer about sorting and selecting students based on how fast they can acquire standards with variations in expectations. Instead, you likely have more if not all students learning to proficient levels. Your school or district embodies what it means to be standards based and learning focused.

Epilogue

Transitioning to standards-based learning is a significant process. It involves all stakeholders and requires much from many. It embodies the many phases of any district change, and it often shifts educational philosophies along the way. In order for this work to solidify into an ongoing part of your system, collaborative cultures and productive structures are necessary. As Heflebower and colleagues (2014) stated, "Teachers need time to process with one another, try new ideas, receive feedback from peers, and—over time—change existing philosophies. A culture of support, trust, and modeling is important" (p. 113).

This work coincides well with the educational initiatives many districts have in progress. Knowing the work to be done is one major task, yet the other involves ensuring that necessary structures function effectively. The structures for *doing* much of this work involve having effective structures for collaboration, up to and including a formal professional learning community process (see DuFour, DuFour, Eaker, & Many, 2016; Marzano, Heflebower, Hoegh, Warrick, & Grift, 2016). Standards-based learning is also a particularly significant topic for schools that are interested in becoming high-reliability organizations. High-reliability organizations are those that "take a variety of extraordinary steps in pursuit of error-free performance" (Weick, Sutcliffe, & Obstfeld, 1999, p. 84). Marzano, Warrick, and Simms (2014) suggested that schools could become high-reliability organizations and detailed five levels of a High Reliability School: (1) safe, supportive, and collaborative culture; (2) effective teaching in every classroom; (3) guaranteed and viable curriculum; (4) standards-referenced reporting; and (5) competency-based education. Levels 3, 4, and 5 of this model specifically address standards-based learning.

The practices, strategies, and guidelines in this book are foundational to making the shifts to standards-based learning, and indeed to a modern, effective educational system that serves all students well. Prioritizing standards leads to a guaranteed and viable curriculum, which ensures students experience the essential content no matter which classroom they are assigned to. Unpacking those standards to form proficiency scales provides a clear progression of learning for teachers and students. Common assessments based on the proficiency scales ensure consistency across classrooms and provide feedback to teachers and students about their instruction and learning. Finally, standards-based grading and reporting structures clearly and accurately communicate what students know and can do. Leading the shift to standards-based learning is hard work, to be sure, but the results for students, families, teachers, and administrators are certainly worth the effort.

APPENDIX A
Additional Resources for Chapter 1

This appendix contains sample materials associated with phase 1 of SBL implementation: specifically, proficiency scales, a consensus-building tool, and staff learning opportunities.

Proficiency Scales

The following examples are from Wichita Public Schools, and include various elementary examples in mathematics and ELA. You will see a third-grade mathematics example (figure A.1, page 156) followed by a fifth-grade mathematics example (figure A.2, page 157). Next are first- and fourth-grade ELA examples written for Spanish speakers (figure A.3, page 158, and figure A.4, page 159), and a second-grade ELA scale in Vietnamese (figure A.5, page 150).

PATTERNS IN MULTIPLICATION AND DIVISION (THIRD-GRADE MATH)

KCCRS Correlation: 3.OA.9 4-22-19

4.0	The student *could*: • Use knowledge of arithmetic patterns to find products or quotients outside the 1–100 multiplication table.	*For example, when given that 9 x 7 = 63, use the fact that doubling the row of a product represented on the multiplication table will double the product to find the product of 18 x 7.*
3.5	In addition to score 3.0 performance, partial success at score 4.0 content	
3.0	**The student will:** **T1-OA.9: Identify arithmetic patterns including patterns in the multiplication table, and explain them using the properties of operations.**	*For example, explain why the product of 4 and a number will always be even or why odd products never sit next to each other on the multiplication table.*
2.5	No major errors or omissions regarding score 2.0 content, and partial success at score 3.0 content	

2.0	**F1: The student will recognize or recall specific vocabulary (for example, *even, odd, numerical expression, associative property, column, commutative property, distributive property, dividend, divisor, equal groups, factor, multiplication table, product, quotient, row*) and perform foundational processes such as:**	
	F1: Foundational Processes	***Clarification or Examples***
	• Multiply and divide whole numbers within 100.	
	• Describe the properties of multiplication.	*Commutative, associative, distributive*
	• Explain the relationship between multiplication and division.	*Explain that the divisor and quotient of a division problem are both factors of the dividend, and that dividing a multiplication product by either factor of a factor pair will result in the other factor.*
	• Explain odd and even.	*With manipulatives, demonstrate how, when working with odd numbers, the manipulatives can paired up; however, there will always be one manipulative left without a partner. Even sets of manipulatives will always be able to be paired up without any left over.*

1.5	Partial success at score 2.0 content, and major errors or omissions regarding score 3.0 content
1.0	With help, partial success at score 2.0 content and score 3.0 content
0.5	With help, partial success at score 2.0 content but not at score 3.0 content
0.0	Even with help, no success

Source: © 2019 Wichita Public Schools. Used with permission.

Figure A.1: Proficiency scale for patterns in multiplication and division.

DECIMALS—PLACE VALUE (FIFTH-GRADE MATH)

KCCRS Correlation: 5.NBT.3, 3a, 3b, 4   6-11-19

4.0	The student *could*: • Compare decimal values to other rational numbers and explain reasoning.	*For example, when given the numbers 0.397 and $\frac{2}{5}$, determine that $0.397 < \frac{2}{5}$ by reasoning that $\frac{2}{5}$ is equivalent to $\frac{4}{10}$ so when comparing them as decimals, .397 is less than .400.*
3.5	In addition to score 3.0 performance, partial success at score 4.0 content	

3.0	**The student will:** **T1-NBT.3a: Read and write decimals to the thousandths using:** • **Base-ten numerals** *(for example, 34.512)* • **Number names** *(for example, thirty-four and five hundred-twelve thousandths)* • **Expanded form** *(for example, [3 x 10^1] + [4 x 10^0] + [5 x $\frac{1}{10}$] + [1 x $\frac{1}{100}$] + [2 x $\frac{1}{1000}$] or [3 x 10] + [4 x 1] + [5 x 0.1] + [1 x 0.01] + [2 x 0.001])* • **Unit form** *(for example, 3 tens + 4 ones + 5 tenths + 1 hundredths + 2 thousandths)* **T2-NBT.3b: Compare two decimals to the thousandths based on meanings of the digits in each place, using >, <, =, and ≠ relational symbols to record the results of the comparisons.** *(For example, when given the decimal values 4.69, 4.1701, 4.069, and 4.6900, compare the numbers using <, >, =, and ≠ symbols.)* **T3-NBT.4: Use place value understanding to round decimals to any place (whole numbers and decimal fractions to the hundredths place).** *(For example, round 18.396 to the nearest hundredths = 18.40)* *Note: Place Value and Powers (NBT 1, 2) is the predecessor to this scale and should be considered before applying this scale.*
2.5	No major errors or omissions regarding score 2.0 content, and partial success at score 3.0 content
2.0	**F1–F3: The student will recognize or recall specific vocabulary (for example, *base-ten numerals*, *number names*, *expanded form*, *unit form*, *decimal fraction*, *decimal place value*, *decimal point*, *decimal value*, *hundredths*, *place value*, *tenths*, *thousandths*, *unit*, *whole number*) and perform foundational processes such as:**

F1: Foundational Processes	*Clarification or Examples*
• Express a whole number as a decimal value.	*Explain that 2 is two 1s as well as 2.0 or 2.00.*
• Identify decimal place values.	*Identify the digit 2 in 1.02 as being in the hundredths place.*
• Identify equivalent forms of a decimal.	*Some equivalent forms of 0.72 are:*

$\frac{72}{100}$	$\frac{7}{10} + \frac{2}{100}$
$7 \times (\frac{1}{10}) + 2 \times (\frac{1}{100})$	$0.70 + 0.02$
$\frac{70}{100} + \frac{2}{100}$	0.720
$(7 \times \frac{1}{10}) + (2 \times \frac{1}{100}) + (0 \times \frac{1}{1000})$	$\frac{720}{1000}$

• Read a decimal in standard form using base ten numerals.	Students would say something like, "This number says two thousand, twelve, and 2 hundredths."
• Read a decimal using number names.	*Read* thirty-two and fifteen hundredths *to represent* 32.15.
• Read a decimal using expanded form.	*Read* 30 + 2 + 0.1 + 0.05 *to represent* 32.15.
• Read a decimal using unit form.	*Read* 3 tens + 2 ones + 1 tenth + 5 hundredths *to represent* 32.15.

F2: Foundational Processes	*Clarification or Examples*
• Identify equivalent decimal fractions.	*Explain that $\frac{206}{100}$ and $\frac{260}{1000}$ represent the same value. Explain that .26 = 0.26 = 0.260.*
• Compare decimal fractions.	*When given the fractions $\frac{7}{10}$ and $\frac{75}{100}$, determine that $\frac{7}{10} < \frac{75}{100}$.*
• Explain that decimal place values represent fractions.	*Explain that the digit 5 in 1.56 represents $\frac{5}{10}$.*

Source: © 2019 Wichita Public Schools. Used with permission.

Figure A.2: Proficiency scale for decimals.

CONOCIMIENTO FONOLÓGICO (1ELA) RF.1.2b-d	
4.0	El estudiante **podría:** • Identificar cuándo se dice un sonido en particular en un pasaje o grupo de palabras (por ejemplo, al escuchar una oración en voz alta, levantara la mano para un sonido de letra o par de letras en particular e identificara la palabra de la que proviene el sonido).
3.5	Además de demostrar un rendimiento de 3.0, el éxito parcial en el contenido de la puntuación es 4.0
3.0	El estudiante **podrá:** **T1—RF1.2b—Mezclar sonidos para decir palabras de una sílaba con mezclas consonantes** (por ejemplo, combinar los fonemas /g/, /r/, /-/ y /n/ en la palabra hablada verde). **T2— RF1.2d—Divida una palabra hablada de una sílaba en sonidos o fonemas individuales** (por ejemplo, separara la palabra hablada verde en los fonemas /g/, /r/, /-/, y /n/).
2.5	No hay errores u omisiones importantes con respecto al contenido de puntuación 2.0, y el éxito parcial en el contenido de la puntuación es 3.0
2.0	**F1**—El estudiante reconocerá o recordará el vocabulario académico general y específico del dominio (por ejemplo, *consonante*, *mezcla consonante*, *sílaba*, *vocal*) y realizará procesos fundamentales tales como: • Mezclar dos consonantes para hacer una mezcla consonante (por ejemplo, combinar /g/ y /r/ en el sonido hablado *gr*). • Mezclar una vocal y una consonante. • Mezclar dos partes de una palabra juntas (por ejemplo, combinar /gr/ y /-n/ en la palabra hablada verde) **F2**—El estudiante reconocerá o recordará el vocabulario académico general y específico del dominio (por ejemplo, *fonema*, *sonido*, *sílaba*) y realizará procesos fundamentales como: • Identificará el sonido inicial en una palabra hablada de una sílaba. • Identificará el sonido de la vocal medial en una palabra hablada de una sílaba. • Identificará el sonido final en una palabra hablada de una sílaba.
1.5	El éxito parcial en el contenido de la puntuación 2.0 y los principales errores u omisiones con respecto al contenido de la puntuación es 3.0
1.0	Con ayuda, el éxito parcial en el contenido de la puntuación 2.0 y la puntuación 3.0 contenido
0.5	Con ayuda, el éxito parcial en el contenido de la puntuación 2.0, pero no en el contenido de la puntuación 3.0
1.0	Incluso con ayuda, no hay éxito

Source: © 2019 Wichita Public Schools. Used with permission.

Figure A.3: ELA proficiency scale in Spanish.

	EDITANDO (4ELA) W.4.10.h-i, 11a-d
4.0	• El estudiante **podría:** • Crear una lista de verificación (por ejemplo, crea una lista de verificación como recordatorio para comprobar si hay diferentes errores en gramática, mayúsculas, puntuación y ortografía).
3.5	Además de demostrar un rendimiento de 3.0, el éxito parcial en el contenido de la puntuación es 4.0
3.0	El estudiante **podrá:** **T1–W4. 11a—Editar para la capitalización** (por ejemplo, capitalizar correctamente los sustantivos y adjetivos apropiados en un párrafo sobre cómo la rotación de la Tierra alrededor del Sol causa estaciones). **T2–W4.10i—Editar la puntuación para que exprese eficazmente el significado y siga las reglas de puntuación estándar** (por ejemplo, incluirá comas en oraciones compuestas y comillas alrededor del diálogo y las comillas directas). **T3–W4.11d—Editar para la ortografía** (por ejemplo, realizara la revisión ortográfica en un documento escrito en un procesador de textos y resaltar otras palabras en el texto que podrían estar mal escritos).
2.5	No hay errores u omisiones importantes con respecto al contenido de puntuación 2.0, y el éxito parcial en el contenido de la puntuación es 3.0
2.0	**F1—**El estudiante reconocerá o recordará el vocabulario académico general y específico del dominio (por ejemplo, capitalizar, pronombre, adjetivo adecuado, sustantivo adecuado) y realizar procesos fundamentales tales como: Indique que la primera letra de una oración debe estar en mayúsculas. • Declarar que el pronombre I siempre está capitalizado. • Lista de tipos de sustantivos y adjetivos adecuados. • Identificara los sustantivos y adjetivos apropiados en una oración. • Demostrara cómo utiliza un diccionario o glosario para averiguar si una palabra necesita ser en mayúsculas. **F2—**El estudiante reconocerá o recordará el vocabulario académico general y específico del dominio (por ejemplo, diálogo, situación) y realizará procesos fundamentales tales como: • Identificara frases imperativas, declarativas, exclamatorias e interrogatorios y el signo de puntuación final utilizado para las oraciones. • Demostrara dónde poner una coma en una oración compuesta. • Colocará correctamente una coma antes de una conjunción de coordinación en una oración compuesta. **(W.11c)** • Colocará comillas alrededor de un cuadro de diálogo o una cita. • Colocará correctamente una coma entre el diálogo y una etiqueta de diálogo. **(W.4.11b)** **F3—**El estudiante reconocerá o recordará el vocabulario académico general y específico del dominio (por ejemplo, homófono, corrector ortográfico) y realizará procesos fundamentales tales como: Demostrara cómo usar conjuntos de homófonos en oraciones. • Anotara palabras o frases en un borrador que puedan estar mal escritas. • Demostrara cómo usar un diccionario o glosario para encontrar la ortografía de una palabra. • Revisará un documento con la revisión ortográfica y corrija las palabras que están mal escritas. • Demostrara cómo utilizar el diccionario de un procesador de textos para comprobar la ortografía de una palabra.
1.5	El éxito parcial en el contenido de la puntuación 2.0 y los principales errores u omisiones con respecto al contenido de la puntuación es 3.0
1.0	Con ayuda, el éxito parcial en el contenido de la puntuación 2.0 y la puntuación 3.0 del contenido
0.5	Con ayuda, el éxito parcial en el contenido de la puntuación 2.0, pero no en el contenido de la puntuación es 3.0
0.0	Incluso con ayuda, no hay éxito.

Source: © 2019 Wichita Public Schools. Used with permission.

Figure A.4: ELA proficiency scale in Spanish.

	NHẬN DẠNG SỐ (TOÁN MẪU GIÁO)	
	KCCRS Sự Tương Quan: K.CC.3	
4.0	Học sinh có thể: • Đọc và viết các chữ số lớn hơn 20.	
3.5	Ngoài hiệu suất điểm 3.0, thành công một phần ở nội dung điểm 4.0	
3.0	**Học sinh sẽ:** **T1-CC.3: Đọc và viết các số 0–20.**	
2.5	Không có lỗi lớn hoặc thiếu sót nào liên quan đến nội dung điểm 2.0 và thành công một phần ở nội dung điểm 3.0	
2.0	**F1: Học sinh sẽ nhận ra hoặc nhớ lại từ vựng cụ thể** (ví dụ: *count, digit, number*), **học sinh sẽ thực hiện các quy trình nền tảng như:**	

F1: Các Quy Trình Nền Tảng	*Làm Rõ và/hoặc các Ví Dụ*
• Phân biệt giữa ký hiệu chữ cái và ký hiệu số.	
• Nói tên số trong phạm vi 1–19 khi được trình bày với các số theo đúng thứ tự.	
• Giải thích rằng mỗi số được viết đại diện cho một và chỉ một số được nói.	
• Giải thích rằng các số có hai con số sẽ luôn xuất hiện ''sau'' các số có chỉ một con số trong dãy số đếm.	
• Giải thích rằng một số bằng chữ viết có thể bao gồm nhiều hơn một con số.	
• Đọc các số 0–20 (không theo thứ tự liên tiếp).	
• Viết các số 0–10 (không theo thứ tự liên tiếp).	

1.5	Thành công một phần ở nội dung điểm 2.0 và các lỗi hoặc thiếu sót lớn liên quan đến nội dung điểm 3.0
1.0	Với sự giúp đỡ, thành công một phần ở nội dung điểm 2.0 và nội dung điểm 3.0
0.5	Với sự giúp đỡ, thành công một phần ở nội dung điểm 2.0 nhưng không phải ở nội dung điểm 3.0
0.0	Ngay cả với sự giúp đỡ, không thành công

Source: © 2019 Wichita Public Schools. Used with permission.

Figure A.5: ELA scale for Vietnamese-speaking students.

Some schools write proficiency scales for nonacademic factors, such as work completion and following classroom rules, which are often considered priorities in a standards-based learning environment. The following scales (figures A.6–A.8) are examples for elementary and secondary learners.

Score 4.0	In addition to score 3.0 performance, the student demonstrates in-depth inferences and applications that go beyond the expectations in score 3.0. *For example*, explains potential problems if classroom rules are not followed. *For example*, self-corrects behavior that isn't in compliance with a classroom rule.
Score 3.0	The student: Follows classroom rules determined by the collective efforts of the teacher and the class. Listens and follows verbal directions. Corrects behavior when redirected by the teacher.

Score 2.0	The student recognizes or recalls specific vocabulary, such as:
	redirected, verbal directions
	The student performs basic processes, such as:
	States classroom rules determined by the collective efforts of the teacher and the class.
	Repeats verbal directions when asked.
Score 1.0	With help, the student demonstrates partial success at score 2.0 and score 3.0

Source: Adapted from Hoegh, 2020.

Figure A.6: Proficiency scale for following classroom rules.

Nonacademic Skill	Score 4.0 Consistently Exceeds Expectations	Score 3.0 Consistently Meets Expectations	Score 2.0 Inconsistently Meets Expectations	Score 1.0 Does Not Meet Expectations
Work Completion Completes work and turns it in punctually	Is punctual or early turning in assignments	Is punctual in turning in assignments	Is not always punctual in turning in assignments	Is not punctual in turning in assignments
Degree of Frequency	No infractions	0–2 infractions	3–5 infractions	More than 5 infractions

Source: Hoegh, 2020.

Figure A.7: Proficiency scale for work completion.

Level 4.0	In addition to Level 3.0 performance, the student will:
	Critique his or her own collaborative behaviors by identifying personal strengths and areas of growth as a collaborative team member.
Level 3.5	In addition to Level 3.0 performance, the student shows partial success at level 4.
Level 3.0	The student will use all level 2.0 collaborative skills with consistency to:
	Engage collaboratively in small-group activities.
	Contribute in a meaningful way to whole-class discussions.
Level 2.5	The student is successful with Level 2.0 elements and partially successful with Level 3.0 elements.
Level 2.0	The student is successful with the simpler details and behaviors such as:
	Define the concept of collaboration.
	Explain why it is necessary for group production.
	Explain specific active listening behaviors for small-group and class discussions.
	Identify conversation prompts for appropriate and productive agreement or disagreement within small-group or whole-class discussion.
Level 1.5	The student is partially successful with Level 2.0 elements without prompting.
Level 1.0	With prompting, the student is partially successful with Level 2.0 elements.
Level 0.5	With help or prompting, the student is partially successful with Level 2.0 elements.

Source: Hoegh, 2020.

Figure A.8: Proficiency scale for collaboration, high school.

Consensus Building

Consensus building takes place near the beginning of a changeover to SBL. Grading and reporting are surely major concerns that require consensus, but ongoing consensus building is also part of any healthy system. With major change such as a move to SBL, building consensus helps establish a firm foundation and then maintains the structure's soundness for the future. A consensus-building guide appears in figure A.9. Leaders facilitating SBL work is the primary audience for this guide.

CONSENSUS BUILDING
Logistics and Protocols

Definition of consensus and the work around consensus:

From the Universal Tier Tools Protocol and Facilitation Guide: What Is Consensus? (Iowa Area Education Agencies, n.d.):

"Consensus is a decision-making process that is widely viewed as more effective than simple voting because it results in all team members 'consenting' to the decision. It means arriving at a decision that each member of the group can accept and support. It may not be everyone's first choice. It may not even be anyone's first choice, but it's a decision everyone can live with."

From the same toolkit:

"Attention to consensus means that staff and administration understand the *why* behind change and have a voice to productively ask questions and participate in decision making. Consensus rests upon the belief that we are better together, and different perspectives make our action planning better. Consensus should be attended to throughout the continuous-improvement process."

Examining the *why* behind the benefits of SBL, including grading and reporting, needs ongoing consensus building as shifts to SBL are a second-order change, a paradigm shift.

Possible practical actions taken:

One action that could be taken in the earliest stages is distributing a beliefs and consensus survey to all involved educators. These types of questions could be adapted to examining beliefs in SBL.

Norms of behavior could be created for teams. Perhaps one norm could be that when issues are discussed or consensus reached, all participants then agree to leave the room united.

Considerations:

Consider that the change to SBL and grading practices is very large. It represents a clear break from past practice. Because of this, it is likely to be a years-long process, and all parties must be patient with that.

Consider that most, if not all, parents and community members went through their schooling with older, more conventional practices, and that's all they've ever known. Patience with and education for them are key. It may be worthwhile to regularly gauge parent and community member understanding of this new system, perhaps via survey or focus group.

Remember that our culture has made frequent reference to "grades" in every manner, for a very long time, for various reasons: in advertising, TV, movies, online, etc. We must keep this in mind as we work to help people know what our own SBL and grading practices are about.

When students are at the center of change, all the effort of a second-order change is worthwhile.

Would this include grading and reporting?

Ideas:

- From the very start, consider doing what it takes to make this a systemic approach involving everyone in the system or district. This includes helping a superintendent know that expressing a vision and a purpose—a *why* for this work—is critical. It is also key for the superintendent to create the conditions for leaders and educators to meet that vision and purpose so the work moves forward. If not systemic in a full district, then systemic within a building. Creating the conditions for systemic change includes designing a plan and prioritizing the work.
  - Then start to build consensus by creating a leadership team(s) that can help guide other leaders and educators in the system to consistently lead the work of learning and doing in order to make forward movement methodically and purposefully, according to the plan. Guiding educators means helping get a belief system in place.

- Train the educators in a system or building using a variety of methods, such as:
  - Reading books and articles or watching clips
  - Visiting a district or building that is doing this work successfully
  - Attending a conference
- Then, discuss ideas from those sources that could work in your own system and that meet your vision and purpose.
- It is true that some districts start their efforts from the teacher level and go upward. There may be challenges here, as district or building leadership needs to come on board at some point and help lead and advocate for the system, but ambitious and thoughtful teachers can cause this to happen if they are organized in their approach.
- Some districts choose to inform and educate their school boards from the very start. Others, in an effort to forestall having to say "I don't know" to any number of questions at the very start, wait a little while to do some reading, investigation, and discussion before they bring their school board members up to speed on the philosophy, the work, and the benefits to students.
  - No matter what, it is key that the superintendent is genuinely on board in some way when the school board is informed or educated. This is important since the board and superintendent communicate directly with one another on these matters, and often communicate outwardly with parents and community members.
- Consider building a webpage or website for your system or district that explains, with specificity and detail, your SBL grading system. Invite someone to be the "keeper" of this website so that items and info are updated regularly. Consider what can and should be public, so that parents, community members, and even visitors can learn about the system. Consider, too, what might be smart to password protect for just district or school staff to access. Then publicize the website.

How do you build consensus on rubrics and grading scales with new staff, veteran staff with strong beliefs, and others?

Ideas:

- Have some sort of systemic, collaborative approach to learning about, creating, and implementing proficiency scales. Ensure understanding the difference between scales and rubrics.
- Involve leaders and classroom teachers in creating proficiency scales. Make a point of inviting those who profess some negativity with the idea of SBL. All voices will learn from all other voices.
- Involve new staff as appropriate. New teachers to the district or building, including those fresh out of university courses or student teaching, may have helpful ideas or practical advice on how their former schools implemented things. Once SBL practices are implemented, figure out some way to onboard new teachers yearly, perhaps through use of collaborative teams or a special leadership team.
- Involve parents and students as appropriate. Sometimes inviting a parent or two onto a leadership committee can help diffuse negativity or can help gain consensus among parents in the community in general. Meeting with a few student leaders regularly to gain their perspective about SBL grading practices can give invaluable insight for clarification or adjusting.

What areas benefit from or need consensus?

Ideas:

- Starting out, establishing a vision and purpose for the work benefits from consensus. When paradigm-shifting, years-long work is undertaken, it may be best to work on educating and gaining consensus with other educators from the start.
- Consensus is important for each aspect of SBL that significantly shifts away from the past, such as moving to a four-level proficiency scale from the traditional hundred-point grading scale.
- Continued agreement and consensus are important for the vision and purpose.
- Continued agreement and consensus are important for professional learning for teachers over a long period of time for consistency.

Figure A.9: Consensus-building questions.

continued →

How do we monitor implementation and progress?

- First, create goals for implementation or for the full operationalization. Think: What was the impetus to even start this work? Were there internal data that compelled looking at the current grading system and seeking a different, better way? Some districts find a mismatch in grades or GPAs and ACT scores, for example, and so want semester grades to be more predictive. Other districts have data showing other discrepancies, such as inflated or deflated grades or too many graduates needing remedial work at college.

- With those goals in mind, what will it look like if the goals are met? What would be the success criteria for the goals?

  – What will it look like for teachers?

  – What will it look like for students? What does success look like in the classroom?

- Think of gauging some social-emotional aspects of undergoing this big change. How do students feel about their learning? How do teachers feel about implementation this semester? Next semester?

No matter what, plan to start with baseline data and then regularly gather data around goals or success criteria and analyze, discuss, compare, monitor, and adjust. Continue to build consensus to do the right work by the students.

What are common misconceptions?

Ideas:

- It is a misconception that the work of establishing SBL, including grading and reporting, is short term; it requires perhaps a year of study and then implementation in the next year.

- It is a misconception for teachers to think they can wait it out because "this too shall pass."

- It is a misconception that this is easy.

- It is a misconception that this is a project or event rather than a new and better way to plan, instruct, and assess for improved learning for all students.

Addressing these misconceptions on a regular basis is key to continuous, ongoing consensus building. Checking on perceptions and misperceptions could be accomplished on a regular basis by surveys or focus group work.

How do we get information out, especially to parents?

Ideas:

- Create an informative website outlining all aspects of a district's SBL implementation

- Consider having one or more parents on a leadership committee.

- At the beginning, especially, consider holding a parent meeting in an auditorium or gym to address the biggest picture items so as to build the case for change.

- Build consensus by having small parent focus groups do periodic book studies for discussing and understanding philosophical and practical shifts.

How do we create or deal with parent or community member perceptions?

Ideas:

- First, ensure that perceptions are clear and that root causes for the perceptions are discovered. Try not to deal with assumptions.

- Correct perceptions by educating parents and community members with clear, accurate examples of what education in an SBL environment looks and sounds like.

- Educate, through meetings, focus groups, websites, publications, and other means, so that parents and community members clearly see differences between past, traditional practices and SBL and grading practices. Ensure people understand that some past practices were actually harmful and unfair to students. Today's practices move toward student partnership in their own learning, greater fairness to students, and more accurate reflection of actual learning in final grades.

Source: © 2019 by Heartland AEA. Used with permission.

Staff Learning Opportunities

Figure A.10 is an example of staff training opportunities from Monett R-1 School District.

2018–19

**Standards-Based Learning Academy
for Classroom Teachers, Grades K–12**

Monett R-1 is excited to announce the SBL Academy series for the 2017–18 school year. Michael Evans, assistant superintendent, will be leading a variety of learning sessions to assist teachers to better understand SBL and how it impacts classroom practice.

Participation is open to any kindergarten through twelfth-grade teacher but will be limited to twenty dedicated participants. Selected participants will receive twenty-five hours of targeted professional development to personalize instruction, analyze data, and become reflective thinkers to enhance instruction. Academy participants will be compensated for their time, effort, and active participation.

Collaboration will begin in early fall and continue throughout the school year. Sessions are designed to include after-school paid time and independent project-based learning.

Topics include, but are not limited to:

- Essential learning outcomes
- Proficiency scales
- Formative and summative assessment
- Tracking student performance
- Providing student feedback
- Personalized competency-based education

Source: © 2019 by Monett R-1 School District. Used with permission.

Figure A.10: Staff learning opportunities.

Additional Resources for Chapter 2

This appendix contains sample materials associated with phase 2 of SBL implementation: specifically, leveled assessments, an implementation plan, a communication toolkit, and support for standards-based reporting in higher education.

Leveled Assessments

The following examples are leveled assessments based on proficiency scales. The first example is for second-grade ELA (figure B.1, page 168). The second example is a set of assessment items related to an algebra I proficiency scale (figure B.2, page 170). The third example is for grade 5 physical education (figure B.3, page 171). Note that items for score 2.0, score 3.0, and score 4.0 are included on each assessment. These assessments would typically be administered toward the end of an instructional unit.

KEY IDEAS AND DETAILS

Ask and Answer Questions

Score 2.0

Read the given passage and then answer questions 1–6.

Importance of Recycling

We use resources from our planet to make things like toys, cars, dishes, houses, and so much more! This is a good thing. Our Earth has been good to us and now it's time to return the favor!

We mix resources like wood, oil, and minerals from the Earth with other things to create the stuff we use every day. The problem is, when we do this, we create something that stays around forever. Items such as plastic won't decompose, or break down. The problem with this is that most people just throw it away when they are finished with it. Where does it all go?

Landfills are places where trash is taken and dumped off. This space is limited, and when we fill it up, we have to find somewhere else to take the garbage. There is a solution, though, and that is to recycle. Recycling means that we reuse it or turn it into a new product. This keeps it from going into landfills and just sitting there.

Many things that we use each day can be recycled. We can turn writing paper or newspapers into new types of paper. An aluminum can can be melted down and turned into a new one. Glass can be melted and used as jewelry, mirrors, counter tops, and many other things.

Recycling is not hard to do. It just takes time to sort the materials into different piles and take them to a recycling center. However, many cities have made it easy by offering a recycling service where they come to your house and pick up the material. What will you do? How do you recycle?

1. Who is the text trying to reach?

   a. everyone

   b. people who already recycle

   c. animals

2. What is the text about?

   a. reusing

   b. recycling

   c. reducing

3. Where does all our trash go?

   a. sewers

   b. landfills

   c. the ocean

4. When was this story most likely written?

   a. in the future

   b. in the present time

   c. a very long time ago

5. Why is it important to recycle?

   a. to add more landfills

   b. so we can use more garbage

   c. to save our land and environment

6. How does recycling help the land?

   a. reduces water use

   b. reduces landfills

   c. increases garbage

Score 3.0

Using the same passage, "Importance of Recycling," write six questions that can be answered by reading the text.

1. Who _____

2. What _____

3. When _____

4. Where _____

5. Why _____

6. How _____

Score 4.0

Read the passage below called "Reusing Trash." As you read, think about how this passage is similar and different to "Importance of Recycling."

Reusing Trash

Have you ever wondered where all the trash goes when the garbage truck comes and takes it away? It is taken to a place called a landfill. A landfill is a place where they pile garbage, smash it up, and then bury it. This can be harmful to us and animals. But what if we could reuse that stuff? Well, the good news is, we can!

If you have something that you don't want anymore or you have outgrown, then you can give it to someone or donate it. Maybe your family is getting new furniture. They can sell the old furniture and someone else can reuse it. Most things do not have to be thrown away.

Another option for our stuff is to recycle it. Most of the things we use every day can be recycled. If you think about it, you can probably put most of your trash items into one of the following categories: plastics, metals, glass, or paper. All of these things are easy to recycle.

Recycling is where the items are melted or broken down and made into something new. We are basically reusing the things that we would have thrown away. This is important because it keeps that stuff from sitting in a landfill and staying there forever!

Can you imagine wearing an empty milk jug as a shirt? Once the milk jugs are cut into tiny pieces, they can be used to make shirts, mittens, and other items made of fabric. Aluminum, like soda cans, can be used for car parts and bicycles. Glass can be made into tiles and used on floors, artwork, and jewelry. Recycling protects our Earth, animals, and us . . . and that is pretty cool!

Now that you've read both passages, use the graphic organizer to record two similarities and two differences between these two pieces of text.

Similarities	Differences
1.	1.
2.	2.

Source: © 2019 by Archdiocese of Chicago. Used with permission.

Figure B.1: Sample leveled assessment items for grade 2 ELA.

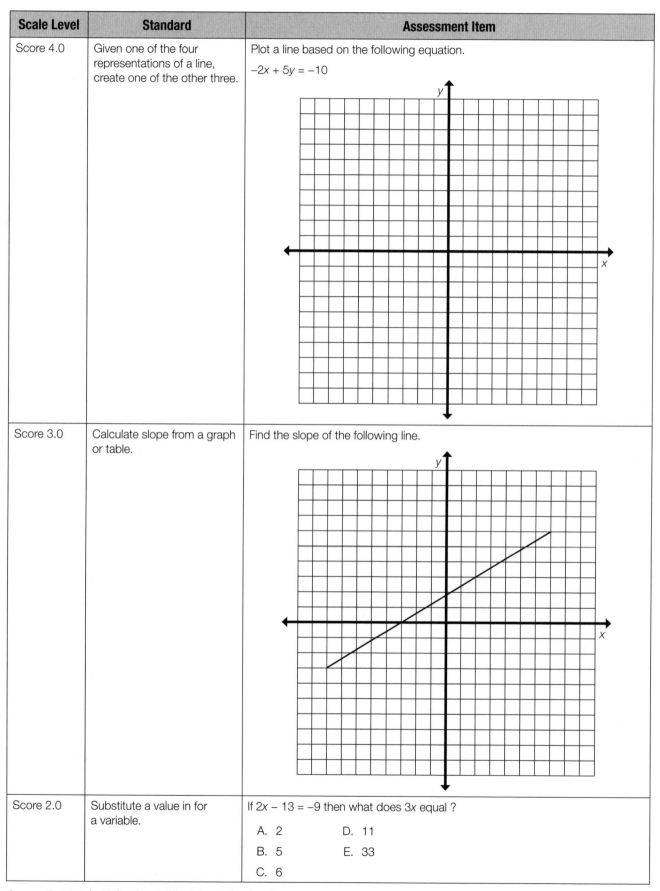

Scale Level	Standard	Assessment Item
Score 4.0	Given one of the four representations of a line, create one of the other three.	Plot a line based on the following equation. $-2x + 5y = -10$
Score 3.0	Calculate slope from a graph or table.	Find the slope of the following line.
Score 2.0	Substitute a value in for a variable.	If $2x - 13 = -9$ then what does $3x$ equal? A. 2 D. 11 B. 5 E. 33 C. 6

Figure B.2: Sample leveled assessment items for algebra I, understanding linear relationships.

SOCCER ASSESSMENT

Standard: PE.5.1 The student will demonstrate grade-appropriate movement skills and patterns in a variety of activities.

Learning Goal: I can demonstrate grade-appropriate movement skills and patterns in a variety of classroom activities.

Student	Dribbling	Passing	Receiving	Throwing	Score	Notes
Student 1	X	X	X	X	3	
Student 2	X	X	X	X	4	Has exceptional skills and has demonstrated the ability to help others with one or more of the required skills.
Student 3			X		2	
Student 4		X		X	2	
Student 5		X	X		2	Reassess this student later in the week as he fell and skinned his knee.

Skill Descriptions

Dribbling: Student keeps the ball moving between his or her feet.

Passing: Student stops, plants one foot on the ground, and kicks the ball using the inside of the free foot to target.

Receiving: Student plants one foot on the ground and stops the ball with the inside of the other foot.

Throwing: Student places both hands on the outside of the ball and overhand throws to target.

Assessment Administration

1. Teacher will provide students with a description or demonstration of the skill prior to students being assessed.

2. Students will be engaged in playing soccer while the assessment is given.

3. All components of the skill must be demonstrated to receive a check.

4. Students demonstrating high skill levels will receive a score of 4.0.

Source: Hoegh, 2020.

Figure B.3: Sample performance assessment of soccer skills, fifth grade.

Implementation Plan

Figure B.4 shows additional portions of the NYOS elementary charter school's implementation plan and progress tracking format (see figure 2.15, page 89). These are additional factors school leaders identified as critical elements needing to be addressed in their move from a standards-referenced to a standards-based grading system, including logistical elements and classroom culture and mindset elements. The first column on the left provides a description of the specific element of operation each teacher in the school needs to have prepared for the transition. The three columns on the right provide a way for each teacher to track and report their progress in each element so school leaders can monitor the transition by individual teacher and get aggregate data regarding specific elements of the transition schoolwide.

LOGISTICAL ELEMENTS			
Set up systems that allow students to easily access concrete and digital resources. • How will students access their resources independently? • Examples: colored buckets, crates with hanging folders, labeled tubs, drawers, class homepage with links, Symbaloo page, Google Drive	All Set!	In Progress	Not Yet
Establish standard operating procedures (SOPs) for common classroom situations and post in a highly visible location. • How will students navigate the materials and activities independently? • Examples: SOPs for choosing an activity, getting help, turning in work, taking assessments, dealing with computer issues, and so on	All Set!	In Progress	Not Yet
Have plan or system for administering assessments and returning feedback. • How will I collect info about a student's progress? • Examples: request a paper assessment on demand or at a certain time during block; give immediate feedback or wait; use observation checklists	All Set!	In Progress	Not Yet
Create systems for students and teachers to track progress toward proficiency. • How will the students' and I track their progress toward proficiency? • Examples: growth calculator, whole class chart, individual student charts, checklists, graphs, scale with checkboxes, FreshGrade or other digital portfolios	All Set!	In Progress	Not Yet
Create plan for celebrating student success. • How will we acknowledge growth and celebrate when students reach proficient level? • Examples: sticker chart, class chants or affirmations, "Ask Me About My Goal" bracelets or stickers, positive notes home	All Set!	In Progress	Not Yet
Have a plan for addressing needs of advanced students. • What happens when a student has mastered all the learning goals in a topic? • Examples: peer tutor, start work on next topic, level 4 task, work on next grade level's goals in same topic	All Set!	In Progress	Not Yet
Establish shared vision to anchor purpose for learning. • How can I help students understand the purpose of attending school? • What goals do we share as a classroom community?	All Set!	In Progress	Not Yet

Identify skills and behavior traits needed for independent learning. Use that list to build a Code of Cooperation. • What traits are required to be successful independent learners? • How can these traits be communicated to students? • What commitment can students make to support their own learning and the learning of others?	All Set!	In Progress	Not Yet
Design a plan for monitoring and evaluating adherence to routines and procedures. • How will students and I evaluate the success of our routines and procedures? • How will I address issues with routines and procedures?	All Set!	In Progress	Not Yet
Have tools ready to support students who need more structure. • How will I structure the learning block for students who need a more gradual release of responsibility? • How will I modify the routines or activities for exceptional learners, such as special education students, English language learners, and students with behavior contracts?	All Set!	In Progress	Not Yet
Integrate growth mindset and goal-setting activities into classroom routines. • How will I teach students to use feedback constructively? • How will my students set personal goals for this unit? • How will I help my students develop a growth mindset?	All Set!	In Progress	Not Yet

Source: © 2019 by NYOS. Used with permission.

Figure B.4: Implementation plan and tracking.

Communication Toolkit

Figure B.5 (page 174) is an example from Wichita Public Schools. This standards-referenced grading communication toolkit lists various communication materials and their purpose, the quantity needed, the audience, and any pertinent notes. For instance, the rack card is a brochure that would be available in the school lobby or office. There are also suggested brochures, banners, and a handbook.

Standards-Referenced Grading (SRG) Communication Toolkit
Contact print shop for Spanish or Vietnamese copies.
All items are available on the SRG website: www.bit.ly/259SRG
Elementary Parent and Family Handbook

Item and Purpose	Quantity	Audience	Notes
Rack Card, One-Pager, FAQ Document: Available in the office	One hundred per school	Parents, families, parent groups, community	Items can be used at kindergarten roundup, PTO events, site council meetings, and so on.
Poster and Banner: Visible in an accessible location such as the school entrance lobby near the office.	Two posters One banner	Parents, families, parent groups, community	Post in locations that are accessible to all, such as school lobbies and common areas.
Brochure: Distribute at Meet the Teacher Night or send home by August 30. Available in the office.	One per student	Parents, families	Students may have taken home a brochure last May. We are sending an additional brochure.
Parent Letter: Distribute at Meet the Teacher Night or send home by August 30.	One per student	Parents, families	Translated copies may be printed from the SRG website or ordered from print shop.
Postcard: Send home by August 30. Available in the office.	One per student	Parents, families	Invitation for stakeholders to learn more about the concept through: Four SRG community Q&A sessions SRG hotline in October District's SRG website
Summary of Standards by Grade Level: Parent-teacher conferences and available in the office.	Twenty-five per grade level, per school	Parents, families, parent groups, community	Items can be used at kindergarten roundup, parent-teacher organization (PTO) events, site council meetings, parent-teacher conferences, and so on.
Progress Report Examples by Grade Level: Parent-teacher conferences and available in the office.	Twenty-five per grade level, per school	Parents, families, parent groups, community	Items can be used at kindergarten roundup, PTO events, site council meetings, parent-teacher conferences, and so on.

Source: © 2019 by Wichita Public Schools. Used with permission.

Figure B.5: SRG communication guide example.

Support for Standards-Based Reporting in Higher Education

A common parent question that districts need to address during the implementation process sounds something like this: "Will this type of grading and reporting be accepted by colleges?" It is a fair question that provides districts with a great opportunity to clarify and strengthen the move to standards-based or standards-referenced grading and reporting. Many districts are reaching out to colleges in their areas and nationally for statements that reaffirm the schools accept transcripts from all types of grading approaches when they consider students for admission. These statements provide a powerful and impactful message when included in parent handouts and on school and district websites. For example, Harvard published the following statement.

> Harvard College, a most selective institution of higher education, accepts applications for admission from students attending secondary schools from across the United States and the world. We admit students from a wide variety of educational settings, rural and urban, private and public schools.
>
> Regarding the New England Secondary School Consortium and its efforts to implement proficiency-based practices and gradation in schools throughout the region and beyond, parents and the public should be advised that Harvard College:
>
> 1. Accepts a wide range of student transcripts if they meet our stated admissions requirements and provide a full and accurate presentation of what an applicant has learned and accomplished
>
> 2. Assures applicants to our institution from schools with proficiency-based transcripts that they will not be disadvantaged in any way
>
> We are pleased to join the New England Secondary School Consortium in support of stronger academic preparation for postsecondary study, leading to increased collegiate enrollments and higher college completion rates. (Harvard College, 2016)

APPENDIX C

Additional Resources for Chapter 3

This appendix contains sample materials associated with phase 3 of SBL implementation: specifically, a vertical alignment tool, a parent's guide to SBL, and a sample presentation to parents.

Vertical Alignment

Figure C.1 (page 178) shows the schedule for a district's vertical alignment workday (described in phase 3 on page 106) that ensures an appropriate progression of knowledge and skills on proficiency scales across grade levels. This process includes three phases that lead to vertical alignment across proficiency scales for a standard that covers the entire K–12 grade band. One teacher per grade level participated in the process. A total of four different sets of proficiency scales were vertically aligned as a result of spending an entire day of working the process repeatedly. Equally important is the fact that the district now knows and understands this process well enough to apply it to additional ELA proficiency scales and other content areas in the future. Worksheets that teachers used in their analysis of standards are provided as reproducibles on the following pages.

ELA VERTICAL ALIGNMENT PROCESS	
8:00 to 8:30	Introduction and overview of the day (Amy)
8:30 to 8:45	Overview of the alignment process (Jan)
8:45 to 9:00	Individual examination of district-chosen priority standard (Elements of Literary Text)
9:00 to 9:30	Grade-band examination of scale (K–2, 3–5, 6–7, 8–12)
9:30 to 10:00	Final examination of scale and revisions made (K–3, 4–6, 7–12)
10:00 to 10:15	Break
10:15 to 10:30	Individual examination of district-chosen priority standard (Author's Purpose)
10:30 to 11:00	Grade-band examination of scale (K–2, 3–5, 6–7, 8–12)
11:00 to 11:30	Final examination of scale and revisions made (K–3, 4–6, 7–12)
11:30 to 11:45	Reflections on the morning
11:45 to 12:30	Lunch
12:30 to 12:45	Individual examination of district-chosen priority standard (Persuasive Writing)
12:45 to 1:15	Grade-band examination of scale (K–2, 3–5, 6–7, 8–12)
1:15 to 1:45	Final examination of scale and revisions made (K–3, 4–6, 7–12)
1:45 to 2:00	Reflection on the process
2:00 to 2:15	Break
2:15 to 3:30	Examine another priority standard (if time allows)

Source: Hoegh, 2020.

Figure C.1: Schedule for vertical alignment workday.

Vertical Alignment Process, Phase I

Phase I: Individual examination of a district-determined priority standard

Time allotment: Fifteen minutes

Please examine your grade-level proficiency scale in relation to the set of criteria provided. Be sure to record anything that will help to determine necessary enhancements to your scale.

Criteria	Yes	No	Comments
Specificity The language of each level on the scales is clear and specific. Each learning target is a single-idea statement of intended knowledge gain.			
Progression Verbs are present, and these verbs and corresponding context represent a progression of complexity from score 2.0 to 4.0.			
Comprehensiveness The proficiency scale is achievable. It has enough depth, yet not so much to warrant an additional scale. Each level on the scale includes one to three related learning targets.			
Measurability Each learning target is observable and quantifiable.			
Format Each learning target is written with the verb first to provide focus on what the student should know or be able to do.			
Vocabulary Key vocabulary has been identified at the score 2.0 level.			
Prerequisites Prerequisite knowledge and skills have been identified at the score 2.0 level.			
Rigor Score 3.0 aligns closely to the standards represented on the scale. The cognitive demand at score 3.0 aligns to the expectations of the standards. The passage of text is grade-level appropriate and is similar to what students will engage in on the state test.			

Source: Hoegh, J. K. (2020). A Handbook for Developing and Using Proficiency Scales in the Classroom. *Bloomington, IN: Marzano Resources.*

Vertical Alignment Process, Phases II and III

This tool guides both phase II and phase III of the vertical alignment process.

Phase II: Grade-band examination of a district-determined priority proficiency scale (K–2, 3–4, 5–7, 8–12)

Phase III: Expanded grade-band examination of the same proficiency scale (K–3, 4–6, 7–12)

Time allotment: Thirty minutes for each phase

Examine each proficiency scale in the grade band in relation to each statement on this page. Be sure to record the information discussed to help ensure that the following statement is true about each scale: *The scale is aligned vertically with previous and subsequent grade levels or courses.*

Scale 1	Scale 2	Scale 3
The scale meets all criteria listed in phase I.		
The verbs at each scale level (2.0, 3.0, 4.0) indicate a progression from one grade level to the next.		
The level of rigor is appropriate on each scale in comparison to the adjacent grade-level scales.		
The text of the correlating common assessment is grade-level appropriate (if applicable).		
The items on the common assessment align to the learning targets on the proficiency scale.		
Please record any proposed changes to any of the scales in this grade band and the reason for the change.		

A Parent's Guide to Standards-Based Grading

Northwood Public School District in Northwood, North Dakota, drafted a guide for parents that explains some the key purposes and details of their standards-based grading system. The following sections present text from that guide.

© 2020 by Northwood Public School. Used with permission.

Why Would We Change From the Traditional Grading System?

Northwood Public School is using a standards-based assessment and grading system in 7–12 English and 7–11 mathematics. We are doing this to measure and communicate students' learning and academic growth and achievement with greater accuracy. This system also allows for clearer feedback to students based on specific learning goals.

In the traditional hundred-point grading system, grades are generated from the work assigned to students (daily work, assessments, participation, and so on) These scores are entered into a gradebook and the student's final grade becomes an average of all of these items. These often include points for things like extra credit or point deductions for behaviors such as turning in work late.

This system doesn't take into account the learning process and doesn't accurately show what a student can do. Because teachers may apply points differently, students often do not know what their grade means, and what a grade means can vary from class to class. Earning points becomes a motivating factor for students, causing them to chase points instead of knowledge.

Standards-based systems, however, focus on mastery of essential content. This is the entire goal. This system is fairer and more accurate and focuses on learning.

How Will Standards-Based Grading Be Different?

We believe that a grade has one purpose: to communicate a student's learning and knowledge of content and skills. Standards-based grading is designed to do that by clearly communicating a student's mastery of a series of critical concepts.

Critical concepts are defined for each course. A critical concept is a big idea that is essential to mastering a course, and each concept may contain multiple standards within it. These critical concepts are then laid out in the form of a proficiency scale. A proficiency scale (see figure C.2, page 182) clearly defines what students should know and be able to do at each level, 1–4.

When students begin a learning opportunity, it makes sense that they would score lower on this scale. As they continue through the learning activities and practice the skills, their scores should reflect that new knowledge. In this system, students would not be punished for not understanding material at the beginning of an opportunity to learn. Their final score will reflect what they know and are able to do at the end of the course.

4.0	Above the standard(s), exceeding mastery
	I am able to apply what I have learned.
3.0	Mastery of the standard(s)
	I get this.
2.0	Simple material understood, approaching mastery
	I am still learning the basics.
1.0	Needing support
	Even with help, I do not get this.

Figure C.2: Critical concept proficiency scale.

A student's final score will be not be an average of all scores. It will instead be the student's current level of understanding. In a perfect system, standards-based grading would work without a final letter grade being necessary. In reality, however, we still need to compute a letter grade in order to provide students the opportunity to send a transcript to colleges. We have created a conversion chart (see table C.1) that teachers will use at the end of an assessment period. It is important to not convert these scores early in the learning process, because at that time students are just beginning to learn. After the opportunity to learn has ended, and mastery of content becomes a reasonable expectation, a final grade can be determined.

TABLE C.1: NORTHWOOD PUBLIC SCHOOL SCALE CONVERSION CHART

	Letter Grade	Percentage
4.00	A+	100
3.16–3.99	A	98
3.00–3.15	A–	94
2.89–2.99	B+	93
2.61–2.88	B	92
2.50–2.60	B–	86
2.40–2.49	C+	85
2.17–2.39	C	84
2.00–2.16	C–	78
1.80–1.99	D+	77
1.56–1.79	D	76
1.51–1.55	D–	70
0.00–1.50	F	69

What About Behavior Assessments?

There is no doubt that the development of a strong work ethic is vital to student success. In the traditional classroom, late work is handled differently by different teachers. In this system, we will be assessing and reporting work habits separately from academic knowledge. For example, if a student turned in an assignment a week late, but showed mastery of content on that assessment, the academic score would not be lowered because of the late work. That behavior would be reported separately and will be referred to as college and career ready practices (see figure C.3).

4	☐ **Work Completion:** All assignments are handed in complete and on time, with no exceptions. ☐ **Participation:** Fully participates in all in-class activities ☐ **Self-Discipline:** No disruptions or off-task behaviors ☐ **Respect:** Respects adults, peers, and property
3	☐ **Work Completion:** Most assignments are handed in complete and on time, with infrequent exceptions. ☐ **Participation:** Participates in most in-class activities ☐ **Self-Discipline:** Infrequent disruptions or off-task behaviors ☐ **Respect:** Almost always respects adults, peers, and property
2	☐ **Work Completion:** Some assignments are handed in complete and on time, with many exceptions. ☐ **Participation:** Participates in some in-class activities ☐ **Self-Discipline:** Some disruptions or off-task behaviors ☐ **Respect:** Sometimes shows disrespect to adults, peers, or property
1	☐ **Work Completion:** Few assignments are handed in complete and on time. ☐ **Participation:** Participates in few in-class activities ☐ **Self-Discipline:** Many disruptions or off-task behaviors ☐ **Respect:** Frequently shows disrespect to adults, peers, or property

Figure C.3: College and career ready practices.

How Is Eligibility Determined?

Eligibility will be determined based on work habits. If a student fails to complete necessary work, he or she could become ineligible for the week.

Sample Presentation to Parents

An additional support the district team from Wichita Public Schools provided to local schools is presentation slides with corresponding scripts for the presentation. Again, this lessened the burden for building-level principals, instructional coaches, and teachers in researching and creating such communication tools. The following is an example of a script for opening the presentation and introducing the need for SBL.

> *Imagine two students in the same class. Student A is a hard worker. Never misbehaves at school but struggles understanding algebra. His parents work with him every night and his work is complete and done on time—clean and neat. However, he hasn't successfully mastered the standards for this course. He participates in every extra-credit activity available, including bringing additional supplies to class and attending school events. Based on his effort, behavior, and completion of work, the student ultimately receives a C on his report card.*

> *Student B isn't a hard worker. She is often tardy to class, completes some of her work, and lacks motivation. She finds herself in occasional trouble due to her attendance and talking out in class. However, algebra comes very easily to her. She is able to successfully answer every question correctly on her assessments and has mastered the standards for this course. However, because of her lack of motivation, attendance, and occasional missing assignment, Student B gets a C on her report card in algebra.*
>
> *When entering Algebra II in the fall, both students are in the same mathematics class. Both students received the same grade in the previous class. Do both students, however, need the same level of support with the content of the class? Do they both understand algebra the same way?*

Figure C.4 is a sample of some of the presentation slides. In the first slide, you see a classroom assessment aligned to the levels on a proficiency scale. This is helpful in two ways. First, it helps parents and students see how assessments are directly linked to the proficiency scales (and thus, prioritized standards); it also implies that everything asked on an assessment is linked to the instruction student receive in class. The second slide is an indication of how a student may proceed with knowledge and understanding on a proficiency scale. At the 2.0 level, the student has 6 out of 6 scale components mastered, whereas at the 3.0 level, a student would have 12 out of 12 mastered.

ALIGNED ASSESSMENT AND INSTRUCTION

Every Student Future Ready — WICHITA PUBLIC SCHOOLS

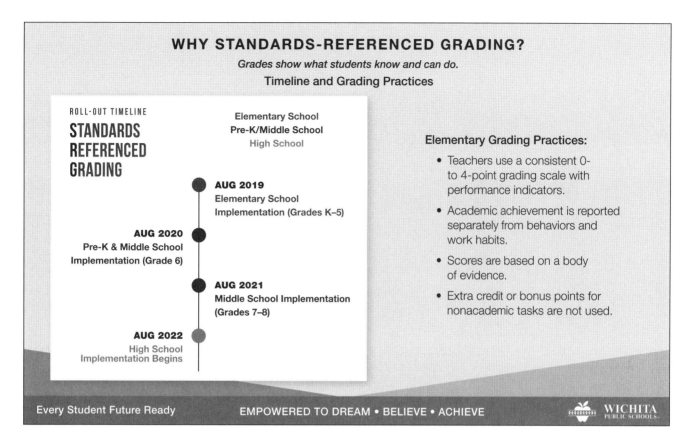

Source: © 2019 by Wichita Public Schools. Used with permission.

Figure C.4: Sample presentation to parents.

APPENDIX D
Additional Resources for Chapter 4

This appendix contains sample materials associated with phase 4 of SBL implementation: specifically, protocols for focus groups, samples of standards-based report cards, and parent FAQs.

Focus Group Protocol

Focus groups are an excellent way to gather qualitative data about components of SBL. For instance, does the group understand proficiency scales and how they are used? Do the focus group participants see a connection between prioritized standards, proficiency scales, classroom assessments, and instruction? This protocol (Krueger, 1994) was revised and adapted by the authors to provide consistent guidelines for planning SBL focus groups. There are three phases to conducting a focus group: (1) planning before the focus group, (2) conducting the focus group, and (3) interpreting and reporting the results. These phases are explained in the following sections.

Phase 1: Planning Before the Focus Group

1. Consider a project plan to identify your overall purpose and outcomes for the focus group.

2. Determine how many focus groups you want to run.

   a. Multiple focus groups will enable you to compare and identify themes that emerge from each discussion.

   b. Focus groups should run between sixty and ninety minutes. If the focus group participants are students, a typical class period is completely fine.

3. Identify your participants.

   a. Determine how many participants you want in each group. Each focus group should have between six and ten participants. Fewer than six participants may limit the conversation and yield poor data while more than ten can be unwieldy.

   b. Develop a list of key attributes to seek in participants based on the purpose you have identified.

    c.   Secure names and contact information and send invitations. We suggest a cross section of students or parents including various socioeconomic groups, course pathways representing a variety of extracurricular interests, and variations of school success thus far.

4.   Generate your questions.

    a.   Based on the purpose and goals of the focus group, identify no more than five questions.

    b.   Revisit the questions to make sure that they will yield the kind of information you are seeking.

    c.   Order the questions from general to specific.

5.   Develop your script.

    a.   *Part one:* welcome participants, explain purpose and context, explain what a focus group is, and make introductions. Explain that information is confidential and no names will be used. You will either have a note-taker or record the proceedings. We suggest taking copious notes is enough, as recording can feel obtrusive.

    b.   *Part two:* ask your questions; remember to use probes and follow-up questions to explore the key concepts more deeply.

    c.   *Part three:* close the focus group. Thank participants, give them contact information for further follow-up if requested, and explain how you will analyze and share the data.

6.   Select a facilitator.

    a.   It is helpful if the facilitator is not someone who directly oversees the issue or topical area you are exploring. This may make participants less open to sharing their thoughts or concerns.

    b.   The facilitator should be knowledgeable about the topic at hand, and can be a staff member from the same department.

    c.   The facilitator should be able to keep the discussion going, deal tactfully with difficult or outspoken group members, and make sure all participants are heard.

    d.   The facilitator should ask the questions and probes, but not participate in the dialogue or correct participants.

7.   Choose the location.

    a.   Choose a location that is comfortable, that is easily accessible, and where participants can see one another. Often a school conference room suffices.

    b.   Choose a setting which does not bias the information gathered.

    c.   Consider refreshments.

Phase 2: Conducting the Focus Group

1. Bring materials.

    a. Notebook, computer, or recording device, if you plan to record proceedings

    b. Flip chart, if no whiteboard is available

    c. Focus group list of participants

    d. Focus group script

    e. Name tags

    f. Watch or clock

2. Arrive before the participants to set up the room, refreshments, and so on.

3. Introduce yourself and the note-taker (if applicable) and carry on the focus group according to the script.

4. Conduct the session, being mindful of the following.

    a. Set a positive tone.

    b. Make sure everyone is heard; draw out quieter group members.

    c. Probe for more complete answers.

    d. Monitor your questions and the time closely: it is your job to make sure you are on track.

    e. Don't argue a point with a participant, even if he or she is wrong. Address it later if you must.

    f. Thank participants and tell them what your next steps are with the information.

Phase 3: Interpreting and Reporting the Results

1. Summarize each meeting.

    a. Immediately after the meeting, the facilitator should write up a quick summary of his or her impressions.

    b. Transcribe handwritten notes or audio recording of the focus group. This should be done as soon as possible after the focus group has been conducted.

    c. If the study involved two or more groups with multiple facilitators, discuss your impressions with the other facilitators before reviewing the transcript.

2. Analyze the summaries.

    a. Read the notes and look for themes or trends. Write down any important ideas that occur more than once.

    b.   Context and tone are just as important as words. If comments are phrased negatively or triggered an emotional response, this should be noted in the analysis.

    c.   Interpret the results.

        i.   What are the major findings?

        ii.   What recommendations might you have?

3.   Write the report.

    a.   Your report should include your purpose, outcomes, process, findings, and recommendations.

    b.   Submit the report to whoever requested the focus groups.

4.   Make adjustments and take action on what you learned.

    a.   Schedule a meeting to discuss the implications.

    b.   Highlight the main themes, issues, or problems that arose in the focus groups. Discuss how you will address these.

    c.   Prioritize the results and make action plans for the most important priorities.

Standards-Based Report Cards

When schools and districts implement standards-based learning, a standards-based report card is typically part of the later stages of implementation. Figures D.1 and D.2 (page 192) show a high school and an elementary school sample, respectively.

RUTLAND HIGH SCHOOL

Rutland, Vermont

Semester 1 Report for Student A

Below you will find a report of your current progress toward meeting the standards in your yearlong classes, and final grades in term and semester-long classes. An "M" indicates that an assessment is missing and a "U" indicates that the standard is unassessed at present. The 0–4 score next to the course name is your course grade and below that you will see your grade for each course standard that has been assessed to date. If you have questions about what you see here, please see your teacher.

Driver Education	2.9
Overall Academic Master (100% of total)	2.9
Achieve and maintain safe behavior on the road	3.4
Apply knowledge of concepts, principles, and tactics related to driving	2.7
Demonstrate competency in a variety of driving situations	2.7
Exhibit responsible behavior that respects self and others	2.8
Overall Habits of Work Mastery	3.2
Demonstrate the habits and behaviors necessary for success	3.2

Earth Science Honors	3.4
Overall Academic Mastery (100% of total)	3.4
Analyze data to claim how a change to Earth's surface affects other systems	3.0
Plan and conduct an investigation of water and its effects on Earth	3.5
Overall Work Habits Mastery	3.0
Demonstrate the habits and behaviors necessary for success	3.0

English 1 Honors	3.5
Overall Academic Mastery (100% of total)	3.5
Acquire and apply domain specific vocabulary in a variety of contexts	3.8
Demonstrate command of grammar and usage	3.6
Engage in collaborative discussions and express ideas clearly and persuasively	3.4
Produce clear, coherent, and organized writing using a process for development	3.4
Read, analyze, and interpret a wide range of literary texts	3.3
Overall Habits of Work Mastery	3.4
Demonstrate the habits and behaviors necessary for success	3.4

Source: © 2018 by Rutland High School. Used with permission.

Figure D.1: Portion of a standards-based report card.

DEEK CREEK GRADE 3 ELEMENTARY REPORT CARD 2020-2021

Student: _____

Student ID: _____

Homeroom: _____

School: _____

Attendance Summary By Term

	Q1		Q2		Q3		Q4		Total	
	Absent	Tardy	Absent	Tardy	Absent	Tardy	Absent	Tardy	Absent	Tardy
	0	0	0	0	0	0	0	0	0	0

Academic Performance Level for Proficiency (Standards-Based)

Name	Score
Beyond mastery of standard	4
Partial mastery of 4.0	3.5
Meets standard	3
Partial mastery of 3.0	2.5
Foundational skills and vocab	2
Partial mastery of 2.0	1.5
Foundational skills with help	1
With help, partial mastery	0.5
Even with help, no success	0
Blank = Not assessed this term	
^ = 4 not possible on this standard	
IE = Insufficient evidence	

English Language Arts

	Term			
	Q1	Q2	Q3	Q4
Determine the meaning of synonyms, antonyms, homonyms, and homophones				
Recognize possessive nouns and pronouns				
Use affixes, roots, and stems to determine meaning of words				
Use text features to understand non-fiction texts				
Recognize verbs (present, past, future, irregular, past participle)				
Interpret the literary elements of a selected passage (character, setting, plot, characterization, and theme)				
Distinguish fact from opinion in a text				
^ Locate the main idea and supporting details				
Identify figurative language				
^ Recognize adjectives and adverbs				
Use reference materials to locate information				
^ Determine the author's purpose (persuade, inform, entertain)				
Compare and contrast story elements to discriminate genres				
Create a well-developed essay				

English Language Arts

	Term			
	Q1	Q2	Q3	Q4
Read and comprehend grade-level text for fiction and non-fiction				
^ Use context clues to determine the meaning of words				
Make inferences by connecting prior knowledge and experience with information from the text				

Social Studies

	Term			
	Q1	Q2	Q3	Q4
Identify Oklahoma state symbols				
Locate information using map skills				
Identify the characteristics of the Five Civilized Tribes				
Demonstrate knowledge of the Trail of Tears				
Determine the purposes of Oklahoma's government				
Describe the events of the Land Run				

Science

	Term			
	Q1	Q2	Q3	Q4
Identify and construct various examples of life cycles				
Construct an argument that some animals form groups that help members survive				
Identify the effects of forces in motion				
Demonstrate and understanding of inherited versus acquired traits				
Describe weather and climate in certain regions				

Mathematics

	Term			
	Q1	Q2	Q3	Q4
^ Model, read, and write up to five digits				
^ Estimate the sum and difference up to five digits				
Add and subtract up to four-digit numbers with regrouping				
Add and subtract up to four-digit numbers to solve real-world problems				
Represent multiplication facts by using a variety of models	■	■		
^ Demonstrate fluency of multiplication facts with factors up to 10	■	■		
Create and compare equivalent and nonequivalent fractions up to the twelfths				
Measure length in metric and customary units to the nearest yard, foot, inch, and half-inch				
Use perimeter to solve problems				
Use area to solve problems	■			
^ Classify angles as acute, right, obtuse, and straight	■			
^ Identify and compare 3-D shapes based on attributes	■			
Summarize and construct graphs and charts				
^ Solve simple elapsed-time problems to the nearest 5 minutes up to one hour			■	
^ Represent division facts by using a variety of models			■	
^ Determine the value of a set of coins or bills			■	

Mathematics

	Term			
	Q1	Q2	Q3	Q4
Describe and create representations of numerical patterns		■	■	
^ Recognize, represent, and apply the number properties for addition and multiplication			■	

Art

	Term			
	Q1	Q2	Q3	Q4
Communicate the elements of art: value and balance				
Use art terminology				
Use conscientious planning and craftsmanship in work	■	■		
Critique and analyze different artists and their works of art		■		

Music

	Term			
	Q1	Q2	Q3	Q4
Demonstrate appropriate audience behavior				
Keep steady beat through movement and singing games	■			
Sing classroom songs using a pentatonic scale (Do Re Mi Fa So La)			■	■
Perform whole note				

Physical Education

	Term			
	Q1	Q2	Q3	Q4
Exhibit responsible personal and social behavior that respects self and others				
Demonstrate competency in a variety of motor skills and movement patterns	■			
Recognize the value of physical activity for health, enjoyment, challenge, self-expression, and social interaction		■		
Apply knowledge of concepts, principles, strategies, and tactics related to movement		■	■	

STEM

	Term			
	Q1	Q2	Q3	Q4
Decompose (break down) the steps needed to solve a problem into a precise sequence of instructions				
Define a simple design problem reflecting a need or want that includes success criteria and constraints	■			
Conduct investigations to produce data as a basis for evidence		■		
Generate a solution to a problem based on the criteria and constraints of the problem		■	■	

Social, Emotional, and Behavioral Skills

	Term			
	Q1	Q2	Q3	Q4
^ Demonstrates self-control				
^ Follows teacher directions				
^ Accepts and assumes personal responsibility				
^ Shows respect to others		■	■	
^ Uses appropriate words and actions to solve conflicts				

Source: © 2020 by Deer Creek Public Schools. Used with permission.

Figure D.2: Third-grade report card.

Parent FAQs

Wichita Public Schools created a document for answering common questions from families. The following questions and corresponding responses may or may not be identical to your implementation questions, but their district-specific work provides an excellent real-life example of implementation. As their standards-referenced implementation began at the elementary level, table D.1 includes a number of questions in relation to the phase 4 activity of implementing new reporting documents for their elementary grades. The left column identifies a topic, and the right column provides sample questions and responses.

TABLE D.1: FAMILY FAQS ABOUT ELEMENTARY REPORTING DOCUMENTS

Category	Questions and Answers
Behavior and Work Ethic	Q: What are the behavior and work habit targets? A: The targets can be found under our Parents & Students tab of our website. At the elementary level, behavior factors (social skills, turning in and completing assignments, and effort) will be reported separately on the report card. WPS maintains that these are important aspects for success in school and life, but should not inflate or deflate a student's academic grade intended to reflect their understanding of what is being taught in class. Q: Why was work ethics removed from grading standards? A: We believe behavior and work habits are so important we are separating them from the academic score. This ensures our academic scores truly reflect what students know and can do academically. This also provides a way for specific, valuable feedback to be given for behavior and work habits. At the secondary level, these types of standards or targets are called Employability Skills.
Consistency in Grading	Q: Will all teachers grade the same? A: Teachers will use both obtrusive (written, formal) and unobtrusive (verbal, informal) assessments. The expectations for meeting mastery of the standards will be the same; however, the way teachers assess may differ. Q: How do we make sure all students are meeting their grade level if each student has different goals by the end of the year? A: All students in a grade level have grade-level standards. The goal for all students is to meet these standards by the end of the year. Q: Will homework be graded? A: In this system, homework is not part of the academic grade. However, completion of work can be scored using the behavior and work habit targets. Q: How many data points will teachers use to determine scores? A: Teachers will collect data that becomes part of a body of evidence for evaluating student progress and growth. The amount of data collected and needed will depend on the student and standard. Q: Will all teachers grade the same? Will information be subjective or objective, based on how they feel the child is doing versus how another teacher feels the child is doing? A: All assessment should be aligned to a standard and a proficiency scale. This will provide a common language when determining student mastery of standards. Professional judgment will still be needed when determining where a student is in his or her progression of learning.

Evaluation of the System	Q: How will the new system be evaluated to assess if it is achieving the desired outcomes?
	A: Assessment of this system will include many staff members (district personnel, building and district leaders, and teachers) analyzing state achievement results and feedback from stakeholders.
	Q: Will there be any follow-up sessions to share how things are going or possibly how the new grading system may be adjusted, if needed?
	A: We will be sharing information such as this with the school board throughout the implementation.
	Q: How do you find or know the average level for each subject?
	A: In this system, the focus is on the progression of learning according to proficiency scales and mastering standards. It is not necessary to focus on averaging scores.
	Q: How can I help my child at home to get him or her more prepared to perform at a 4.0 level?
	A: Content will be taught at the foundational level (2.0) and mastery level (3.0). Anything a student does that is above and beyond the standard might be considered at the 4.0 level. Focusing first on mastery of the standards is key.
	Q: Is there research to support the use of standards-referenced grading?
	A: Yes. Please visit www.usd259.org/grading to view documents.
	Q: Are the learning standards available online? If so, where? For all grades?
	A: Yes. Please visit www.usd259.org/grading to view documents listing the standards for each grade level.
Fine Arts and PE Grading	Q: Will art and music be part of this work? Will they undergo similar proficiency scale development and use?
	A: Yes. All elementary music, physical education, and art courses will have targets and scales, and students will be able to set goals in each class based on the proficiency scales.
Fundamental Questions	Q: What are standards?
	A: Standards are statements about what students should know and be able to do at each grade level. The Kansas State Department of Education posts adopted standards at the following site:https://www.ksde.org/Agency/Division-of-Learning-Services/Career-Standards-and-Assessment-Services/CSAS-Home/Standards-and-Fact-Sheets.
	Q: How is this different from the way students used to be assessed in elementary school?
	A: Students will continue to have assessments as they have in the past. However, assessments will now focus on certain standards and targets and students will know where they are in their progression of learning the target.
	Q: Is this new grading system going into effect in middle schools and high schools?
	A: Yes. This system will begin to be implemented in the following years at the middle school and high school levels.
	Q: How will other districts understand the grades?
	A: When a student transfers, his or her records are sent upon request from the previous school. Each student's progress report will include a section explaining how to determine what an SRG number score means for the student's letter grade at the new school.

continued ➞

| Grade Conversion (GPA, College, Scholarships) | Q: Will students have GPAs in middle school and high school?

A: Yes. Student scores on standards will be shown on progress reports. All scores on standards in a content area will then be converted to a letter grade. Letter grades in all subject areas can then be used to determine a grade point average (GPA).

Q: How will I know how my child is doing without letter grades? What does a 2 mean? Is a 2 a C?

A: It will be important to look at the performance indicators on the progress report. We will not convert to letter grades in elementary.

Q: How is this going to be different from an A–F scale?

A: Traditionally, students received an overall letter grade indicating their performance in class. This included both academic and behavior and work habit performance. Now, students will receive feedback regarding their performance toward mastering standards. The academic performance will be graded separately from the behavior and work habit performance.

Q: How will SRG be distinguished from letter grades as there are five numbers on SRG scales and five traditional letter grades? How do I not equate a *4* to an *A* or a *1* to a *D*?

A: The district will adopt a secondary conversion to letter grades chart that will help answer this question.

Q: What are the criteria for mastery?

A: *Mastery* is the term used when students have met the grade-level standard or target.

Q: How are high school transcripts going to look for universities?

A: Transcripts will have all necessary information needed for students applying to colleges and universities.

Q: What is the decaying average formula?

A: This formula calculates a student grade with more weight given to the most recent assessment scores; the higher the decay rate, the more heavily recent assessments are weighted. This method acknowledges that students learn over time, whereas a simple average does not.

The most recent assessment defaults at 65%.

For example, if there are two assessments, the most recent assessment gets 65% weight, and the first gets 35%. For each additional assessment, the sum of the previous score calculations decays by an additional 35%. If you have three assessments, the weighting would be 12% for the first assessment, 23% for the second assessment, and 65% for the third assessment.

The mathematics behind the 65% decaying average works like this.

Let's say you have four assessments that receive the following scores: 1, 2, 3, 4 (this last one being the most recent).

$(1 \times .35) + (2 \times .65) = x$ $(x \times .35) + (3 \times .65) = y$

$(y \times .35) + (4 \times .65) = z$ (this being the current standard score: 3.48)

An example:

A student receives a score of 2, 3, and 4 (most recent) on a single standard. Using decaying average the student receives a 3.5. The formula calculates to a 3.5275 and rounds down.

If a student receives a score of 2, 4, and 4, the decaying average formula calculates to a 3.755, so it rounds up. |
| Progress Report | Q: How will I know prior to the end-of-the-year report if my child is falling behind?

A: Teachers will continue to monitor students who may be struggling or need enrichment and communicate specific needs with parents. Progress reports at the elementary level will go home each quarter. |

Other	Q: How is one classroom teacher supposed to equitably keep track of each student?
	A: Keeping track of student progress is not new. It has always been an expectation we have. With scales, it will be a streamlined process.
	Q: Is .5 a part of the grading?
	A: Yes. We want to celebrate progress. Having a half-point score between each level helps us do that.
	Q: Why are there so many more standards in areas like PE and art as opposed to science and social studies? Does this distribution change over time in different grades?
	A: For this year, there will be fewer science and social studies standards required to be taught and assessed each quarter, even though there are units being taught.
Retaining Students	Q: Will students be retained if they have not mastered a certain percentage of content in their current grade?
	A: No. We are standards-referenced, not standards-based. In our system, students continue to progress to the next grade level. Research has shown that retention is not an effective practice. Our time and energy are better spent working to support students throughout the school year providing quality core instruction and both enrichment and intervention courses.
Student Impact	Q: How will this affect students with special needs?
	A: Students will continue to receive the support they have had previously. Students will continue to work on their identified goals. All students will use proficiency scales.
	Q: Is this less stressful for students?
	A: Yes. In this system, students know what they need to learn and have ownership of their learning when they set goals and track their own progress.
	Q: How are you advising the students about the change?
	A: Students are learning from their teachers. At the secondary level, some students have been engaged in the change process through focus groups and feedback sessions.

Source: © 2019 by Wichita Public Schools. Used with permission.

Additional Resources for Chapter 5

This appendix contains sample materials associated with phase 5 of SBL implementation: specifically, information on active progress monitoring.

Active Progress Monitoring

The following staff development material was created by school leader Carrie Swanson and instructional coach Vanessa Valencia as they worked with teachers in Aurora Public Schools (Colorado). They developed the document specifically for the purpose of training teachers how to connect proficiency scales to daily formative assessment practices, which in turn informs instructional planning.

Source: © 2017 by Carrie Swanson and Vanessa Valencia. Used with permission.

What Is Active Progress Monitoring?

In the standards era, it is imperative that teachers not only know and teach the standards but also know specifically what students need to do to demonstrate mastery of the standards and have a method for measuring proficiency and growth. Active progress monitoring is an instruction and assessment strategy that allows teachers to collect formative data on students in relation to the standard and proficiency scale. Proficiency scales identify the success criteria the teacher is looking or listening for to determine if students have learned the content and skills required to demonstrate mastery. Active progress monitoring involves the use of unobtrusive assessment and can occur at any point during instruction—while students are independently working or working collaboratively, in small groups, and even during the closure, debrief, or summary. The data collected during active progress monitoring is used to gauge a student's current level of skill and make decisions for future instruction, intervention, or extensions of the learning.

How Do I Implement Active Progress Monitoring?

Active progress monitoring is implemented once the standard has been determined by the teacher or team of teachers and success criteria have been identified by teachers or reviewed in the proficiency scale levels. For a particular lesson, a teacher may only be teaching a part of the standard rather than the entire standard. For example, a teacher may decide to teach Common Core State Standard RL2.2: *Recount stories, including fables and folktales from diverse cultures, and determine their central message, lesson, or moral* (NGA & CCSSO, 2010a) in two different parts. The teacher first decides to teach students to recount or retell a story, and then later to retell it with the theme. If the standard is taught across multiple lessons, the success criteria would be identified in the proficiency scale for the specific parts of the standard being taught. In the preceding example, the success criteria for retelling might include:

1. Telling the important parts from the beginning, middle, and end in sequential order

2. Identifying the problem and solution or major event

3. Referring to characters by name

4. Identifying a logical theme or lesson the main character learns

When implementing active progress monitoring, it is important to consider the tool and method used. The monitoring tool could be a seating chart, a class list, a table, or another format to record unobtrusive assessment data. The method you identify may be determined by the success criteria for that particular chunk of information. It could be a plus or minus, a check, or a numeral system. The data may also be recorded as a proficiency scale level such as 2.0, 2.5, or 3.0. In the following example (figure E.1), you will see the standard and learning target, the success criteria, and the numerical system that will be used to identify which components of the success criteria students are demonstrating during class. For example, you'll notice Julia has a *1* and a *3* listed by her name because she is currently demonstrating that she can tell the important parts from the beginning, middle, and end in sequential order and is referring to characters by name. Julia is not yet demonstrating, however, that she can identify the problem and solution or major event and identify a logical theme or lesson the main character learns. You'll notice Juan, on the other hand, has a *1, 2, 3,* and *4* by his name because he has demonstrated mastery of all the success criteria and thus also has a *P* circled by his name indicating that he demonstrates proficiency on this standard.

How Do I Use Active Monitoring to Plan for Instruction?

While you are actively monitoring, you may quickly realize that few students are hitting the mark. Rather than missing a teachable moment, you can now make on-the-spot decisions to provide immediate feedback and correct misconceptions. You may decide to call students back to the whole group for a quick reteach (often called *catch and release*), clarify any misconceptions or stuck points, and then release them to apply the learning again.

After the class period, you will want to begin analyzing and evaluating your data to make instructional decisions for tomorrow or another point in the future when you are teaching that particular standard again. Notice how the teacher noted this in figure E.1 under the heading Implications for Instruction. After looking at the data, the teacher determined a need for four small groups to reteach parts of the success criteria that

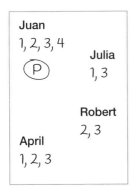

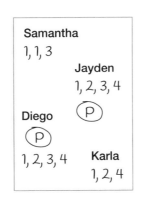

Implications for Instruction:

Small Groups:

#1: B, M, L—David, Vanessa, Ella, Aaliyah

#2: Problem and Solution—Julia, Samantha, Sarah, Christy, Carrie

#3: Names—Karla, James, Maddison, Lily

#4: Theme and Lesson—April, Robert, Eliseo, Kate, D'Angelo, Larry, Jesus

Learning Target: The student will be able to recount stories, fables, and folktales and determine the theme.

Success Criteria:

1. Tell the important parts from the beginning, middle, and end in sequential order.
2. Identify the problem and solution or major event.
3. Refer to characters by name.
4. Identify a logical theme or lesson the main character learns.

Eliseo	Carrie
1, 2, 3	4
1	
Christy	David

Lily	Larry
1, 2	1, 2, 3
1, 2, 3	
Jesus	Ella

Vanessa	Maddison
	1, 2
1, 2, 3	2, 3, 4
D'Angelo	Aaliyah

James	Sarah
2	3
1, 2, 3	(P) 1, 2, 3, 4
Kate	Delores

Figure E.1: Active progress monitoring.

students had not yet demonstrated. The teacher marked students who met all the success criteria as proficient; students not meeting all the success criteria were grouped based on their specific learning needs.

For example, Juan demonstrated all the success criteria while Larry was grouped with other students who need instruction or practice with identifying theme.

When looking at all the student data, you may ask yourself, "What percentage of students demonstrated proficiency in the success criteria or standard?" If the answer is less than 80 percent, you may reflect with some of these questions.

- Did I model for students how to demonstrate the success criteria?
- Do I need to reteach this learning target with a different approach?
- Were my success criteria clear to students?
- Do I reteach this standard through whole-group or small-group instruction?

If 80 percent or higher demonstrated proficiency, you may decide to provide small-group or one-on-one support for those who didn't reach proficiency. This might be done the following day or sometime in the near future. You might also group the students according to your data collection method. If you numbered the success criteria, then you may group students by skills they demonstrate and skills they still need to acquire.

What Is the Difference Between Monitoring and Roving, and When Do I Do Each?

Active monitoring involves collecting and recording unobtrusive assessment data while students work in relation to the success criteria. Active monitoring is done throughout the entire instructional block. *Roving* is a separate instructional strategy in which the teacher makes quick rounds throughout the classroom right after smaller lesson segments and during independent practice. The teacher might clarify the task or directions, monitor for behavior and engagement, or support students with quick check-ins. Roving could look like quick "coaching in the moment" where you might say, "Great job on _____. Now I want you to think about _____."

How Do I Write Success Criteria So That I Can Actively Monitor Them?

You can write success criteria as learning targets to identify exactly what you expect students to demonstrate by the end of your instructional time. Proficiency scales written for your priority standards identify the success criteria as learning targets organized in a progression of learning based on the standards identified in level 3.0 of the scale (see figure E.2). In order to have success criteria that you can monitor, you will want to write them in a way that is straightforward, clear, and concise so that there are no questions about what students must do to demonstrate mastery. It helps if students see models, examples, and demonstrations of what success criteria look like and how to apply the success criteria.

What Teachers Said About Active Progress Monitoring

- "The monitoring tool was effective to group students and/or showcase student exemplars as well as discuss next steps."
  —Kindergarten teacher

- "It is important that the team comes together and comes to an agreement on what the success criteria are so we all are measuring the same thing."
  —Second-grade teacher

- "Active monitoring lightened my after-class grading load."
  —Third-grade teacher

- "Active monitoring allowed me to make on-the-spot decisions as well as decisions for future instruction."
  —Third-grade teacher

Standard			
CCSS.ELA-LITERACY.RL.2.2: Recount stories, including fables and folktales from diverse cultures, and determine their central message, lesson, or moral.			

Grade: Second			
Score 4.0	**In addition to score 3.0, the student demonstrates in-depth inferences and applications that go beyond what was taught.** • The student will apply the score 3.0 criteria to write a book review, make book recommendations on the class book blog, or write a literary analysis. • Book or movie review (written or video essay) • Book recommendations on class book blog		Sample Activities
	3.5	In addition to score 3.0 performance, in-depth inferences and applications with partial success	
Score 3.0	The student will be able to recount stories, fables, or folktales and determine the theme. Success criteria: • Tell the important parts from the beginning, middle, and end in sequential order. • Identify the problem and solution or major event. • Refer to characters by name. • Identify a logical theme or lesson the main character learns.		Written or oral assessment
	2.5	No major errors or omissions regarding 2.0 content and partial knowledge of the 3.0 content	
Score 2.0	**There are no major errors or omissions regarding the simpler details and processes as the student:** 1. Can retell the story with important details 2. Knows story elements like characters, setting, plot, problem, and solution 3. Can relate the story in sequential or chronological order 4. Understands a central message or lesson 5. Knows key vocabulary such as *theme*, *folktale*, *story*, *fable*, *sequential*, *chronological*, *characters*, *setting*, *plot*, *problem*, *solution* **However, the student exhibits major errors or omissions regarding the more complex ideas and processes.**		Oral assessment
	1.5	Partial knowledge of the 2.0 content, but major errors or omissions regarding the 3.0 content	

Figure E.2: Sample second-grade ELA proficiency scale.

- "Having criteria for above and below proficiency increases awareness and accountability for learning."
  —Middle school teacher

- "The teacher knows specifically what they are listening for and looking for."
  —Middle school social studies teacher

References and Resources

Ames, C. (1992). Classrooms: Goals, structures, and student motivation. *Journal of Educational Psychology, 84*(3), 261–271.

Bangert-Drowns, R. L., Kulik, C. C., Kulik, J. A., & Morgan, M. (1991). The instructional effects of feedback in test-like events. *Review of Educational Research, 61*(2), 213–238.

Berry, B., Daughtrey, A., & Wieder, A. (2010, January 1). *Teacher leadership: Leading the way to effective teaching and learning.* Accessed at https://files.eric.ed.gov/fulltext /ED509719.pdf on September 25, 2020.

Biggs, J. (1998). Assessment and classroom learning: A role for summative assessment? *Assessment in Education: Principles, Policy and Practice, 5*(1), 103–110.

Brookhart, S. M. (2011, November). Starting the conversation about grading. *Educational Leadership, 69*(3), 10–14.

Brookhart, S. M. (2014). *Grading* (2nd ed.). Upper Saddle River, NJ: Pearson.

Brookhart, S. M. (2017). *How to give effective feedback to your students* (2nd ed.). Alexandria, VA: Association for Supervision and Curriculum Development.

Butler, D. L., & Winne, P. H. (1995). Feedback and self-regulated learning: A theoretical synthesis. *Review of Educational Research, 65*(3), 245–281.

Chapman, C., & Vagle, N. (2011). *Motivating students: Twenty-five strategies to light the fire of engagement.* Bloomington, IN: Solution Tree Press.

Charantimath, P. M. (2006). *Total quality management.* Singapore: Pearson Education.

Covey, S. R. (2004). *The seven habits of highly effective people: Powerful lessons in personal change.* New York: Simon & Schuster.

Dodson, C. (2019). *The critical concepts in social studies.* Centennial, CO: Marzano Resources. Accessed at www.marzanoresources.com/critical-concepts-social-studies on May 12, 2020.

DuFour, R., DuFour, R., & Eaker, R. (2008). *Revisiting Professional Learning Communities at Work: New insights for improving schools.* Bloomington, IN: Solution Tree Press.

DuFour, R., DuFour, R., Eaker, R., & Many, T. (2016). *Learning by doing* (3rd ed.). Bloomington, IN: Solution Tree Press.

DuFour, R., & Eaker, R. (1998). *Professional Learning Communities at Work: Best practices for enhancing student achievement.* Bloomington, IN: Solution Tree Press.

Eaker, R., & Marzano, R. J. (Eds.). (2020). *Professional Learning Communities at Work and High Reliability Schools: Cultures of continuous learning.* Bloomington, IN: Solution Tree Press.

Erickson, J. A. (2011, November). How grading reform changed our school. *Educational Leadership, 69*(3), 66–70.

Every Student Succeeds Act of 2015, Pub. L. No. 114–95, 20 U.S.C. § 1177 (2015).

Fisher, D., Frey, N., & Pumpian, I. (2011, November). No penalties for practice. *Educational Leadership, 69*(3), 46–51.

Forbes Quotes. (n.d.). *Alfred North Whitehead quote.* Accessed at https://forbes.com/quotes /341 on May 12, 2020.

Fullan, M. (2008). *The six secrets of change: What the best leaders do to help their organizations thrive and survive.* San Francisco: Jossey-Bass.

Gareis, C. R., & Grant, L. W. (2008). *Teacher-made assessments: How to connect curriculum, instruction, and student learning.* Larchmont, NY: Eye on Education.

Garmston, R. J., & Wellman, B. M. (2016). *The adaptive school: A sourcebook for developing collaborative groups* (3rd ed.). Lanham, MD: Rowman & Littlefield.

Gobble, T., Onuscheck, M., Reibel, A. R., & Twadell, E. (2016). *Proficiency-based assessment process, not product.* Bloomington, IN: Solution Tree Press.

Guskey, T. R. (2000, December). Grading policies that work against standards . . . and how to fix them. *NASSP Bulletin, 84*(620), 20–27.

Guskey, T. R. (2006, May). Making high school grades meaningful. *Phi Delta Kappan, 87*(9), 670–675.

Guskey, T. R. (Ed.). (2009a). *The principal as assessment leader.* Bloomington, IN: Solution Tree Press.

Guskey, T. R. (Ed.). (2009b). *The teacher as assessment leader.* Bloomington, IN: Solution Tree Press.

Guskey, T. R. (2009c). *Practical solutions for serious problems in standards-based grading.* Thousand Oaks, CA: Corwin Press.

Guskey, T. R. (2011, November). Five obstacles to grading reform. *Educational Leadership, 69*(3), 16–21.

Guskey, T. R., & Bailey, J. M. (2001). *Developing grading and reporting systems for student learning.* Thousand Oaks, CA: Corwin Press.

Guskey, T. R., & Jung, L. A. (2006, Winter). The challenges of standards-based grading. *Leadership Compass, 4*(2), 6–10.

Guskey, T. R., & Jung., L. A. (2013). *Answers to essential questions about standards, assessments, grading, and reporting.* Thousand Oaks, CA: Corwin Press.

Harvard College. (2016). *Collegiate statement regarding proficiency-based education and graduation.* Accessed at www.newenglandssc.org/wp-content/uploads/2016/06/MA _Harvard.pdf on September 21, 2020.

Hattie, J., & Timperley, H. (2007). The power of feedback. *Review of Educational Research, 77*(1), 81–112.

Heflebower, T. (2009). A seven-module plan to build teacher knowledge of balanced assessment. In T. R. Guskey (Ed.), *The principal as assessment leader* (pp. 93–117). Bloomington, IN: Solution Tree Press.

Heflebower, T. (2020). A multiyear plan for standards-referenced reporting. In R. Eaker & R. J. Marzano (Eds.), *Professional Learning Communities at Work and High Reliability Schools: Cultures of continuous learning* (pp. 191–218). Bloomington, IN: Solution Tree Press.

Heflebower, T., Hoegh, J. K., & Warrick, P. (2014). *A school leader's guide to standards-based grading.* Bloomington, IN: Marzano Resources.

Heflebower, T., Hoegh, J. K., & Warrick, P. (2017). Get it right the first time! *Phi Delta Kappan, 98*(6), 58–62.

Heflebower, T., Hoegh, J. K., Warrick, P. B., & Flygare, J. (2019). *A teacher's guide to standards-based learning.* Bloomington, IN: Marzano Resources.

Heritage, M. (2008). *Learning progressions: Supporting instruction and formative assessment.* Washington, DC: Council of Chief State School Officers.

Hoegh, J. K. (2020). *A handbook for developing and using proficiency scales in the classroom.* Bloomington, IN: Marzano Resources.

Hoerr, T. R. (2014). Principal connection / goals that matter. *Educational Leadership, 72*(1), 83–84.

Iowa Area Education Agencies. (n.d.) *Steps 2 & 3: Beliefs and Consensus.* Accessed at https://sites.google.com/view/utt/steps-2-3consensus on September 21, 2020.

IvyPanda. (2020, February 12). *Factors critical to the implementation of second order change.* Accessed at https://ivypanda.com/essays/factors-critical-to-the-implementation-of-second-order-change September 25, 2020.

Jung, L. A., & Guskey, T. R. (2007, November). Standards-based grading and reporting: A model for special education. *Teaching Exceptional Children, 40*(2), 48–53.

Jung, L. A., & Guskey, T. R. (2010, February). Grading exceptional learners. *Educational Leadership, 67*(5), 31–35.

Jung, L. A., & Guskey, T. R. (2012). *Grading exceptional and struggling learners.* Thousand Oaks, CA: Corwin Press.

Kagan, S., & Kagan, M. (2009). *Kagan cooperative learning.* San Clemente, CA: Kagan.

Kansas State Department of Education. (2011). *Kansas college and career readiness standards.* Accessed at https://community.ksde.org/Default.aspx?tabid=4754 on September 3, 2020.

Kohn, A. (2011, November). The case against grades. *Educational Leadership, 69*(3), 28–33.

Kotter, J., & Rathgeber, H. (2005). *Our iceberg is melting: Changing and succeeding under any conditions* (New ed.). New York: Penguin.

Krueger, R. A. (1994). *Focus groups: A practical guide for applied research* (2nd ed.). Thousand Oaks, CA: SAGE.

Marzano, R. J. (2003). *What works in schools: Translating research into action.* Alexandria, VA: Association for Supervision and Curriculum Development.

Marzano, R. J. (2006). *Classroom assessment and grading that work.* Alexandria, VA: Association for Supervision and Curriculum Development.

Marzano, R. J. (2010). *Formative assessment and standards-based grading.* Bloomington, IN: Marzano Resources.

Marzano, R. J. (2017). *The new art and science of teaching.* Bloomington, IN: Solution Tree Press.

Marzano, R. J. (2018). *Making classroom assessments reliable and valid.* Bloomington, IN: Solution Tree Press.

Marzano, R. J., & Heflebower, T. (2011, November). Grades that show what students know. *Educational Leadership, 69*(3), 34–39.

Marzano, R. J., Heflebower, T., Hoegh, J. K., Warrick, P., & Grift, G. (2016). *Collaborative teams that transform schools: The next step in PLCs.* Bloomington, IN: Marzano Resources.

Marzano, R. J., Warrick, P. B., Rains, C. L., & DuFour, R. (2018). *Leading a High Reliability School.* Bloomington, IN: Solution Tree Press.

Marzano, R. J., Warrick, P. B., & Simms, J. A. (2014). *A handbook for High Reliability Schools: The next step in school reform.* Bloomington, IN: Marzano Resources.

Marzano, R. J., Waters, T., & McNulty, B. A. (2005). *School leadership that works: From research to results.* Alexandria, VA: Association for Supervision and Curriculum Development.

Marzano, R. J., Yanoski, D. C., Hoegh, J. K., & Simms, J. A. (2013). *Using Common Core Standards to enhance classroom instruction and assessment.* Bloomington, IN: Marzano Resources.

McTighe, J., & O'Connor, K. (2011, November). Seven practices for effective learning. *Educational Leadership, 69*(3), 10–17.

Moss, C. M., & Brookhart, S. M. (2009). *Advancing formative assessment in every classroom: A guide for instructional leaders.* Alexandria, VA: Association for Supervision and Curriculum Development.

National Governors Association Center for Best Practices & Council of Chief State School Officers. (2010a). *Common Core State Standards for English language arts and literacy in history/social studies, science, and technical subjects.* Washington, DC: Author. Accessed at www.corestandards.org/assets/CCSSI_ELA%20Standards.pdf on July 28, 2020.

National Governors Association Center for Best Practices & Council of Chief State School Officers. (2010b). *Common Core State Standards for mathematics.* Washington, DC: Authors. Accessed at www.corestandards.org/assets/CCSSI_Math%20Standards.pdf on August 14, 2020.

National PTA. (n.d.). *National standards for family-school partnerships.* Accessed at https://pta.org/home/run-your-pta/National-Standards-for-Family-School-Partnerships on May 14, 2020.

No Child Left Behind Act of 2001, Pub. L. No. 107–110, 20 U.S.C. § 6319 (2002).

O'Connor, K. (2009a). *How to grade for learning K–12* (3rd ed.). Thousand Oaks, CA: Corwin Press.

O'Connor, K. (2009b). Reforming grading practices in secondary schools. *Principal's Research Review, 4*(1), 1–7.

O'Connor, K. (2018). *How to grade for learning: Linking grades to standards* (4th ed.). Thousand Oaks, CA: Corwin Press.

O'Connor, K., & Wormeli, R. (2011, November). Reporting student learning. *Educational Leadership, 69*(3), 40–44.

Oliver, B. (2011, January). Making the case for standards-based grading. *Just ASK, VIII*(I). Accessed at https://justaskpublications.com/just-ask-resource-center/e-newsletters/just-for -the-asking/making-the-case-for-standards-based-grading/ on July 15, 2020.

Popham, W. J. (1999). *Classroom assessment: What teachers need to know.* Needham Heights, MA: Allyn & Bacon.

Popham, W. J. (2001). *The truth about testing: An educator's call to action.* Alexandria, VA: Association for Supervision and Curriculum Development.

QuoteHD. (n.d.). *Tim Pawlenty quotes.* Accessed at www.quotehd.com/quotes/tim-pawlenty -quote-hope-is-not-a-plan on May 19, 2020.

RAND Corporation. (2014, November). *Early progress: Interim research on personalized learning.* Seattle, WA: Bill & Melinda Gates Foundation. Accessed at http://k12education .gatesfoundation.org/2p-content/uploads/2015/06/Early-Progress-on-Personalized -Learning-Full_Report.pdf on August 26, 2020.

Rath, T., & Conchie, B. (2008). *Strengths-based leadership: Great leaders, teams, and why people follow.* New York: Gallup Press.

Reeves, D. B. (2004, December). The case against the zero. *Phi Delta Kappan, 86*(4), 324–325.

Reeves, D. B. (2008, February). Effective grading practices. *Educational Leadership, 65*(5), 85–87.

Reeves, D. B. (2011, December). For effective leadership, limit initiatives and link professional development [Video]. *ASCD Express, 7*(6). Accessed at http://www.ascd.org/ascd-express /vol7/706-video.aspx on September 28, 2020.

Rooney, J. (2008). The principal connection / taking hold of learning. *Educational Leadership, 66*(3), 82–83.

Rutland High School. (2020a). *A parent's guide to proficiency based learning.* Accessed at https:// rhs.rutlandcitypublicschools.org/academics/proficiency-based-learning-practices on July 23, 2020.

Rutland High School. (2020b). *What do grades mean at RHS?* Accessed at https://rhs .rutlandcitypublicschools.org/academics/proficiency-based-learning-practices/the -meaning-of-a-grade/ on September 25, 2020.

Scherer, M. (2011, November). What we learn from grades. *Educational Leadership, 69*(3), 7.

Schimmer, T. (2016). *Grading from the inside out: Bringing accuracy to student assessment through a standards-based mindset.* Bloomington, IN: Solution Tree Press.

Scriffiny, P. L. (2008). Seven reasons for standards-based grading. *Educational Leadership, 66*(2), 70–74.

Simms, J. A. (2016). *The critical concepts.* Centennial, CO: Marzano Resources. Accessed at www.marzanoresources.com/the-critical-concepts on April 6, 2020.

Stiggins, R. J. (2001). *Student-involved classroom assessment* (3rd ed.). Upper Saddle River, NJ: Prentice Hall.

Stiggins, R. J. (2008). *An introduction to student-involved assessments for learning* (5th ed.). Upper Saddle River, NJ: Prentice Hall.

Townsley, M., & Buckmiller, T. (2016, January 14). *What does the research say about standards-based grading?* Accessed at http://mctownsley.net/standards-based-grading-research on May 14, 2020.

Turkay, S. (2014). *Setting goals: Who, why, how?* Accessed at https://academia.edu/10363659 /Setting_goals_who_why_how on May 12, 2020.

Tyre, P. (2012, February). Making the grade: When do kids deserve As? *Family Circle.* Accessed at https://curriculum.rsdmo.org/reporting/Documents/Making%20the%20Grade% 20Family%20Circle%202012.pdf on July 15, 2020.

U.S. Department of Education. (n.d.). *Every Student Succeeds Act (ESSA).* Accessed at https:// www.ed.gov/essa?src=rn on July 15, 2020.

Vatterott, C. (2015). *Rethinking grading: Meaningful assessment for standards-based learning.* Alexandria, VA: Association for Supervision and Curriculum Development.

Weick, K. E., Sutcliffe, K. M., & Obstfeld, D. (1999). Organizing for high reliability: Processes of collective mindfulness. *Research in Organizational Behavior, 1*, 81–123.

Wichita Public Schools. (n.d.) *WPS standards-referenced grading FAQs.* Accessed at https:// www.usd259.org/cms/lib/KS01906405/Centricity/Domain/4768/SRG%20FAQ.pdf on July 20, 2020.

Wiggins, G. P. (1996). Honesty and fairness: Toward better grading and reporting. In T. R. Guskey (Ed.), *Communicating student learning: The 1996 ASCD yearbook* (pp. 141–177). Alexandria, VA: Association for Supervision and Curriculum Development.

Wiggins, G. P., & McTighe, J. (2005). *Understanding by design* (2nd ed.). Alexandria, VA: Association for Supervision and Curriculum Development.

Winger, T. (2005, November). Grading to communicate. *Educational Leadership, 63*(3), 61–65.

Wormeli, R. (2006a). Accountability: Teaching through assessment and feedback, not grading. *American Secondary Education, 34*(3), 14–27.

Wormeli, R. (2006b). *Fair isn't always equal: Assessing and grading in the differentiated classroom.* Portsmouth, NH: Stenhouse.

Wormeli, R. (2011, November). Redos and retakes done right. *Educational Leadership, 69*(3), 22–26.

Index

A

accommodations, 8, 107–108
accountability, 99–100
active progress monitoring, 144, 199–203
AEAs. *See* area education agencies (AEAs)
alignment, 61, 71–84, 104
    activities for, 8, 9–10
    assessment literacy training and, 77–78, 106
    feedback and goal setting and, 76–77
    in multiphase implementation plan, 9
    of prioritized content and standards, 19
    of proficiency scales, 72–75, 106–107
    in rollout, 126–129
    vertical, 104, 177–180
anchor documents, 35
Anoka-Hennepin Public Schools (Minnesota), 113
area education agencies (AEAs), 52
assessment, 3
    aligning with instruction, 61, 71–74, 79–81
    aligning with standards and scales, 104
    definition of, 8
    digital storage of, 57–59
    expanding implementation of common
        classroom, 144–145
    implementing common, in selected grade
        levels, 127–129
    inter-rater reliability in, 81–83, 85, 130
    intra-rater reliability in, 82, 83–84, 85,
        130–131
    leveled, 79–81, 167–171
    literacy training on, 77–78, 106
    in non-core content areas, 129–130
    priority standards and, 16
    resources on developing, 78
    rollout of, 126–129
    teacher feedback on, 125–126
    terminology related to, 6–7
    tracking correlations among, 140–141
Aurora Public Schools (Colorado), 149, 199–203

B

Barnes, B., 147
behavior assessments, 182–183
belief statements, 132–133
boards of cooperative education services (BOCES),
    52
boards of education, 91–92
    communicating with, 48–49
    educating and updating, 114–117
    observation opportunities for, 134–136
    training incoming, 150
BOCES. *See* boards of cooperative education
    services (BOCES)
Burger, Sarah, 92–93, 96
Bush, George W., 48

C

calibration, 82. *See also* reliability
capacity building, 9
    core beliefs and, 89–90
    educating parents and, 92–99
    information sharing and, 87–99
CBE. *See* competency-based education (CBE)
celebrating success, 9, 150–151
    activities for, 8, 9
Charlotte High School (Michigan), 147
collaborative cultures, 153
collaborative scoring, 81, 82
collaborative teams, 49–53
college acceptance of standards-based grading,
    98–99, 175
Columbia Public Schools (Missouri), 108–109
Columbus Public Schools (Nebraska), 106, 120,
    125–126
communication. *See also* feedback
    about grading, 56–57
    activities for, 8, 9
    with all staff, 127

of belief statements, 132–133
with boards of education, 48–49
with constituent groups, 131–136
on implementation plans, 114
information sharing, 87–99
matrix, 132
in multiphase implementation plan, 9
planning, 38, 40–47, 51–52
on reporting systems, 137–139
strategic, 40–41
terminology clarification for, 2–3, 5–8
toolkit for, 173–174
communications directors, 47–48
competency-based education (CBE), 2
competency-based learning and reporting, 2
complex content, 27
Conchie, B., 54
consensus building, 8, 55
resources for, 162–164
consistency, 4–5
constituent groups
communicating with, 131–136
communication with, 38, 40–47
educating, 91–99
training incoming, 147–150
consultants
in alignment, 101
in curriculum design, 58
in implementation, 123, 140–141
in monitoring, 151
continuation, revision, and expansion phase, 9
activities for, 8, 9–10
core beliefs, 89–90
core content areas
capacity building in, 9
curriculum design for, 13–37
feedback on classroom assessments in, 125–126
pacing guides for, 34–37
priority standards for, 14–15
proficiency scales for, 84–85, 106–107
rolling out standards/scales for, 61–71
correlation tracking, 140–141
Covey, S. R., 49
COVID-19 pandemic, 1
Critical Concepts. *See* Marzano Resources Critical Concepts
critical thinking, 76–77
curriculum, 1, 13–37
guaranteed and viable, definition of, 13
intended, enacted, assessed, 8
modifying, 3
in multiphase implementation plan, 9
pacing guides and, 34–37
proficiency scales and, 29–34
terminology related to, 6
curriculum and communication phase, 8, 9

D

data, student achievement, 146–147
data analysis, 100–101
Davis, D., 146
Deer Creek Public Schools (Oklahoma), 92–95, 97, 98, 192–193
design teams
field-testing by, 104–105
member selection for, 15
priority standards identification by, 15–37
standards evaluation criteria for, 16
training on assessment literacy, 77–78
digital portfolios, 49, 150
documentation
for common assessment scoring, 81–82
storage and access of, 25, 49, 57–59, 76–77, 86–87, 119–120
dual enrollment trends, 147, 148
DuFour, R., 99

E

elevator speeches, 41
eligibility determination, 183
Empower Learning, 58, 59, 120–122
endurance, 16
English-learner services, 47
Every Student Succeeds Act (ESSA) (2015), 49, 92
exceptional learners, 4–5, 107–112
definition of, 107
proficiency scale levels and, 28

F

FAQ. *See* frequently asked questions (FAQ) documents
feedback, 1, 3, 4–5
on classroom assessments, 125–126
field-testing and, 105
reviewing and incorporating teacher, 67, 68–69
revision and, 105–106
on standards and proficiency scales, 61–67
field-testing, 67–71, 104–105, 120–123
file naming, 58
Flygare, J., 42, 72, 76, 111
focus groups, 133–134, 145–146
protocol for, 133–134, 187–190
Formative Assessment and Standards-Based Grading (Marzano), 87
frequently asked questions (FAQ) documents, 25, 137, 194–197
Fullan, M., 54–55

G

Gateway High School (Aurora, Colorado), 146
goal setting, 76–77
Google Drive, 57
Google Forms, 62
grading
analyzing existing practices and beliefs in, 56–57

need for reform of, 1
parent's guide to, 181–183
parents' questions about, 98–99
standards-based, 2
standards-referenced, 2
grading tools, electronic, 86–87, 119–123
document storage in, 58, 59
field-testing, 120–123
training incoming staff on, 149
guiding teams, 53–55

H

A Handbook for Developing and Using Proficiency Scales in the Classroom (Hoegh), 29, 111
Harvard, 175
Heartland Area Educational Agency (Iowa)
definitions document by, 5, 8
staff leader education at, 52–53
Heflebower, T., 2, 5, 16, 42, 72, 76, 79, 87, 111, 153
high reliability schools, 99, 153
Hoegh, J. K., 2, 16, 29, 42, 72, 76, 79, 87, 111, 153

I

implementation
activities for, 8, 9
analyzing existing grading practices/beliefs and, 56–57
boards of education and, 48–49
communication in, 38, 40–47, 88–89, 114–117
educating parents and, 92–99
expanding, 84–87, 143–146
field-testing in, 67–71
guiding teams in, 53–55
monitoring, 99–101
multiphase plan for, 4, 8–12
plan examples, 172–173
planning, 38–40, 114
rollout, 112–117, 126–129
time line for, 42, 47
universal, 103–112
information sharing, 61, 87–99. *See also* communication
instruction, aligning with assessment, 61, 71–74, 79–81
instruction planning, 4–5
active progress monitoring in, 200–202
proficiency scales in, 25–26, 70–71, 72–75
instructional coaches, 47
instructional supports, 107–112
inter-rater reliability, 81–83, 85, 130
interventions, 8
intra-rater reliability, 82, 83–84, 85, 130–131
Iowa Area Education Agencies, 55

J

Jefferson County Public Schools (Colorado), 17, 111–112
categories of priority standards from, 21, 23–24

Learning Network leadership at, 53
proficiency scales, 29, 31, 32
proficiency scales description by, 64–65

K

Kotter, J., 53

L

lagging indicators, 99
leaders
accountability of, 99–100
additional learning for, 87
in alignment and capacity building, 61–101
building knowledge and understanding of SBL, 4–5
communicating implementation plans to, 88–89
core beliefs and, 89–90
educating key, 47–53
monitoring by, 119–120
multiphase plan development by, 4, 8–12
staff, in implementation, 49–53
Leading a High Reliability School (Marzano, Warrick, Rains, & DuFour), 99
leading indicators, 99
learning. *See also* standards-based learning (SBL)
for boards of education, 91–92
opportunities for all staff, 131–132
opportunities for learning leaders, 87
from other schools/districts, 90
personalized/online, 1
proficiency scales in, 25–26
for staff leaders, 49–53
taking ownership of, 76
what constitutes, 1
Lenz, Jaci, 92–93, 96, 134–135, 136
leveled assessments, 79–81, 167–171
leverage, 16
life skills, 119
Lincoln Elementary School (St. Charles, Missouri), 146
Lindahl, B., 52–53

M

Marzano, R. J., 2, 13, 87, 99, 153
Marzano Resources Critical Concepts, 17, 20, 22
proficiency scales, 29–31
McKeel Academy Charter Schools (Lakeland, Florida), 41
Measure of Academic Progress (MAP), 140, 141
measurement topics, 20, 22
meetings
guiding team, 54
for standards prioritization, 17–18
mentoring, 149
Microsoft OneDrive, 57
modifications, 8
Monett R-1 School District (Missouri), 73, 74–75

monitoring, 4–5, 9, 13, 143–152
    activities for, 8, 9
    implementation, 61, 99–101
multiphase plan, 8–12

N

newsletters, 96
No Child Left Behind Act (2002), 48, 92
non-core content areas, 103–106
    alignment of assessments in, 129–130
    expanding implementation to, 143–146
    proficiency scales in, 127, 129
Northwood Public School (North Dakota), 92–93, 96, 134–135,
    136, 181–183
Not Your Ordinary School (NYOS) (Austin, Texas), 88, 89, 149,
    150, 172–173
Novato Unified School District (California), 38–40

O

Obama, Barack, 49
"open chair" protocol, 54–55

P

pacing guides, 34–37, 72
parents
    communication with, 41–42, 44–47
    educating, 92–99
    FAQ for, 194–197
    focus groups with, 133–134, 145–146
    grading information for, 56–57, 175
    report cards and, 118
    reporting systems and, 137–139
    sample presentation to, 183–185
    training incoming, 147–150
presentation slide decks, 93–94
principals, 49–50, 87
priority standards, 4–5, 14–37
    agenda for developing, 17
    aligning assessments with, 104
    analyzing standards documents and, 18
    approach to selecting, 15–16
    categorizing, 20, 22–24
    creating proficiency scales based on, 31–33
    criteria for determining, 16
    definition of, 14
    differentiating the process for, 16
    digital storage of, 57–59
    documentation of, 86–87
    electronic storage of, 25
    expanding efforts with, 84–86
    field-testing, 67–71, 104–105
    need for choosing, 13–14
    in non-core content areas, 129–130
    for other content areas, 85–86

    ownership of, 62
    proficiency scales based on, 25–34
    reviewing final categories of, 25
    rolling out, 61–71
    selecting preliminary, 19–21
    teacher feedback on, 61–67
professional development days, 104
proficiency scales, 3, 4–5, 25–34
    agenda for developing, 17
    aligning assessment with, 78
    aligning assessments with, 104
    aligning for core content areas, 106–107
    aligning with instructional activities/resources, 72–75
    creating new, 31–33
    creation by content area, 17–18
    customizing existing, 29–31, 32
    digital storage of, 57–59
    documentation of, 86–87
    examples of, 156–161
    expanding implementation of, 85–86, 144
    feedback on, 76–77
    field-testing, 67–71, 104–105
    five-step creation process for, 33–34
    format of, 27–28, 29
    gaps between grade bands in, 107
    generic form of, 26, 29
    importance of understanding, 26
    levels in, 27
    in non-core content areas, 127, 129–130
    for other content areas, 85–86
    ownership of, 62
    pacing guides and, 34–37
    parent communication about, 95–96
    progression of knowledge in, 27, 28
    requiring teacher use of, 114
    resources on, 155–161
    revising, 84–85
    rolling out, 61–71, 126–129
    student-created, 96–97
    teacher feedback on, 61–67
    translation guides for, 139
proficiency-based learning and reporting, 2
progress tracking, 1, 4–5, 9, 119–120, 143–152
    activities for, 8, 9
    definition of, 8
    of implementation, 99–101
    resources on, 199–203
    student goals and, 76–77
protocols
    for consensus building, 162–164
    for feedback, 125–126
    focus group, 133–134, 187–190
    guiding team operation, 54–55

Q

quick data, 100–101

R

Rains, C. L., 99
Rath, T., 54
Rathgeber, H., 53
readiness, 16
reflection, 13
    student goal setting and, 77
reliability
    inter-rater, 81–83, 130
    intra-rater, 82, 83–84, 130–131
report cards, 117–119, 190–193
reporting systems, 92–93, 95, 117–123
    ensuring student/family understanding of, 137–139
    expanding implementation of, 145
    implementing for selected grades, 136–141
    report card development and, 117–119
    support for, 175
resources
    on active progress monitoring, 199–203
    on assessment development, 78
    communication toolkit, 173–174
    on consensus building, 162–164
    focus group protocol, 187–190
    on implementation plans, 172–173
    on leveled assessments, 167–171
    parent FAQs, 194–197
    parent's guide to standards-based grading, 181–183
    on proficiency scales, 155–161
    sample presentation to parents, 183–185
    for staff leaders, 50–51
    on standards-based report cards, 190–193
    on vertical alignment, 177–180
reteach, reassess schedule, 135, 136
review and revision
    of pacing guides, 35
    of priority standard categories, 25
    of proficiency scales, 84–85, 105–106, 107–108
rollout, 112–117, 126–129
Rooney, J., 87
roving, 202
Rutland High School (Vermont), 133, 139, 191

S

SBL. See standards-based learning (SBL)
scaffolding, 73, 107–108
A School Leader's Guide to Standards-Based Grading (Heflebower, Hoegh, & Warrick), 29, 42, 79, 87, 111
scouts, 90
second-order change, 3–4
simple content, 27
slide decks, 93–94
staff leaders, 49–53
    assessment literacy for, 106
    buy-in from, 62
    communication with, 127

learning opportunities for, 87, 131–132, 165
    training incoming, 147–150
stakeholders. See constituent groups
standards
    analyzing for prioritization, 18
    boards of education and, 48–49
    creating proficiency scales based on, 31–33
    curriculum based on, 3
    digital storage of, 57–59
    priority, identifying, 4–5, 13–37
    sequencing for instruction planning, 72
    supporting, 15
    terminology on, 5
standards-based learning (SBL)
    components of, 4–5
    implementing, 3–4
    multiphase implementation plan for, 4, 8–12
    terminology for, 2–3, 4, 5–8
    training incoming stakeholders in, 147–150
state assessments, 140–141
Strengths-Based Leadership (Rath & Conchie), 54
students
    communication with, 41
    focus groups with, 133–134
    goal setting by, 76
    report cards and, 118
    reporting systems and, 137–139
    understanding proficiency scales by, 76
superintendents, 48
supplementary standards, 15
supporting standards, 15, 19, 20, 21
SurveyMonkey, 62
surveys
    on grading practices and beliefs, 56
    for teacher feedback on standards and scales, 62, 63
sustaining initiatives, 100–101
Swanson, C., 149, 199–203
Synergy, 138

T

target content, 27
teacher leadership teams, 38–40
    core beliefs and, 89–90
teachers
    on active progress monitoring, 202–203
    assessment literacy for, 77–78, 106
    communication with, 41
    core beliefs and, 89–90
    of exceptional learners, 107–112
    feedback from on classroom assessments, 125–126
    goal setting and, 76–77
    judgment of, 16
    norms sharing by, 134–136
    as scouts to other schools/districts, 90
    seeking feedback from, 61–69
    on special assignment (TOSAs), 29–30

training in inter-/intra-rater reliability, 130–131

training incoming, 147–150

A Teacher's Guide to Standards-Based Learning (Heflebower, Hoegh, Warrick, Flygare), 42, 76, 111

teachers on special assignment (TOSAs), 111

technology

directors of, 48

document storage and, 25, 49, 57–59, 86–87

electronic grading tools, 58, 59, 86–87, 119–123, 149

fine-tuning needs in, 139–140

guiding teams and, 54

personalized learning, 1

reporting systems, 117–123

survey tools, 62, 64

terminology, 2–3, 4, 5–8

time

for collaboration, 104

for feedback collection, 64

for standards prioritization, 16–17

to teach priority standards, 20

TOSAs. *See* teachers on special assignment (TOSAs)

transparency, 54–55

U

unit planning, 72–75

U.S. Department of Education, 49

V

Valencia, V., 149, 199–203

vertical alignment, 104, 177–180

W

Warrick, P., 2, 16, 29, 42, 72, 76, 79, 99, 111, 153

Whitehead, A. N., 3

Wichita Public Schools (Kansas), 155–161

communication plan, 42–47, 173–174

parents FAQ, 194–197

Wiggins, G., 2

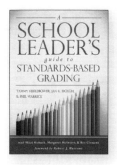

A School Leader's Guide to Standards-Based Grading
Tammy Heflebower, Jan K. Hoegh, and Phil Warrick
Assess and report student performance with standards-based grading rather than using traditional systems that incorporate nonacademic factors. Learn to assess and report performance based on prioritized standards, and gain effective strategies for offering students feedback on their progress.
BKL019

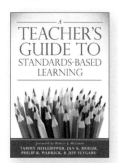

A Teacher's Guide to Standards-Based Learning
Tammy Heflebower, Jan K. Hoegh, Philip B. Warrick, and Jeff Flygare
Designed specifically for K–12 teachers, this resource details a sequential approach for adopting and implementing standards-based learning. The authors provide practical advice, real-world examples, and answers to frequently asked questions designed to support you through this important transition.
BKL044

A Handbook for Developing and Using Proficiency Scales in the Classroom
Jan K. Hoegh
Discover a clear path for creating and utilizing high-quality proficiency scales. Through this practical handbook, you will gain access to a comprehensive toolkit of strategies, methods, and examples for a variety of content areas and grade levels.
BKL045

A Handbook for High Reliability Schools
Robert J. Marzano, Phil Warrick, and Julia A. Simms
Transform your schools into organizations that take proactive steps to ensure student success. Using a research-based five-level hierarchy along with leading and lagging indicators, you'll learn to assess, monitor, and confirm the effectiveness of your schools.
BKL020

A Handbook for Personalized Competency-Based Education
Robert J. Marzano, Jennifer S. Norford, Michelle Finn, and Douglas Finn III
Ensure all students master content by designing and implementing a personalized competency-based education (PCBE) system. Explore examples of how to use proficiency scales, standard operating procedures, behavior rubrics, personal tracking matrices, and other tools to aid in instruction and assessment.
BKL037

Visit MarzanoResources.com or call 888.849.0851 to order.

Professional Development Designed for Success

Empower your staff to tap into their full potential as educators. As an all-inclusive research-into-practice resource center, we are committed to helping your school or district become highly effective at preparing every student for his or her future.

Choose from our wide range of customized professional development opportunities for teachers, administrators, and district leaders. Each session offers hands-on support, personalized answers, and accessible strategies that can be put into practice immediately.

Bring Marzano Resources experts to your school for results-oriented training on:

- ▶ Assessment & Grading
- ▶ Curriculum
- ▶ Instruction
- ▶ School Leadership

- ▶ Teacher Effectiveness
- ▶ Student Engagement
- ▶ Vocabulary
- ▶ Competency-Based Education

LEARN MORE at MarzanoResources.com/PD